To Josh & Beth
Enjoy.
Richard Harris

MEATBALLS & STICKBALL

Growing up in "The Neighborhood" Little Italy

AN ANTHOLOGY
COMPILED AND EDITED BY
RICHARD J. RINALDO

Printed in the United States of America at McNally Jackson Books, 52 Prince Street, New York, NY 10012.

www.mcnallyjackson.com/bookmachine/meatballs-stickball

First Edition

ISBN 978-1-938-02217-3

A ogni uccello il suo nido è bello.
(To every bird, his own nest is beautiful.)

–Italian Proverb

People work much in order to secure their future.
I gave my mind much work and trouble to secure the past.

–Isak Dinesen, *Shadows on the Grass*

CONTENTS

Foreword 9

Preface 11

Introduction 17

PART 1: Ethnicity and Identity 23

PART 2: The Neighborhood 43

PART 3: Nobility 93

PART 4: A Saint, a Psychic, and a Sculptress 121

PART 5: Religiosity 133

PART 6: Sports and Pastimes 187

PART 7: Celebrity 229

PART 8: Patriotism 239

Epilogue 259

Acknowledgements 263

Credits 265

Contributors 267

Materials for Further Reading 275

FOREWORD

"The Neighborhood"—Little Italy is not dead. Meatballs still please our taste buds, and those little rubber pink balls used in the game of stickball still bounce on occasion. Immigrants still seek its opportunity. You cannot kill an idea. Nor is it true that you can never go home again. Italian-Americans continue to come, joining those still here, to make Little Italy the vibrant, sophisticated community it has become. They come to pray, to eat, and to celebrate their heritage. This book is another piece of that celebration.

I call those who come from their new places "the diaspora." They are flung wide across the nation. But to them this place remains special, even a sacred place, including its church, the recently inaugurated Basilica of St. Patrick's Old Cathedral. They are joined here in this book by others who see value in the culture and achievements of this colorful piece of the Big Apple.

Some 40 contributors give us essays, vignettes, and memories about the past. They share more than 300 photographs, on the cover and inside this book. They reminisce and ponder, and sometimes share humor and hurt. Theirs is the human journey of struggle, hope, kinship, and friendship. I welcome them and their story. I know that it will give the reader enjoyment and understanding of "the neighborhood."

Monsignor Donald Sakano
The Basilica of St. Patrick's Old Cathedral
263 Mulberry Street
New York, NY 10012
www.oldcathedral.org

PREFACE

By Richard J. Rinaldo

I keep my friends as misers do their treasure because;
of all the things granted us by wisdom none is
greater or better than friendship. ~Pietro Aretino

CIAO, LITTLE ITALY

Ciao, Little Italy, a tightly knit, though loosely organized group of friends of more than half-a century put together this book with the help of many others. It is a tribute to Italians and Italian-Americans, who have departed this life, moved from Little Italy, New York City, or still live there. The Italian word "ciao" means both "hello" and "goodbye." So those who said goodbye to the "old neighborhood" in a "diaspora" (as Monsignor Donald Sakano, current Pastor of the Basilica of Old St. Patrick's Cathedral, once referred to us) now return to say hello in these pages. We tell stories about our lives and the people and places we still love. We enlisted others, too, who found grist for expression of their talents in our world and others who lived amongst us and made an impression on us and the wider world.

Ciao, Little Italy serves the memory of this special place, a neighborhood, more like a village, where we lived in our youth. With the cooperation of the National Italian American Foundation, we emplaced a plaque on the wrought iron fence of the parish house of the Basilica of St. Patrick's Old Cathedral on Mulberry Street between Prince and Houston Street to commemorate the use of that street as a "Play Street." This book is our second major project. In it we hope to give the reader a

flavor of the vibrancy of the "old neighborhood," to share our memories and experiences of that special place.

Our approach to putting together this book is simple; it is nostalgic and sentimental. This is not a history or sociology book, though it contains some of each. There are so many good books like that about Italians in America. And we have included some references in an appendix or referred to them elsewhere herein for anyone interested. It is also not fiction, though we cannot vouch for the veracity of all the stories we have included. Maybe some are just tall tales based on some real facts. Again, we have listed some fiction and movies in an appendix. Finally, we do not seek glory, fame, money, or power. All net proceeds from the sale of this book will go toward further projects.

But, where is this Little Italy besides Mulberry Street? Barry Moreno, in his book, *Italian Americans*, part of the Barron's *Coming to America* series, says, "The first important Italian settlement in New York was located in the notorious Five Points neighborhood in the 1840s. But as more Italians arrived, the community slowly crept northward and finally found its **richest cultural expression in the immigrant world of Little Italy**." (Our emphasis.) This is our old neighborhood, bounded by Bleecker Street on the north, the Bowery on the east, Canal Street on the south, and Lafayette Street on the west. Some will call parts of it NOLITA for north of Little Italy. However, for us it will always be the "old neighborhood," our Little Italy. Significantly, the image for our next plaque, shown on page 14, was used as a front cover of *U.S. News and World Report* on August 6, 2001, for its cover story, "America 1900-2000: Who We Were, Who We Are, How an Epic Century Changed a Nation." The article seeks to understand who we are as Americans. It points out, "The picture that emerges is one of a nation that continues to be defined in many ways, by its immigrants...."

Of course, our neighborhood was just one of many "Little Italies" in New York City. They were collectively called at one time "the Colonia." Still, it is probably the place where most Italians came on departing Ellis Island. God only knows how many of the nearly 26 million Italian Americans in the United States can trace their roots to this neighborhood.

And how we all loved our neighborhood and its extended family, the games we played, the rituals we repeated, the seasons and feasts we celebrated. It is always a wonder to go back there and listen to the whispers of the past, the music of the feasts, the barking iceman, the Gregorian chants, and your mother calling from the window. We go back to see the columns of the Basilica of Saint Patrick's Old Cathedral, to remember tar beach; to see what we called Jersey Alley, which really isn't an alley, Play Street, the Judson Center, St Michael's Russian Catholic Church, the Puck building; and to recall Puerto Rican bodegas. We remember Spaldeens, stickball and meatballs, Chinese laundries and linoleum floors, pushcarts and pizza with anchovies—memories of youth, learning, loved ones and places.

In all of this, we know, we hope and we believe. We know that in the long run we are all dead, as someone once said. Yet, hopefully, we leave good memories. We leave love. We leave values. We empower and inspire those we leave. We enrich the future. We believe that what we choose to remember often defines who we are. We believe that if you cannot preserve your past, you cannot prepare well for your future or fully enjoy your present. This is not a unique thought. Timothy Cardinal Dolan, Archbishop of New York, reminds us of memories. He cites scholarly research. It tells us that any institution—family, neighborhood, Church, country, organization, or club—needs memories in order to survive and flourish. The Cardinal speaks excellent Italian by the way, having spent some time in Rome. Nice to have God's representative on our side.

A note on style:

Materials in this book come from a variety of contributors. Some are professional writers with published works to their credit. Others are accomplished people, who have written as part of their professional duties. Others have no writing experience. Some of the materials are from transcripts of oral story telling. Some are from emails.

In some cases there was minimal editorial effort in order to preserve the voice of contributors. Therefore, we ask for the readers' indulgence, generosity, and forebearance. Withhold the red pen of your mind, sit back and enjoy the flavor of the variety of our communications. Ed.

The Next Plaque
Immigrants in "The Neighborhood" Little Italy

Most came from Southern Italy from 1900-1914. There were some 4 million. Many stayed here in Little Italy. And it became "The Neighborhood," from Bleecker St. on the north to Canal St. on the south, Lafayette St. on the west to the Bowery on the east. Most had no money, no education, and no special skills. But they had their families and friends, their church, their wits, and a fierce determination to thrive. They did.

Little Italy Is Mine *by Gerard Marinaccio* – PAINT ON WOOD

My whole family is from Little Italy. It was safe for us back then. I used to play on my block with my friends, smoking and hanging out on the church steps getting chased by the older kids. The blocks were a huge playground for us. I attended St. Patrick's School on Mott Street, there I was always punished. I had to clean my desk after class because I would always draw all over. It was bad to them, but WONDERFUL for me! I have been low key about my Art, my whole life. It was not easy growing up in a neighborhood like that, being an artist.

I was born an artist, it's in my veins. People from my neighborhood would not really accept it. They didn't understand it. My father would say: "Get a Job!!! You would never be discovered! Go to work! Art is for the rich!" But I never lost faith and kept creating. I met people that helped me and encouraged me to pursue my dreams. I participated at different events and shows during my journey. I like to refer my Art as a MODERN-DAY-CALLIG-RAPHY. I create pictures within pictures within pictures in a story line format. My compositions express my journeys, pain, joy, and prayers on scraps of metal and wood. The mediums that I work with are marker, spray paint, house paint, watercolor markers, gold leafing, oil markers and pastels. I have also worked on concrete walls with multiple mediums. I show my Art in underground spaces primarily in downtown Manhattan and have a substantial following since 1995. I have participated in over 20 shows between the years 2000 and 2011.

Editor's note: Gerard's grandparents came from Sicily, and his mother is Angel Marinaccio, author of a wonderful book about our neighborhood, Be Home on Time When I Put the Water Up for Pasta. An excerpt is in this book.

INTRODUCTION

By Richard J. Rinaldo

And there is something in human beings that yearns to keep
and nourish that which it values in the past...You can't go home
again; true. But there are layers of tradition at the core of our
being which compellingly seek expression even as we seek to
nurture the next generation. ~Richard Gambino

Here is the recipe for Cousin Marietta's meatballs, which she is
teaching to her granddaughter Alyssa in the picture.

Meat Balls

½ lb. ground pork chop meat
½ lb. ground beef chop meat
4 cloves of garlic
Italian bread that has been
hardened at least 2 days or
more, about the size of a hero
loaf. Use about 1/3 of the loaf.
3 sprigs of parsley
1 ½ cups grated pecorino Romano cheese
2 extra-large eggs
Salt and pepper to taste

Put the Italian bread in a bowl and let it soak in water till it falls apart. Remove the brown crust and discard.
Mix the pork and beef chop meat. Break up the bread into
little pieces and mix very well until it is all incorporated.
Add cheese, eggs, finely chopped parsley and garlic, salt,
and pepper. Mix thoroughly.

Heat 3/4 cup of olive oil in a frying pan. Roll the meat
into balls and fry on high to medium heat. When brown on
one side, turn them and brown the other side.

So there it is. You can skip the rest of this book. You have something valuable and enduring.

For sure, this book is about leaving something behind, passing on those aspects of our lives that we want to share with our descendants. It is also about meatballs as a metaphor for the diversity of all the people that that lived in the neighborhood and their way of life. Now, you will not find a meatball in Gerard's painting. However, in its way it also reflects the timbre of this book, one of variety, complexity, and simplicity at the same time. In addition, this book means to be a bit playful, we hope, though it deals with some serious topics. It is also about sports and games, ways to play, especially stickball. It describes how the game was played, who played where on the field of play and the rules of the game. Stickball, too, is a metaphor—for a wider image of the neighborhood as a place where many played by the rules and all had a chance to play and excel.

The title of Gerard's paintings is telling—"Little Italy is Mine." He's right. It is our neighborhood, always. Maybe there are many new people living there and exciting new places—restaurants, cafes, boutiques, and the great bookstore McNally Jackson, our collaborator in this book. Our Little Italy, however, is a state of mind. I know that I can go anywhere in the world and run into someone who looks vaguely familiar and ask, "Are you from the neighborhood?" If they are, they will automatically know what neighborhood we are talking about. I don't think there is any other place with such an indelible imprint. Moreover, its golden age was when we lived there, a simpler time in so many ways. And yes, we all love New York City then and now.

Back to meatballs: each family in the neighborhood had a special recipe for their meatballs, maybe a little more salt, pepper, and other spices. Maybe they used a different blend of cheeses, bread crumbs, or meats. Maybe some used canola or sunflower oil instead of olive all. Who knows? And that's how the people were. They were Italians and Italian-

Americans, but also as different as any person can be from the next. In one family, you might have one son become a priest and another son a gangster.

Concerning stickball the great scholar of human play, Johan Huizinga talks about "beauty, tension, poise, balance....Play casts a spell over us; It is invested with the noblest qualities we are capable of perceiving in things: rhythm and harmony." It is "outside the range of good and bad" and despite the desire to win, the player "must still stick to the rules of the game." In these ways of play, the field was set and level. Huizinga also extended the notion of play to rituals, and we had a lot of them from christenings to communions, feasts, funerals, and family dinners on Sunday afternoon. In sport, you participated willingly, you played hard, you were allowed to play no matter who you were, and the outcome depended on how you played, not on your place in this or that enterprise. For all the rest, you got to eat. Who could resist?

Saying that this book is about the Golden Age of Little Italy is another point not without controversy. Some who lived in the neighborhood want to forget about it. They look at it as a trailer park and the Italians and Italian-Americans who lived or still live there as trailer park trash. They are happy to have fled to better neighborhoods and are ashamed of their background. To them, the time they lived in the neighborhood was more like the decline and fall of civilization at worst and living in medieval times at best.

I know that many of the people who contributed to this book have a different view—one of thankfulness for the opportunity to live in a special place where generosity, abundance, and simple good times were prevalent.

As for the trailer park, people in our neighborhood did live in crowded tenements. Sometimes there were fewer garbage cans than needed to accommodate the amount of garbage generated by the population. Or the pickup schedule was not as much of a priority for us as it was for Park Avenue. Sometimes the sidewalks overflowed with debris. You could call it the Garbage Age instead of the Golden Age and not be incorrect. There were a lot of rough kids, and you had to watch your step among them. The walls of the apartments were not thick, and you could hear many follies and foibles of family life. Sometimes the coal did not arrive on time to replenish the boilers that generated the steam for the radiator system of heating or for hot water. Apartments rarely had more than one bathroom, and some had bathrooms in the hallway to be shared by several families of tenants. The neighborhood had no public library then. One had to walk to St. Mark's Place and Second Avenue or below Chinatown to take out a book or look at magazines or newspapers.

In 1968, Nicholas Pileggi wrote about the neighborhood in an article in *New York Magazine*. Its title was, "Little Italy: Study of an Italian Ghetto." He described Little Italy as "…a neighborhood of grim men….a withdrawn community in which petty vices are indulged and all indulgences are tolerated, a community so isolated from the main currents of American thought and progress that the traditionally rigid social structure of Mafia-ridden Sicilian mountain village is even today, to many of its inhabitants, the only pattern of existence known." "At one time or another," he tell us, "it has successfully fought against public housing, overhead expressways, indoor pushcart markets, compulsory education, American food and the English language. It has also, as a result of this battle, assumed responsibility for a number of characteristics that the great majority of Italian-Americans would rather forget."

Unfortunately, many of Pileggi's indictments may have been correct. Many of us knew about those "grim men" he described. We showed them respect and ignored their failings, maybe even obtained their assistance in one way or the other to improve our own lives. What choice did we have? Who were we to judge based on hearsay or speculation? Some of them were neighbors, parents or other relatives of our friends, maybe even our own relatives. And we accepted or even cherished them without judgment. Maybe in this way we were too accepting and less than innocent. So, this book tells mostly nice stories, leaving out most of the transgressions, poor behavior, and sinfulness that is part of growing up. The book tries to avoid most of the dirty linen.

Nevertheless, Pileggi missed a lot beneath the surface. He also miscalculated, especially about the influence on the neighborhood and its inhabitants of the Catholic Church embodied in St. Patrick's Old Cathedral, its elementary school, and its priests and nuns. (See Testimonial Dinner photo at right.) His discussion of resistance to education as "the single most important factor in isolating the Italian immigrants, but also a large portion of subsequent generations from American society" is just baloney.

Testimonial Dinner to Msgr. Filitti, 1949

In 1968, Martin Scorsese, for example, who directed the movie *Goodfellas*, based on Pileggi's book, *Wise Guys*, was just starting his cinema career after graduating from New York University. By this time, some of us had already graduated from colleges like Columbia, Fordham, or Manhattan or from graduate school and well on our way to productive careers in law, finance, cinema, or government. He missed many great love stories, a host of local sporting legends, and funny people amidst those "grim men" he chose to feature in his story. He missed a million lessons of race relations and charity, of inspiring role models, and dedicated parents and teachers. He missed vibrant discussions of philosophy,  theology, cinema, art, and great books. Pileggi also makes the common mistake, as do so many of our organizations, of focusing on the most successful Italian-Americans. We have some among us. This book is not only about them. It is mostly about the average Italian-American, those who became policeman, engineers, and firefighters, those who handle your insurance, investments, or your bank accounts, who fight your wars, teach your children or build your ports. In some cases it is a story of the extraordinary nobility of the ordinary person.

Pileggi saw the Little Italy he chose to observe and write about. And it is the one many of us want to see or read about. In a review of a new book, *The Godfather Effect*, by Tom Santopietro, Laura Landro of the *Wall Street Journal* explains some of this. She says, "Mr. Santopietro perhaps rightly worries that the new caricatures of Italian-Americans found in the popular media are as bad as the old images of Italian organ grinders." She adds, "But when it comes to the continuing appeal of Italian mobsters like Tony Soprano, he aptly quotes Italian-American author Bill Tonelli: "'There are many more Italian-American CPAs than hit men, not that I want to watch a cable TV series about accountants.'" Landro does not mention, by the way, that Mario Puzo may have considered *Fortunate Pilgrim* his best work and lamented that *"The Godfather, a fiction he never lived, outshone the novel of his mother's honest immigrant struggle for respectability in America and her courage and filial love."* (Wikipedia.)

Yes, there was another Little Italy, one whose full story is not yet complete, a story in some instances perhaps as dramatic and exciting as that of Tony Soprano or Don Corleone. We hope this book helps tell that story.

PART 1

ETHNICITY AND IDENTITY

"THERE ARE SOME GOOD ITALIANS"

By Richard J. Rinaldo

A NEW YORK TIMES ARTICLE on April 18, 2012, says that a Little Italy tradition has returned to the Feast of San Gennaro in the neighborhood—Mafia corruption. We all knew that the neighborhood had some who chose the way of life of an enterprise known as the "syndicate," "the mob," or "Cosa Nostra." We called them "wise guys," "button men," "made men," or "dunskies" (derived from the honorific Italian word "Don").

Let's get this aspect of the neighborhood out of the way at the outset. There was a suggestion that I talk to someone reputed to be a member for this book, but I declined. I did say that we had something in common besides the neighborhood. We were both soldiers but in different armies.

The military is a good analogy for both recruitment and commitment to this organization. In fact, some scholars trace organized crime back to the days of the Roman Empire and some of its errant legionnaires. It is the dynamic of any gang, the idea of becoming part of something with strong bonds of loyalty and discipline, even the necessity of overcoming or killing enemies. In *The Warriors,* philosopher J. Glenn Gray lists "the delight in seeing, the delight in comradeship, the delight in destruction." Of course, the analogy falls apart with the notion of the legitimacy of your organization and its authorities. For those who joined the mob, there was probably no such issue. There was also an element of *Realpolitik*, to include an underlying aura of violence or its threat as a way to intimidate, control, or placate. John Bivona's vignette about that is below.

Some of those who joined may have been acutely aware of the discriminations, inequalities, vicissitudes, and tribulations of life in a not entirely immigrant friendly America. Indeed, in her monumental work, *The Journey of the Italians in America*, author Vincenza Scarpaci points out that the "indifference and hostility of the American population" were among the factors that fostered the growth of Little Italies." We include later in this book an article, "The Sin of the Slums," in which the author states, "The slum is a symbol of injustice...." Whether the neighborhood was a slum or not is hardly the real issue, but it had some of the characteristics of one, including many people living on low incomes.

Into this milieu came the Mafia, according to one idealistic extrapolation of those facts, self-appointed rebels, their progenitors the Mafia of Sicily that rejected the power of various rulers of that often-colonized island. In *The Italians,* Luigi Barzini discussed "Sicily and the Mafia," and how the Sicilians "had beaten the Arabs, the Normans, the Anjou Kings, and the Spanish, the Austrians, the Bourbon kings, and the Piedmontese...." A less generous view is that the Mafia grew out of the 19th century system of land ownership in Sicily, where rich landowners hired gangs of bandits to be their intermediaries and overseers of the peasants. These gangs also colluded with and represented the peasants with the landowners, for a price of course, on both ends. It was a no-lose business arrangement. Barzini himself recognized that the American Mafia had abandoned the "feudal pretenses of their fathers...in justice for the oppressed"–for dollars.

Mario Puzo described the rebel theory in his novel, *The Godfather.* Members of the Five Families and other families from throughout the country meet. "They were those rarities," Puzo tells us, "men who had refused to accept the rule of organized society, men who refused the dominion of other men." The one known as the Godfather, Don Corleone, says, "Let me say that we must always look to our interests. We are all men who have refused to be fools, who have refused to be puppets dancing on a string by the men on high...."

However, there is another side to them also. The Godfather continues, "None of us here want to see our grandchildren follow in our footsteps...they can be as others, their position and security won by our courage...who knows be a governor or a President, nothing's impossible here in America...." To add fact to fiction, I remember a reputed high-level figure once asking what I would like to do after college. My reply that I would like to be a lawyer was met with a resounding "Great. They take all my money!" And legend has it that one of the pastors of Old St. Patrick's Cathedral made a deal with them to keep away from the students who showed promise in school.

Many of us have experienced both the fruits and the poisons of the efforts of such men in some of our life experiences. Our neighborhood, for example, was the safest in New York City for many years. No one dared invade this protected space with burglaries, muggings, or drugs. They also settled disputes in ways perceived as just. J.J. Anselmo in his novel, *The Newsstand*, describes such an intervention in an extracted story that is in this chapter.

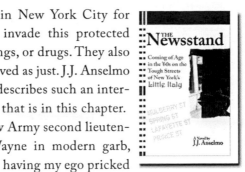

I can remember as a new Army second lieutenant, in dress blues, John Wayne in modern garb, having my ego pricked

by the one-star general in a receiving line who said, "Rinaldo, that's Italian. There are some good Italians." My good friend Anthony Viglietta tells a similar story. At a business meeting, he was asked if Viglietta was a Mafia name! Another excerpt from Anselmo's novel, which describes such a situation follows. On the other hand, maybe sometimes there was that fear that you were not to be trifled with either. And, today, it gives me personally no small pleasure that the son of an Italian immigrant is the Secretary of Defense, and the Chief of Staff of the Army, the grandson of one.

Tell me Johnny

By J.J. Anselmo

"Tell me Johnny, what is your full name?" Mr. Birnbaum inquired.

"My name is John Cara."

"That's Italian, isn't it?"

"Yes. Sicilian to be exact."

"Where do you live?"

"On Mulberry Street in Little Italy."

"Oh, don't tell me that your family's in the Mafia!"

"No. Not everyone in Little Italy is in the Mafia."

"Um…okay, young man," he nodded, "You don't look like the Mafia type…"

Excerpted from the novel, The Newsstand, *© 2011, by J.J. Anselmo, printed at McNally Jackson Books*

You did the right thing

By J.J. Anselmo

SALVATORE "BIG SAL" TUSA was a *Capo* in one of New York City's Five Families. The 65-year–old Mafioso was always impeccably dressed in a finely tailored Italian suit. He usually wore a tie and a white-on-white, cuff-linked shirt with a heavily starched collar. When the weather was cold he would don a wool topcoat and a fedora with a wide brim. His deportment was that of a "man of respect"—and he was accorded great respect by everyone in the neighborhood. Big Sal was very congenial and he displayed Old World manners. He was particularly respectful to the older ladies of the neighborhood, always tipping his hat to them as they walked by, and occasionally exchanging pleasantries. In short, Big Sal was the prototypical *Don*—right out of Hollywood's central casting.

Everyone knew that there was a dark side to Big Sal; one doesn't become a *Capo* by being an altar boy. Big Sal's rap sheet was quite long. He had "made his bones" in the Roaring Twenties but he had apparently continued his rise to the top by committing various crimes in the 30's and 40's. The latest entry on his rap sheet was an acquittal on a homicide charge in 1946.

Big Sal got a great deal of gratification out of doing favors for neighborhood people. If somebody's son needed a job, Big Sal, who had much influence on the waterfront and in the construction industry, would usually find a decent job for that son; some were even given "no-show jobs." Big Sal asked for nothing in return, although it was tacitly understood that should he ever need a favor in return, it had better be done with alacrity.

When John-John reached the two men he said, "Good afternoon, gentlemen."

"Good afternoon, John-John," they both replied in unison. Then, Big Sal added, "How ya doin' up at Columbia…you know I'm really proud of you. Imagine, Gappy, an Ivy Leaguer comin' out of this neighborhood."

"Thanks, I'm doing good, so far…By the way, there's something going on that I think you should know about."

"What's that?" Big Sal responded.

"Well, you know Joe, the blind newsman on Lafayette…"

"Of course we know him," replied Big Sal. "What's the problem?"

"Well, Seymour, the owner of the luncheonette next to the news-stand, wants to raise Joe's electric bill from $10 a month to $20 a month. Also, he wants Joe to give him $40 as a security deposit. Seymour says that if Joe doesn't pay him the security plus the twenty bucks by November 1st, he'll shut off his electricity…plus he won't allow him to use the luncheonette's toilet if he doesn't pay him the entire $60 by November 1st."

"That's really low…shakin' down a blind man. First of all, I'm sure Joe uses very little electric, especially durin' the summer."

"There's nuttin I hate more than a connivin' chiseler," added Gappy in an angry tone.

"What kinda miserable low-life prick withholds a terlit from any-one, especially a blind man?" questioned Big Sal in an even angrier tone.

"I hope I wasn't out of line by telling you about Joe's problem."

"What, are you kiddin'? You did the right thing by tellin' us," reas-sured Big Sal.

As John-John entered his building, Big Sal and his loyal underboss, Gaspare "Gappy" Serra started walking to the luncheonette. By the time they reached it, they had fire in their eyes and their blood was boiling. They simply couldn't fathom how Seymour could be so heartless to a poor blind man.

Once inside the luncheonette, Big Sal and Gappy "nudged" Sey-mour into the back room and had a "very meaningful conversation" with him. For sure, they put the fear of God in him. When the two men exited the luncheonette, they told Joe that the newsstand's monthly electric bill had actually been reduced—from $10 to $5—and that he didn't have to give Seymour a security deposit; plus, he could use the toilet whenever he needed to.

Excerpted from the novel, The Newsstand, *© 2011, by J.J. Anselmo, printed at McNally Jackson Books*

Hit Him

By John V. Bivona

GROWING UP IN OUR NEIGHBORHOOD, of course, we all knew of any number of "connected" people, some of whom were some type of boss. This is a story about an incident involving one of them.

It was a Friday night in the spring, and I was waiting on the corner for my then girlfriend, now wife Anne. We were going out that evening. A friend of ours was going out with a girl who lived in the same building as Anne, and he was waiting for her as well to go out. He had his car parked off of the corner where we could see it, and we were talking. All of a sudden a big black Cadillac made a turn from another street pretty fast and hit our friend's car. The driver knew he hit it but he took off. It was an African-American guy driving the car, a big heavy-set guy. We got the license plate number and, figuring we'd be good citizens, we went down to the 5th Precinct on Elizabeth Street. You have to remember now that my friend was Irish and as Irish-looking as you can imagine.

We reported the accident to the desk sergeant, and as we were talking to the desk sergeant about it a plain clothes cop came out and he also was a very Irish looking guy and, in fact, he was Irish and he asked what we were talking about and the desk sergeant told him it was an accident and gave him the whole description we had given and he started to really get on us. This plain clothes cop, he started saying, "Ahaaaa you 'guineas'... a black guy... sure... if he would have stopped... I don't blame him for not stopping, if he would have stopped you probably beat him up" and he just went on and on like that and as I said it was funny because my friend was Irish and he was calling us "guineas." We left, it was kind of upsetting, but we left anyway.

Well, about two months later, I had my car parked right in front of what was arguably a restaurant. It really wasn't, it was a front for where this boss used to hold court. I never saw anybody eat anything in there, but in any case the doors were open, and there was a front room—it had been originally a grocery store, luncheonette and they had a kind of room where you could sit and eat your sandwich in the back and that is where the boss would sit. So as I crossed the street to get into my car I looked in. Sitting at the table with him was the same cop, the plain clothes cop who had given us all the problems, my friend and I.

Anyway, I became agitated and the boss came out and he said, "Hey kid, what's the matter, what's up?" So I told him the story, which was a big mistake as it turns out. He said, "Are you sure that's the guy?" I said "Yea, I am sure it's him." "That son of a bitch," he said "I got him in my pocket, come in, I want you to tell him the story," and I thought, "Oh boy, what did I get myself into." Anyway I went into the restaurant in the back; of course the cop did not recognize me, so the boss says to me, "Tell him the story." So now I start telling him the story and this cop gets white, he is just getting absolutely white, and he now starts saying, "Oh, I didn't know, but if I had known, blah, blah, blah."

Well the boss starts cursing at him and calling him all kinds of names and then turns to me and he says, "Hit him" and I looked at him and he said, "Hit him, he won't do anything, do anything you want to him." He said, "Hit him, kick him, punch him, the son of a bitch." he said, "You m……." while he kept cursing. I said, "Really, it's OK, you know I don't want to do that, please, you know," and he kept on with that, "Go ahead, go ahead slap him in the face, anything you want to do him." The poor guy was pleading. I thought, "God knows what he was going to do." Anyway I got out of there without ever having to hit the cop and you know, I don't know what happened after that, but that was one of the stories that I remember very well.

MARTY: A REFLECTION

By Richard J. Rinaldo

AS A YOUTH, MARTIN SCORSESE lived on Elizabeth Street between Prince and Houston Streets. He hung out with a lot of us from the neighborhood, and his best friend was Joe Morale, whose short anecdote about Marty appears below. Marty's mother and father, Catherine and Charlie, (rest their souls) were like aunts and uncles to all his friends, and fondly remembered by all. As an asthmatic,  Marty could not play sports, and in an interview noted some regret at not experiencing that part of growing up in the neighborhood. So he went to the movies a lot, and made film aficionados of many of us, whom he influenced by his great passion and love of the art, especially during our college days when he studied cinema at New York University. We frequented such film haunts  as the Bleecker Street Cinema in Greenwich Village and the New Yorker uptown on the West Side, where we watched such classics as D.W. Griffith's *Intolerance,* Eisenstein's *Potemkin,* and Bergman's *The Seventh Seal,* as well as a host of Italian neorealist and French New Wave genres, too numerous to list. We also loved John  Ford and John Wayne as did Marty, and most still do. We learned about dissolves and montages and how actors said "rhubarb" at the same time in order to sound like a crowd. Many of us appeared in his student films, and his breakthrough hit, *Mean Streets,* was based on some neighborhood tales.

Father Frank Principe, our young parish priest discussed elsewhere in this book, was a major influence on all of us, especially Marty, who at one time felt a vocation for the priesthood. Father Principe often reflected on the earthy, incarnational quality of the Italian view of Catholicism and Christ's humanity as the Son of God who came on earth as a man to redeem us. This was also a theme in Marty's film, *The Last Temptation of Christ*, one that did not endear him to those who viewed Jesus in plastic images of purity and Anglo-Saxon appearance and dignity. It was, after all, a story that included a Passion.

Marty has been criticized for his depiction of the neighborhood in *Mean Streets*. There is also a dubious tale that he was banned from the neighborhood for making that film. Actually, in 2001 Marty returned to do a short film titled, *The Neighborhood* following 9-11 as a segment for *The Concert for New York*.

In some of his other films, Marty showed a side of Italians and Italian-Americans that some people would rather ignore, but those of us who grew up in little Italy know these things to be true. At the same time in *The Departed* and *Gangs of New York* he showed that organized crime in the United States was not limited to Italian-American enterprises. Its entrails, in fact, can be read in ancient history thousands of years ago in examples of banditry, extortion, and criminal-like states. (See Hopwood, Keith Ed., *Organised Crime in Antiquity*, (London: Gerald Duckworh and Co, ltd). 1999).

Marty's 1974 documentary "Italianamerican" is telling in its title. He once said that he deliberately chose it to get rid of the hyphenated American label. Accordingly, as most artists do, Marty is kind of a poster boy for the ambivalence of many Americas of Italian descent in regard to their backgrounds of marginality in the immigrant community and their desire to retain their ethnicity at the same time as they embrace the main stream of American life. Today, many us would not object to be called Italian-American, but might also say that we are Americans of Italian descent. In a 2008 public service announcement for the NIAF, Marty said, "I am an Italian-American , and I'm proud of it," and with his great smile and laugh, "I'll give you a second take, I'm a Sicilian American, and I'm proud of it."

Sociologist Richard Gambino, in *Blood of My Blood*, (1974) addressed the ambivalence, citing the so-called miracle of Roseto, a small Italian immigrant town in Pennsylvania where researchers in the 1960's found unusual cardiac health and longevity. The inhabitants patterned their lifestyles after those of the small town in Italy where most of them or their ancestors came from. It is also the opening story in Malcolm Gladwell's *Outliers: the Story of Success* (2008). Both Gladwell and Gambino point out that the secret of such longevity lies in the inhabitants' adherence to Old World life patterns. Among them, Gambino tells us, were "…a unique and strong family, work, pragmatism, pazienza, serietà, humanistic life orientation, and a Realpolitic stance toward authority and power." Gambino points out too that in 1973 the town's heart attack rate soared. The reason, some surmised, was that Rosetans became "Americanized" (see "Living Longer in Little Italy").

The prescription to avoid such results, Gambino suggests, is for Italian-Americans to use those Old World life patterns to fashion a creative ethnicity to help America stay in touch with human values. In the final paragraph of his book, he cites Professor Robert Pietro, who "is fond of pointing out, Americans typically say a person is 'good as gold. The standard Italian expression has a fundamentally different, more humanistic meaning. In Italian a person is said to be *buono come il pane*—As good as *bread*." Marty has proven that he is such.

In an interview, Marty admitted that he felt "not as smart" as many of his friends who went to Fordham College. We did not ask him for his favorite saying, but it could be, "He who laughs last, laughs best." His family traces its forbears to Sicily. We think his favorite expression might be, "Action."

Tom Aiello and Joe Morale add these short vignettes about Marty:

Tom:

> Marty of course grew up with us. And we spent a lot of time at his apartment on Elizabeth St. It was one of those buildings that had the four garbage cans in front. That's how I knew where to go and one of the chores we all always had was to bring down the garbage. Our lives revolved around St. Patrick's Old Cathedral. One of the jobs we had was going up there because Marty's mother Catherine (rest her soul) was a very devout Catholic. And Marty had a very difficult time getting up in the morning.

So we would go up there to get him up and take him to church. He suffered from asthma or allergies and he spent at least a half hour in the morning sneezing.

Joe:

From the earliest times, Marty exhibited some artistic qualities. When we were very young he would make his homemade movies on paper. They were usually about the Roman army fighting in Britain and the Roman army always won! So he had that pride in some of our ancestors from Italy. For sure, he was always interested in what he is doing now. He would go page by page and when he flipped them the soldiers were moving. It took a lot of time for him to do what he did then. He had it in his blood when he was young. Yes, I was in some of his student films, in which two of us were detectives and a few other guys were burglars. And we would go up to the country to a camp in Columbia County, in Copake when it was closed and we had the place to ourselves. There was a lake for swimming and canoeing. And I remember the film we made there, which was kind of a war movie. There was a fellow in a business suit, which was kind of out of place, and he was executed, but we didn't use live ammunition, so he is still around putting this book together.

LIVING LONGER IN LITTLE ITALY

By Richard J. Rinaldo

MY SON BRIAN GAVE ME A BOOK FOR CHRISTMAS—*Outliers*, by Malcolm Gladwell, a staff writer for *The New Yorker* and bestselling author of the *Tipping Point* and *Blink*. Gladwell begins the book with a discussion of Italian immigrants from the town of Roseto Valfortore, in Foggia, who built a new Roseto in Pennsylvania. Most came to America around the same times as our grandparents, near the turn of the 20th century. Gladwell relates how a doctor found that the people of this new Roseto had a health profile, which was way beyond the norm of folks in the rest of the nation.

This Doctor Wolf and a team of sociologists and medical students did a study of the residents in the late 1950s. According to Gladwell, "The results were astonishing. In Roseto, virtually no one under 55 died of a heart attack, or showed any signs of heart disease. The death rate from all causes in Roseto, in fact, was something like thirty or thirty-five percent lower than it should have been."

Moreover, according a member of the study team, "There was no suicide, no alcoholism, no drug addiction, and very little crime. They didn't have anyone on welfare. Then we looked at peptic ulcers. They didn't have any of those either. These people were dying of old age. That's it."

Roseto was, according to Gladwell, "a place that lay outside every-day experience, where the normal rules did not apply. Roseto was an out-lier." Why? Well, they looked and found it was not diet, exercise, genes, or even the climate of Roseto. Instead, it was because of the place they created for themselves in America.

Gladwell provides more details of the study—"how the Rosetans visited each other, stopping to chat with each other in Italian on the street, or cooking for each other in their backyards....about the extended family clans that underlay the town's social structure.... how much respect grandparents commanded." The researchers also found that "they went to Mass at Our Lady of Mt. Carmel Church and saw the unifying and calming effect of the church."

Gladwell sums it up: "In transplanting the paesani culture of southern Italy to the hills of eastern Pennsylvania, the Rosetans had created a powerful, protective social structure capable of insulating them from the pressures of the modern world. The Rosetans were healthy because of where they were from, because of the world they had created for themselves in their tiny little town in the hills."

Now I have no precise idea about what such a study might have discovered about our Little Italy of the 1950s and 1960s, but we all know that it shared many of the characteristics of Roseto. Our neighborhood was, to say the least, a special place. For example, we all remember the support that our church enjoyed in those days from parishioners despite the fact that their parents or grandparents might have been denied entrance to the upper level of the church in earlier days. We all have seen the stained glass windows donated by the Guidetti's, the Viglietti's and others who comprise our list of contributors.

We all used the Youth Center, built from donations of our parents and grandparents. We remember the Holy Name Society, whose members were our family members and neighbors. We remember, too, the extended family of our neighborhood—friends or parents of friends who were and are like our very own relatives. I was looking through a suitcase of records I kept from my father, among them a list of folks who came to my mother's wake, some 17 pages from one of those long yellow pads. In death as in life, the neighborhood was there.

Incidentally the June 3, 2012 celebration of the Bicentennial of the Basilica of St. Patrick's Old Cathedral included a special recognition of longtime resident Ann Messina, one of our nonagenarians.

I am an Italian-American

by Angelo R. Bianchi

My roots are deep in an ancient soil, drenched by the Mediterranean sun, and watered by pure streams from snow-capped mountains.

I am enriched by thousands of years of culture.

My hands are those of the mason, the artist, the man of the soil.

My thoughts have been recounted in the annals of Rome, the poetry of Virgil, the creations of Dante, and the philosophy of Benedetto Croce.

I am an Italian-American, and from my ancient world, I first spanned the seas to the New World. I am Cristoforo Colombo.

I am Giovanne Caboto, known in American History as John Cabot, discoverer of the mainland of North America. I am Amerigo Vespucci, who gave my name to the New World, America.

First to sail on the Great Lakes in 1679, founder of the territory that became the State of Illinois, colonizer of Louisiana and Arkansas, I am Enrico Tonti.

I am Filippo Mazzei, friend of Thomas Jefferson, and my thesis on the equality of man was written into the Bill of Rights.

I am William Paca, signer of the Declaration of Independence.

I am an Italian-American; I financed the Northwest Expedition of George Rogers Clark and accompanied him through the lands that would become Ohio, Indiana, Wisconsin, and Michigan. I am Colonel Francesco Vigo.

I mapped the Pacific from Mexico to Alaska and to the Philippines, I am Alessandro Malaspina.

I am Giacomo Belinimi, discoverer of the source of the Mississippi River in 1823.

I created the Dome of the United States Capitol. They call me the Michelangelo of America. I am Constantino Brumidi.

In 1904, I founded in San Francisco, the Bank of Italy now known as the Bank of America, the largest financial institution in the world. I am A.P. Giannini.

I am Enrico Fermi, father of nuclear science in America.

I am Steve Geppi, founder of Diamond Comics, the largest distributorship of comics on the planet.

I am the first enlisted man to earn the Medal of Honor in World War II; I am John Basilone of New Jersey.

I am an Italian-American.

I am the million strong who served in America's armies and the tens of thousands whose names are enshrined in military cemeteries from Guadalcanal to the Rhine.

I am the steel maker in Pittsburgh, the grower in the Imperial Valley of California, the textile designer in Manhattan, the moviemaker in Hollywood, the homemaker and the breadwinner in over 10,000 communities.

I am an American without stint or reservation, loving this land as only one who understands history, its agonies and its triumphs, can love and serve it.

I will not be told that my contribution is any less nor my role not as worthy as that of any other American.

I will stand in support of this nation's freedom and protect against all foes.

My heritage has dedicated me to this nation. I am proud of my heritage, and I shall remain worthy of it.

I am an Italian-American.

 Angelo R. Bianchi, Esq., was born in the City of Newark; was married to the late Dorothy Pilone; and has two children: Jean Ann and Robert. He is the son of the late Anthony R. Bianchi and Jean Santoro; and grandson of the late Angelo R. Bianchi, M.D., who was made Cavaliere della Corona d'Italia on April 18, 1932, and Professor Alfonso Santoro, who was made Cavaliere della Corona d'Italia on March 23, 1911. He graduated from St. Vincent's Academy, Seton Hall Preparatory School, Seton Hall University, and Seton Hall School of Law. He is the founder of the Law Offices of Angelo R. Bianchi, LLC, in Bloomfield, New Jersey; former Banking Commissioner of the State of New Jersey; and the author of "I Am an Italian-American."

PART 2

THE NEIGHBORHOOD

Passport Please!

By Richard J. Rinaldo

IN A TELEPHONE CONVERSATION, J.J. ANSELMO reminded me that when you ran into someone from the neighborhood from the time you lived there that you really did not know well, you had to prove your identity. Yes, you had to have kind of a passport, just like a nation. It was a memory passport or you would not be granted true admittance. So you had to know a lot about the neighborhood. You had to know some of the neighborhood characters, for example. Did you know Mikey Broke the Drum, Calabrese, Garlick (yes, that was a nickname too)? Did you know Allie Cat? Bull Ryan, Joe Slugger, Casey?

If you claimed to participate in sports, you had to know all about stickball, the Youth Center, Play Street, James Center, Jersey Alley, the tower and the Puck Building. You had to know how much a spaldeen ball cost in 1960. Do you remember how to climb the wall into the graveyard of St. Patrick's Old Cathedral? (More on these later.)

Did you ever drink a Manhattan Special? An egg cream? What were its ingredients? You had to have an opinion about the feast. The current residents, who would like to see it ended, would find support from some who lived there in the past, who hated the crowds, the garbage, the smell, and the noise. Was a calzone baked or cooked in hot oil? Guys might need to know how to build a scooter from the old-style roller skates, a 2 X 4, and an orange or milk crate. How did you play "skelsie?" Where was Jone's Diner?

You might get by with some more generic information if you lived more than a few blocks from one another. With the old spirit of *campanilsmo* (from the Italian word for bell), you only wandered as far as you could hear your church bell. But, as time went by, that idea evolved. You might hang out in different places and with others whose heritage was from different places in Italy. So you could get a pass on some things you did not know. Of course, there remained some residual prejudices and stereotypes and ribbing, the hard–headed Calabrese, for example. But, for the most part the neighborhood was still a big Italian village.

Hopefully, this section of the book captures more of the color and character of the neighborhood.

HISTORY

By Emelise Aleandri

The following is a "Short History of the Neighborhood" provided courtesy of the author Dr. Emelise Aleandri and Arcadia Publishing. It comes from the Introduction to her book, Images of America: Little Italy *(2002). The book has recently been printed by Arcadia in Italian under the title* La Piccola Italia. *Arcadia has also published Dr. Aleandri's* The Italian-American Immigrant Theatre of New York City *(1999). All of the books are available from the publisher online at www.arcadiapublishing.com.*

IN NEW YORK CITY, LITTLE ITALY, "La Piccola Italia," is now, and always has been, a state of mind much more than just a geographical location. The Italians and the East European Jews who arrived after the 1880's, tended to live in ghettos much more than the immigrant groups who had preceded them earlier in the century, partially because of language. The late 19th Century Italians thought of themselves collectively as an Italian colony, "La Colonia." The colony included the Italians of all five boroughs where many "Little Italies" eventually emerged (i.e., Arthur Avenue in the Bronx, South Brooklyn and Bensonhurst), and even towns in nearby New Jersey that had frequent and daily contact with the Italians of the city. Manhattan's Italian neighborhoods were localized but spread out all over the island: Italian East Harlem; West Greenwich Village and what is now Soho; the pocket in the vicinity of West 110th Street and Amsterdam Avenue; East Greenwich Village, and of course, *the* Little Italy, the downtown area of the Lower East Side, straddling Canal Street, east and west. Today, it is this neighborhood that common parlance identifies as Manhattan's Little Italy, and which is the subject of this book's pictorial presentation.

At the center of what became Little Italy there was originally a 135 acre farm owned for most of the 18th century by the Holland-born French Huguenot Nicholas Bayard and his family. Their homestead was situated on a hill just above what is today the intersection of Hester and

Mott Streets, and overlooked the sylvan setting of the Collect (from the Dutch "Kalchhook") fresh water pond, a five acre lake just to the west. As the city expanded, the region surrounding the lake became occupied by pottery works, tanneries, tobacco merchants, rope works, slaughterhouses and Coulthardt's Brewery (which in a few decades would become a noxious five-story tenement slum turned mission house). The industries polluted the Collect and the Common Council had the pond filled with soil, from the years 1802 to 1817, by leveling Bunker Hill, just north of what is now Grand Street between Mott Street and Broadway. The year 1817 saw the extension eastward of Anthony Street (now Worth Street) to meet Orange Street (now Baxter Street) and Cross Street (formerly Park, now Mosco Street), thus forming the five-spoke intersection known as the Five Points, an eventually notorious name which came to refer to the entire surrounding neighborhood, also described as the "Bloody Ould Sixth Ward." Its loose boundaries were Canal Street, Broadway, and points east of Chatham Street (later Park Row) and the Bowery to the East River – in other words, a large portion of the future Little Italy.

The Collect business owners, among them the Lorillards, the Schermerhorns, the Ashdors (later known as the Astors) kept their land and went into real estate, building two-story wooden houses that served as both living and working space for an artisan class that would soon become obsolete as industrial mass production took hold. The land, essentially a filled in swamp, was unsteady, flooding in rain, disturbing building foundations and festering disease, no longer the location of choice for the upper class. 25% of Five Points residents were unskilled immigrants by 1825, and 15% were African-Americans (living mainly on Little Water Street). The 1830's, 40's and 50's saw increased immigration to the city, among them first Germans, then the Irish Catholics, all of whom needed inexpensive lodging near their work. They gravitated toward the Five Points. To accommodate them, cheap crowded tenement houses replaced the frame houses, as the more prosperous residents of earlier days moved up and out, leaving the neighborhood to the poor. The vicinity became rife with saloons, brothels, basement lodging houses, gambling dens, abandoned children, cholera epidemics, thieves, drunks, the unemployed, pickpockets and street walkers.

By 1855, only 28% of the residents were native born Americans, and 3% were Italian born, living mainly on Anthony and Orange Streets. In the early part of the 19th century, a number of Northern Italian political and religious refugees, among them Lorenzo Da Ponte and Giuseppe Garibaldi, emigrated to New York City but for the most part lived on the borders of the Five Points, while many of the poorer early Italian immigrants lived within. As immigration increased, former immigrant groups that had become more established moved on. By 1870, the U.S. Census counted 2,790 Italians already in residence in New York City. The Italian newspaper *L'Eco d'Italia* dubbed the Five Points "Le Boulevard des Italiens." In the 1870's a trickle began that would become the Italian and Eastern European Jewish mass migration of the next 50 years, completely changing the sounds, sights and character of the entire Lower East Side. By 1890, 52% of New York's Italians inhabited what was now a thoroughly entrenched "Little Italy." The 1900 census showed that over 225,000 Italians lived within New York City's boundaries alone. That was at the time greater than the population of Rome.

Throughout the first quarter of the 20th century, immigration statistics reveal a steady flow of new immigrant arrivals. But the immigration quota laws of 1924 restricted the annual importation of new Italian immigrants into the United States and the neighborhood gradually began to see the effects of the restrictive quotas. Furthermore, as the second and third generations of Italian-Americans became acculturated, they moved to "the country," in sufficient numbers to form little Italian enclaves, i.e. Staten Island, Bensonhurst Brooklyn, the "farms" in the Bronx and Queens; as well as New Jersey, Long Island and Westchester. Today, Little Italy, "La Piccola Italia," is more *piccola* than ever. What remains Italian is primarily the full length of Mulberry Street between Canal Street and Houston Street, and the streets either side of the intersections at Hester, Grand, Broome, Spring and Prince Streets. The majority of the rest of the neighborhood has accommodated the new Chinese and Asian immigration, thus continuing the practice the area has followed for the last two centuries.

 Further information about Dr. Aleandri:
Dr. Emelise Aleandri, a native of Riva Del Garda, Italy, is a producer, director, writer, actress, and singer. She is Artistic Director of Frizzi & Lazzi, the Olde Time Italian-American Music and Theater Company and winner of the Elena Cornaro and CSJ Awards from the New York State Grand Lodge Order Sons

of Italy in America for her work in Italian-American culture. She performs both traditional and contemporary Italian and Italian-American music and theatre in both Italian and English. A TV and film actress, she starred in the title role of the new film, *Sister Italy*, and was featured in the recently released *Vito Bonafacci*, the Spike Lee films *Crooklyn* and *Summer of Sam*. She also starred as the famous 19th century Italian actress, Eleonora Duse opposite Lilianne Montevecchi in *Of Penguins and Peacocks*. She performed in the Walnut Street Theatre production of *Italian Funerals and other Festive Occasions* and in the Off-Broadway productions of *Sweatshop* and *SHHHHH!* For ten years she was the Producer/Host of *Italics: The Italian-American Magazine*, a nationally-aired cable TV show she created. She has produced two documentaries for television: *Teatro: The Legacy of Italian-American Theatre, Festa: Italian Festival Traditions* and *Circo Rois*. She scripted and produced the children's musical, *The Legend of La Befana*, and the Edwin Mellen Press has published her multi-volume encyclopedic history, *The Italian-American Immigrant Theatre of New York City: 1746-1899*. Learn more about Emelise and the theatre at http://www.frizzilazzi.com/index.htm.

LITTLE ITALY 1980

The following article from Attenzione, *September 1980, is provided courtesy of its publisher, the late* Jeno Paulucci, *and its author* Anthony Mancini. *The article provides a good look at and great discussion of the neighborhood as it existed in 1980 with many aspects of the tectonic shifts in its population, appearance, and character that would come to fruition later. It was, nevertheless, pretty much the Little Italy we knew and many of us will recognize the people and places in the article, like our beloved Anna Sceusa, Sal the Barber, and others, bless their souls. The article was skillfully written by Professor Mancini, director of the journalism program of Brooklyn College. Professor Mancini is a seasoned educator and versatile professional writer of both fiction and non-fiction works. Mancini spent his early career as a reporter and editor for 20 years at the* New York Post, *mostly pre–Rupert Murdoch. He started as a copy boy at age 19. He has contributed free-lance articles to many national and local newspapers and magazines. Mancini also is the author of seven novels appearing in trade hardcover and paperback editions, many of which have been reprinted in foreign lands, including Japan, Finland, Romania, Spain, France, Germany, Holland and other countries. His first novel,*  Minnie Santangelo's Mortal Sin, *published in 1975, was a Reader's Digest condensed book selection. Another novel, Talons (1991) was a Literary Guild selection. His novel* Menage *was reissued in September, 2011, by Tolmitch Press on Kindle. Mancini, a native New Yorker, was born an identical twin to Italian immigrants and is a Fordham College graduate. He is married to actress Maria Cellario. They live in Manhattan and have two grown children, Romy and Nicholas. Why does he write? Because it is a curse, addiction and compulsion. And, once in a while, a pure joy.*

LITTLE ITALY NOW: NE

The city's oldest Italian settlement still represents the human core of the Big Apple. But there are also some fears that the community contains the seeds of its own destruction.

BY ANTHONY MANCINI

They call the area around Mulberry and Grand Streets "the neighborhood," and in the geography of the Italian-American heart, this section of Lower Manhattan holds a firm place as the prototype of all the Little Italys that are peppered across the country. It is where our grandparents first arrived when they emigrated from Campania, Basilicata, Sicily, Calabria, or the Abruzzo. It is where our grandfathers, indebted to the *padroni*, went to work in factories making machine parts, where our grandmothers did piecework in their fifth-floor walk-ups and cooked pasta and chick peas on cast-iron stoves, and where our aunts sewed sleeves in the sweatshops of Eldridge Street and our uncles played clarinet in the Bowery Band.

The oldest Italian settlement in New York is a rectangle of about 125 acres just north of City Hall. Roughly, it is bounded by Canal Street on the south, Bleecker Street on the north, Lafayette Street on the west, and the Bowery on the east. Italians, as Carlo Levi once observed, are sensitive to the pang of separation. This may explain why Manhattan's Little Italy, though besieged by the Saracens of social change and no longer the Italians' portal to America, endures.

John Fratta was born 27 years ago in a cold-water flat on Baxter Street. Today he lives only a few blocks away, on Mulberry. And he won't budge. "My wife wanted us to move," he says, sitting behind his desk in the wood-paneled clubhouse of the local Democratic club, where he is a district leader. "But I told her when we got married, 'I was born here and I'm gonna stay here.' It's crazy, this love for the area, when there are so many better-looking places to live. But there's something about it that makes you never want to leave."

The tenacity of Fratta and others like him makes today's Little Italy more than just a quaint collection of bocce courts and restaurants, more than just a stage set for the annual Festa di San Gennaro. (The patron saint of Naples, though toppled by the Vatican, still reigns on Baxter Street, where the Church of the Most Precious Blood maintains a "national shrine" to him.) These people make it a real community. "We're staying," says native Anna Sceusa of the Neighborhood Council to Combat Poverty. "We're like the Rock of Gibraltar, we are. What am I gonna do—twiddle my thumbs in Staten Island? No, I'm staying here to see the finale."

NEIGHBORHOOD NEWCOMERS

Such references to the area's imminent demise recur often in conversation, because like many communities in New York, this one is beset by the usual urban problems: an aging population, penury, and decayed housing. Almost everyone lives in the original old-law tenements, five-story walk-ups with toilets in the hallways and bathtubs in the kitchens. The last census put the median income at $7,000 and the population at 15,112. Of this number, about 60 percent are Italian, and 5 percent are Hispanic and black. The rest are Chinese.

"The patron saint of this neighborhood," says one resident, "should be Marco Polo." It is a common lament among the Italians. Landlords from Chinatown, whose northern boundary was once defined by Canal Street, have long been buying buildings in Little Italy and renting apartments to their

54

W YORK

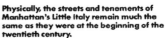

Physically, the streets and tenements of Manhattan's Little Italy remain much the same as they were at the beginning of the twentieth century.

compatriots. When old-time Italian residents describe the process, they make no effort to hide their resentment and distrust. "The Chinese buy on the spot," says one resident melodramatically, "with satchels full of opium money."

Affluent newcomers from the nearby lofts of SoHo have also made inroads. They are drawn to Little Italy by the celebrated safety of the streets and the redolence of the shops. They have renovated neighborhood warehouses and townhouses, thereby driving up the rents. "But these people also reinforce the ethnicity of the neighborhood," insists Annamaria Lepore of Ferrara Foods and Confections, an Italian bakery, liquor store, and nationwide wholesaler of Italian foods. "They're very pro-Italian—they're looking to speak Italian, they want to go to the greengrocer's. Many of them have a more direct, intellectual interest in Italian culture than people from the neighborhood."

Meanwhile, the locals have been doing their part to spruce up the streets. The vaunted *risorgimento* began six years ago with the founding of the Little Italy Restoration Association (LIRA) and the opening of a crop of restaurants and cafés. The decor was done by Florentine architect Antonio Morello. Preening recently on Mulberry Street, Morello boasted, "I made Little Italy what it is today."

The *risorgimento* has sparked tourism on Mulberry Street, which sports fresh coats of paint, sidewalk cafés, potted trees, and elegant and pricey restaurants like Il Cortile and S.P.Q.R. Old-timers regard all the

changes with both pride and cynicism.

"*Madonna,*" exclaims Anna Capparella of LIRA, "look at the crowds who come here on the weekends. We put Little Italy back on the map."

"*Beh,*" replies Anna Sceusa, "the money they make here doesn't help the neighborhood at all. Look around you. What do you see? Do we live glamorous? The money goes out to Scarsdale and Massapequa, where the restaurant owners live."

Restaurant owners like Ferrara's Lepore insist that much of the money stays in Little Italy. "Take a look at what we're doing, for example, at Ferrara. We've been putting exorbitant sums of money into Grand Street to restore and refurbish. I know that's true of a number of other restaurateurs—they're putting the money into their buildings."

Despite the improvements, life in the neighborhood still means hardship for many. Teenagers drop out of school. Young married couples, lacking adequate housing, move to the suburbs. And the elderly are still climbing five flights, clutching their bundles, to dilapidated apartments which are

often without heat in the winter. "It breaks your heart," says Assemblyman Paul Viggiano. "I remember this winter visiting some old people huddled in a storefront, trying to keep warm by the candles of the saints."

"Some of these apartments," says Anna Sceusa, "are worse than the caves of Matera. They're older than Balboa. But you should see how the hippies are buying them up."

Delivering food stamps and other government benefits to the neighborhood's residents is often difficult, because the government doesn't target Italian areas for poverty

A pet project of community organizers is the conversion of the old Centre Street police headquarters (top) into an Italian-American cultural center.

programs and because the residents themselves shrink from accepting handouts. "They won't take what they're entitled to," says Fratta with a shrug. "They think it's charity."

Another common urban problem—one that haunts many other neighborhoods, but was unthinkable until lately in Little Italy—has reared its head: street mugging. In one

recent incident, an old woman was mugged on her way home from the bank to her apartment building on Prince and Elizabeth streets. "Now you're taking our last reason for living here away from us," said Fratta, who immediately raised the matter with the local police captain. Action was swift: The anticrime unit was enlisted, and within a few days the mugger was arrested.

Despite such isolated cases, the neighborhood remains one of the safest in the city thanks to what the local sociologists call "the value system." "There's still no fear here," says LIRA's Anna Capparella, whom some locals have dubbed the "Mayor of Mulberry Street." "You can walk home from a bingo game in the Fourth Ward to Prince Street and be nonchalant about it. Everybody knows each other, everybody helps each other. The doors are open in the hallways. On a dark night, if you drop your pocketbook in the street, people watching from their windows come to help you pick it up."

THE RETURNING SUBURBANITES

Capparella, a native of Mott Street who now lives on Mulberry, is openly scornful of those who move away. "They want the backyard, the swimming pool. They say, 'I don't want to raise my kids on the street.' So they move out. But they find when they get to Westchester or Long Island that they've lost the value system. Neighbors don't make a neighborhood. And they leave something behind that gives them an excuse to come back—they leave the old folks."

These emigrants from the urban village to the New World of suburbia have another excuse to make the trip back to the city at least once a year: the Feast of San Gennaro. Even as they fill their stomachs with sausage-and-pepper heroes and hum to the strains of wandering accordion bands, they take the opportunity to lord it over the ones who stayed behind. And that makes the local residents' blood boil.

"When they say, 'How can you stay in this neighborhood?'," says Capparella with fire in her eyes, "I wanna kill."

John Fratta is equally emphatic. "I tell them, 'You rat bastard, how can you say that? You grew up in this neighborhood. To criticize it is worse than changing your name.'"

Life in Little Italy still mirrors life in the *paesi* and *quartieri* left behind a generation or two ago in the Mezzogiorno. Certain streets are inhabited entirely by people from the same regions, or even the same towns, of Italy: The Sicilians occupy Elizabeth Street, the Neapolitans Mulberry Street, the Baresi and Abruzzesi share Mott Street, and the Northern Italians Baxter Street, according to an informal poll of local historians. The pantheon of neighborhood saints is as

crowded as the sidewalks in summer: San Gennaro, San Antonio, San Cataldo, San Donato, San Francesco di Paola, and the Virgin in all her incarnations, to name but a few. The most famous processions are those in honor of San Gennaro and San Antonio, but some dimmer lights of the firmament, such as San Calogero the Hermit of Sciacca, have also bobbed down the narrow streets followed by proud, kerchiefed women with tear-stained cheeks.

In warm weather, life spills like sparkling wine into the streets. The men visit

DeSantis Meats is one of the neighborhood's many family operations.

"members only" social clubs—male enclaves with names like "The In Crowd" or "The Andrea Doria Association"—all uniformly outfitted with espresso machines and imitation wood paneling. There they play cards or watch a ball game on television. The women gossip in sidewalk cafés, butcher shops, and bakeries, and around fruit stands. Teenagers gather on street corners or in littered Columbus Park. And everywhere there is the sound of voices booming, because, as novelist Pietro Di Donato observed, "It is Italian to expound, to not agree."

Grand Street in the summertime is an old-fashioned tintype of promenading humanity. Serenaded by the voices of Carlo Buti or Massimo Ranieri from the loudspeakers of the record shops, natty men in sunglasses walk arm-in-arm, florid tourists buy lemon ices at Ferrara's, and chauffeured limos park in front of favorite restaurants like Benito's or, farther north, Lombardi's, where Enrico Caruso once consumed epic

portions of pasta. Storefront windows are adorned with posters plugging movies such as *Eboli* or exhorting golden glover Michael Trapani to victory. All around there are portraits of neighborhood heroes—a gallery which includes Frank Sinatra and Pope John Paul II, Mario Cuomo and Benito Mussolini, Dean Martin and Mother Cabrini.

North of Kenmare Street, however, the "piazza atmosphere" fades and the neighborhood looks dingier.

"The houses," wrote Viola Roseboro in *Cosmopolitan* as far back as 1888, "are chiefly tumble-down old rookeries not originally built as tenements, and are therefore worse than the worst of those constructed for the purpose. Ancient one-story stables have been converted into cheap shops and drinking places and everywhere steps lead down from the sidewalk to various low dives in the cellars...."

Five years after Roseboro penned that description, the city began demolition of Mulberry Street, but the area remained blighted until 1895, when the Board of Health condemned it. After the old-law tenements were built through the efforts of reformers like Jacob Riis, conditions improved somewhat. But by 1910 the area was again overcrowded, and not a brick of new housing has been put up since.

CITY HALL SUBSIDIES

A gaping symbol of the neighborhood's long quest for residential development is the littered lot on Spring Street between Mott and Elizabeth—the so-called P.S. 21 site. Since 1975 LIRA has been trying to get city approval for a subsidized apartment project of 159 units on the location. But the plan has been haunted by bureaucratic delays and budget cuts.

"How come," asks Anna Sceusa, "the city always runs out of money when it comes to this neighborhood?"

"The people are naturally skeptical," observes Monsignor Nicola Marinacci, pastor of the original St. Patrick's Cathedral, built in 1909. "And a little bit rebellious. Now for seventy-five years there has been no kind of new building here. They envy Confucius Plaza [a nearby Chinese-American highrise]."

LIRA president Oscar Ianello, owner of Umberto's Clam House, sees an end in sight. He points out that the commitment drawings are already on the boards with plans to begin work by late summer. Ianello, hopes the project will prompt neighborhood landlords to renovate existing apartment buildings and attract Italian families back from the suburbs. "With the gas situation, the subway situation, and the economic situation, the old neighborhood looks better and better."

Although the tenant selection procedure for the project has not yet been formulated, state and federal housing authorities have set a 73 percent quota of Italian Americans, with priority going to present residents of Little Italy now in substandard housing. Competition for the apartments is expected to be keen.

Another pet project of LIRA was the proposed conversion of the beautiful old Police Headquarters on Centre Street into an Italian-American Cultural Center, for which the community got a $20,000 grant

from the National Endowment for the Arts to conduct a feasibility study. The project committee was studded with the names of prominent New Yorkers, including Jackie Onassis and sculptor Louise Nevelson, a longtime Little Italy resident known affectionately to many as "Donna Luisa."

The building was also coveted by neighborhood real estate developers, who saw its potential as luxury housing or office space. Last March, after LIRA failed to raise enough money for the cultural center, the city took back the lease to the baroque landmark. But

a compromise was struck between the community and the Board of Estimate, which promised to require any developer to reserve a portion of the building's 100,000 square feet of space for use as a cultural center. What portion? Ianello says that LIRA would accept "no less than fifty percent," but other neighborhood leaders regard the Board's promise as a token gesture to appease the community.

The neighborhood's lack of success in getting a fair slice of government aid is complicated by internal strife. "Put two

In warm weather, the community's European flavor becomes more pronounced, as life moves outdoors and fruit vendors take to the streets.

Italians in a room and they'll argue about a glass of water," comments Anna Capparella. "Is it half-full or half-empty?"

Such problems are compounded by widespread political apathy. When John Fratta, a popular and energetic local boy, first ran for a seat on the Democratic state committee, he managed to win with only 350 votes from the 3,000 registered party members in Little Italy. When he ran for district leader a year later, he got 750 votes. Fratta helped depose former Assemblyman Louis De Salvio, an old-style politician who for many years was the leading political power in the community, esteemed for individual favors to constituents, but with little influence with city and state power brokers.

Monsignor Marinacci, for one, thinks that the community's problems—in fact, the problems of Italian Americans nationally—stem from a failure to produce political leaders of any real stature. "It's part of our

blood," the dour clergyman says, standing in an anteroom of the rectory overlooking north Mulberry Street. "Look at the national scene—whom do we have to look up to?" Like many local residents, Marinacci, who came to Little Italy from the Abruzzo ten years ago, takes a fatalistic view. "You cannot change things," he says. "You have to be resigned and take it all in your stride."

But the community can point to one success story—the recent opening of a new senior citizens' center in a five-story renovated factory at 180 Mott Street. It took LIRA no less than five years of winding through the city's bureaucratic maze to get the center's doors to open last April. The inbred skepticism of the residents was somewhat assuaged. "Ci dà speranza," said an old lady in the building lobby. "It gives us hope."

More senior citizens' centers are likely to be going up in Little Italy, if population trends are any indication. The 1970 census showed that 10.5 percent of the residents are over 65 years of age. Unofficial estimates place the current figure at over 25 percent. What is more disturbing, in 1970 only 6.5 percent of the population was under 5 years of age—and that figure is undoubtedly lower now. The flow of new immigrants from Italy has ebbed to a trickle and those who do come soon move on to greener pastures in Brooklyn or Staten Island. "These new greaseballs are very smart," comments the outspoken Anna Sceusa. "They make money quickly and move out fast."

Of the 715 students at Saint Patrick's School, only 20 percent are of Italian heritage. The playground on Spring Street is often quiet, and on almost every block stands a funeral parlor.

Yet there are those who see cause for optimism. "My two sons disliked the neighborhood," recalls Anna Capparella. "At least they said they did. They always complained there was no place to play. Now they're nineteen and twenty-one, and they want to stay."

"It has nothing to do with economics," says Assemblyman Viggiano. "The people here care. Will we wake up one morning and find that it's all gone?"

On a recent spring morning, the sun spread balm over the tenements on Hester Street. An old woman with snowy hair draped a dish towel over the sill of her second-story kitchen window to rest her elbows as she leaned out to watch the activity below. Soon a young mother appeared, with two small children in tow and another in a stroller. She greeted the older woman: "We're coming up to visit you."

The expression on the old lady's face seemed to warm the morning air, and it was hard not to be glad that Little Italy had survived to see another day. ∎

MEMORIES OF SIMPLE TIMES

By Joseph Graziano

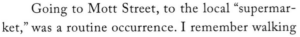

AS I THINK ABOUT GROWING UP in the neighbor-hood, I recall fond memories of a simple lifestlyle. At age five, a friend and I were given free milk at a "milk station" on Cleveland Place Park across the street from where I lived. In those days, this was a special event that made the newspapers.

Going to Mott Street, to the local "supermarket," was a routine occurrence. I remember walking with my mother or grandmother past the vendors and shops, many selling the same items. But the women had their favorites, and would only buy from them. Everything you needed was available; produce, for example. Everyone looked forward to the special fruits and vegetables when they were in season. Meats came from the many butcher shops. They advertised the daily special by hanging a lambskin or pigs head outside—that would cause quite a stir today.

The preferred place to buy a chicken, however, was the chicken market, where you picked out a plump bird and watched as its head was cut off and the feathers removed—a bigger stir, today's shopper might even faint. Many bakeries were available, Neapolitan or Sicilian style, but they didn't make cake. For cakes, jelly doughnuts, or crullers you had to go to "Moderna" on Kenmare St. or "Piccolo" on Spring St., especially on Sunday morning after Mass, to buy "buns."

There were stores selling butter and eggs, cheese, pasta, nuts, and dried fruit. And, especially on Friday, fresh fish of all kinds. Who could forget the *baccala* (cod fish) store on Spring Street, where salted cod fish lay in big sinks filled with water to soften them and remove the salt. Now if you needed housewares, dishes, etc., they were available as well at the neighborhood "Home Depot"—Benigno's, a little hardware store which seemed to stock just about anything for the home.

If this shopping trip made you hungry, there was our version of fast food....the bakery that sold a slice of Sicilian "abeets" for a nickel. I never knew anyone who said pizza.

When you were sick the doctor would make a house call, but you often just went to the druggist, described your symptoms, and he would give you a remedy. Today that might result in an arrest and lawsuit.

We also had home delivery.... not just groceries....I was a delivery boy for Joe Darconte's grocery store on Prince Street, as was our editor. But some families needed ice, kerosene, coal, and "javell" (bleach), all delivered to your door. (Fox's U Bet chocolate syrup and seltzer water for egg creams too. Ed.) Needed your knives sharpened? No problem. No one needed a car; everything was within walking distance.

I remember childhood activities, none of which involved special equipment or electronic devices....except a radio where we listened to the serial shows.

We played on the street, roller skating, stickball, stoopball, kick the can, hockey, using a spaldeen, Johnny on the pony, skellsie, pitching pennies. Sometimes we played cards...Brisk (*briscola*), Hearts, Bankers and Brokers....yes, we did play for nickels and dimes.....if we had any. I never remember being bored or deprived,

We had fun doing simple things. How about playing in the back room of Guidetti's funeral parlor? Among the coffins!

When we were old enough some of us were picked to be altar boys....a great honor. And there were perks involved; the nun's gave us special treatment. And if you were picked to assist at a wedding, you would get a "tip" from the groom. Getting up early to "serve" the 7:00 a.m. Mass was not a plus, however. As I recall, there are a few memorable stories; we got to sample the sacramental wine....Muscatel, I think. It wasn't very appealing.

Louis Frezza, a friend who died very young, managed to set his eyeglass frames on fire when he held a candle too close.....fortunately no serious injury. And then there was the morning that I was serving a Mass for Father Sansaverino, a priest who had been recently transferred to St. Pat's from the Vatican. He was not very tall and the priest that said the earlier Mass was very tall, so when he reached into the tabernacle the chalice was beyond his reach. So, I had to get a chair for him to stand on. I remember hearing a few new Latin words that morning......none of them were in the Missal.

We didn't realize it at the time, but the neighborhood was truly a special place. Our kids and grandkids are fascinated by the stories.

WINDOWS

by Richard J. Rinaldo

I LIVED IN A FOUR ROOM WALKUP tenement apartment at 213 Mott Street. It was called a "railroad" apartment because the rooms were lined up like railroad trains from the front of the building to the rear. A lot of the neighborhood had these buildings. There were two windows, one set on the street side of the building

and one set in the rear overlooking a back yard and with a view of a building on another street. During the summer, a fan at one end could, when set in reverse direction, pull air through the entire apartment, along with soot. It was better than being hot, though. But some times even the fan did not work well, and some daring neighbors might sleep on the fire escapes, which most buildings had. On a nice day during the summer we could go to "tar beach," the roofs

which were covered by some type of tar. There we would sun ourselves.

Windows were also a means of receiving food or ice from the street. Who could forget the cries of "ice man, ice man," and your mother throwing a burlap bag tied to a rope out of the window to pull up a block of ice just unloaded from the ice man's horse and cart. Or maybe a watermelon from the watermelon man. These were delicate procedures to ensure that the product did not swing into the building or windows below. Windows were also a means of communication. I can still hear my Uncle Jimmy Frisco's whistle as he signaled for me to join him for a walk or a visit

to the doctor. Or my mother calling me to supper. Or my friends calling me to play. During the feasts, a band would parade through the feasts with the saint carried, adorned with cash donations. If you threw down the right amount, they would stop and play the *Marcia Reale Italiana,* an old, Italian national anthem, while facing the saint's statue toward your window.

Roofs were a place of adventure where we could explore previously unknown routes from one building or one street to another to another. Francis Coppola captured the latter in a scene from "Godfather" where Vito Cor-

leone negotiates several roofs to get to the apartment of an enemy whom he will kill. Meanwhile we see from that roof a typical Italian feast, in this case the Saint being San Rocco. Well, San Rocco's feast is in August and Vito is wearing an overcoat. Sorry Francis, but your verisimilitude slipped on that one. Back yards were another place for mischief and exploration. Secret passages might be found by going through them while braving darkness and rats or climbing over barbed wire fences, glass-lined walls, or the like. How did we survive?

The neighborhood in the old days was always sooty. As students at St. Patrick's Old Cathedral School, we had to wear uniforms, and that meant a white shirt with blue pants and a blue tie with an embroidered SPS in a triangle. The white shirt stayed sparkling clean for a few hours. In the evening rush hour, southbound traffic lined Mott Street in a huge jam headed downtown somewhere, probably Kenmare Street, where a left turn would take them to the Williamsburg Bridge to Brooklyn, and there was a lot of horn blowing—very annoying.

Windows also served as a place for observation or even voyeurism. A

classic image in the neighborhood would be an elderly person peering from a window into the street, sharing in its intimacies, action, or mischief, sometimes overtly, sometimes surreptitiously through blinds or barely moved curtains. Martin Scorsese, discussed elsewhere in this book, used the window from his apartment at an early age to watch other children play, since as an asthmatic, he was unable to participate. Maybe windows honed his observational skills and ability to view people and events from a perspective not shared by the average person—an artistic ability certainly germane to filmmaking. These windows often became a pulpit for admonishments to errant youth for crossing a street they were forbidden to cross or cursing or fighting or worse. One often hears, "If these walls could talk." If these windows could talk! Writer, poet, and playwright Vito Gentile captures this aspect of the neighborhood with this story reprinted with his permission:

WHY GOD MADE LITTLE ITALY

By Vito Gentile

"What do you think is up there?" spouted an over-ripe woman stuffing a cannoli into her mouth, while her eyes gazed up at the tenement apartments hidden in the autumn night way, above the noise and glare of the annual street festival.

"People!" a woman's voice yelled down from a darkened window. "What do you think, we only live here for the few weeks of the feast? We're here all year!"

Stunned, the cannoli-stuffing woman turned to her friend, "They got good ears down here in Little Italy!" Ears? Forget ears – eyes are what they've got. Whoever was up in that window was reading lips. You can't rent an apartment on Mulberry Street unless you can see a block away from your front stoop. And that's just the men; the women must be able to read the figures on a grocery receipt in a shopping bag from a fourth-floor window. And the real pros can do it thought a lace curtain.

You think they were born with this extraordinary eyesight? They were trained – trained by their mothers from the day they were married and the apartment was passed on to another generation so the rent wouldn't' change—the way God intended it to be. And why the good eyesight? It's their job, their duty to watch what and who comes and goes on their block. They are the unspoken official deputies of their street, sometimes like the old west; except there are no sheriffs in Little Italy, only mothers—guardian angels, beacons in the night patrolling the perimeters of their stone stoops, always watching —

Always protecting their family from epidemics, ("The kid next door didn't go to school today, what do they got?"); another depression—God forbid!—("You're husband ain't working?"); famine, ("Hey, Commara, how come you didn't' buy any fruit in the grocery store? What happened, nothing ripe?"); and most important, an invasion, ("Who's that man standing on the corner? He's been there since I started saying my Rosary.")

No one hides in Little Italy. It's simpler to just make a good excuse for what you do. I would wager that had the Watergate complex been on Grand Street instead of in Washington, D.C.—even before the night-watchman found a taped lock on a hallway door, everybody in the neighborhood would have known what was going on in the Democratic Headquarters. So much for your Woodwards and Bernsteins! The only difference, that's as far as it would have gone.

These innocent women might know your business, but it's their cross in life to carry your secrets. "It's not my business," a favorite expression of a truly professional mother of Little Italy. "Do what you got to do!," "Go where you got to go!," "See what you got to see!"

Do you think they care about what you're doing, "I got my own troubles!," "You should only know…!," and the song of the crucified mama, "Don't even let me say it!!!" But they do, to their neighbors and to their sick bedridden mothers. Despair has always been known to be better for curing a mother than medicine—"I had my cross, you have yours!" Nice, real nice!

They tell their commaras, who also tell them, and the doctors who take care of their varicose veins – even the boys who carry groceries four flights for a quarter. They'll cry to anyone – anyone who'll listen; and what do they say? Nothing! Again, it's the eyes. Look at them closely if you dare. Look and you'll see the scars brought on by the disgrace of a daughter who smokes cigarettes in the bathroom; sons who don't come visiting on Sunday anymore because of their wives' families who the lady next door happens to know; and women their husbands might have once looked at forty years ago while playing cards down at the club.

"What is my life?!" these eyes cry out. And you must listen to these eyes and take pity on them. How can you help it when a woman walks around with that much despair on her make-up-less face surrounded by black hair, black dress, black shoes and socks?

Are they all in mourning? Well, not really. Some wear it for an uncle who might have died a year ago in Italy and you know, their neighbors expect them to. It could also be that they had been in church that morning helping a com-mara bury her second husband. Could they go to a funeral mass wearing red? Come on! Or even better, they were either out at the cemetery visiting, or possibly they went to pay a friendly visit to someone in the hospital. Did you ever see the expression on a dying person's face when one of these women comes paying a visit in her Zorro outfit?

See, black is a wonderful color to wear. It goes with nothing and reminds you of so much. And just in case— God forbid—something "serious" should happen, they're ready. It's the color that can't be seen from a distance in case someone's watching them; and most of all, it's a respectful color; a color to wear to Mass, to Novena, to devotion.

Yes, church is the only place they go when they're not cooking, cleaning, shopping, spying—no, correction; sometimes you can't help noticing someone spending an extra two minutes in the confessional—why? And better yet, it's where they go to pray so their fellow spies can watch them as they watch each other, seeing who can hold out the longest before they have to rush home to stir the sauce and pull in the laundry.

Praying comes as natural to these women as observing the good deeds and the bad ones of others. But back to praying; you think they're selfish and go praying for themselves? Never! They pray Mama gets well so she can go out to Long Island and visit Dominick, that Sonny's wife will quit that job and stay home and have kids, and "Maybe my Josie will meet a nice man and settle down." For that miracle they'd take off their black dress and carry a candle in a festa for twenty years.

And there are other types of prayers, "Maybe that club my husband goes to ten times a day will blow up with all its card tables and smelly cigars?" Unselfish women like this don't pray for themselves. They don't need it, they're saints already— they became saints the day they married "Don't let me say it; him!" and gave birth to "Him" and "Her!" And martyrs the day they moved in with Mama – the way God intended it to be.

What can one say for these wife-mother-daughters who are so giving, so understanding, so over-protecting. There are not enough basilicas in Italy or churches in all of the five boroughs of New York to house this many living saints. That's why God made Little Italy, to enshrine these dear little ladies in one community to dwell in harmony, while keeping a watchful eye on the rest of us.

"What do you think, I have all day to sit by the window?!"

VITO GENTILE BIOGRAPHY

Vito Gentile, a native New Yorker of Italian decent, has written more than thirty plays, screen-plays, and teleplays, as well as non-fiction books, numerous articles for periodicals, and seventeen (and counting) volumes of poetry.

During his near fifty-year writing career, Vito has honored his Italian heritage many times through his work, beginning with his well-received urban trilogy, *Francine in Black and White,* which consists of *Amidst the Gladiolas, Confetti and Italian Ice,* and *Cold Manhattan Special.* There is also an autobiography, *Little Christmas* – a memory piece of Christmas holidays seen through the eyes of an inquisitive child, and a screenplay, *In the Shadow of a Saint,* a slice-of-life epic in need of a producer.

Through his poetry, Gentile has written extensively about growing up among his wonderful parents and his six brothers and sisters. These family-inspired poems run the gamut from hunting for mushrooms in cold December woods, through the aroma of his mother's cooking, to listening to the third act of Tosca on his father's lap.

Gentile taught dramatic writing at New York University for several years and is published by Samuel French.

Recollections of the Monroe

By Marie Elaine Graziano

My early recollections of living in our old neighborhood would have to include growing up in the Monroe. It was the largest apartment house in Little Italy located on the corner of Prince and Lafayette streets. (The name comes from the fact that it was the location of the Monroe House built by Gouveneur Morris in the early 19th century. Morris was a nephew of James Monroe-Ed.) The building was divided into four sections – the A, B, C, and D sides. It had 92 apartments in it.

(Donald Napoli at right next to front door and window in the '50s, while the new look is at left. Photos courtesy of Donald and John Buffa respectively).

The huge entrance hall was beautifully tiled and led the way to each section of the five story walkup. It was a year round meeting place for our

neighbors. Some of the people were lucky enough to get a seat on the extra wide marble window sills. Others just stood. Some sat in chairs that they stored in the "carriage room," a generic storage area in the back of the hallway for just about anything that you couldn't fit in your apartment. All for the sake of catching up on the gossip of the day. (Photo of current hall courtesy John Buffa)

During the winter months, even if you didn't have a particular reason for leaving your apartment, you could spend some time chit chatting because the oversized radiators that were constantly clanking away kept the hallway toasty warm. They also, by the way, provided a quick dry for wet gloves during snowball fights! In the summertime all the marble and tile of the hallway made it feel a lot cooler than the hot steamy sidewalks outside.

We had two doctors in the building. One doctor's office had a smoke-filled waiting room with clouded windows and old newspapers piled up all over the place. It wasn't too inviting. The doctor himself always greeted his patients with a cigarette in his mouth that had an ash as long as your finger. Then we had a dentist on the first floor of the "D" side. His office looked like something out of a horror movie to me. One day he actually straddled the chair I was sitting in to remove a tooth that was growing in towards my tongue.

I think my family held the record for moving around the most – from one section of the building to another – but always for very good reasons. Our first apartment was two rooms on the fifth floor that consisted of a large kitchen and bedroom. The kitchen-living room was divided by a huge porcelain table in the middle. One side naturally had all the kitchen appliances. The other, our "living room," had a Castro convertible sofa and a TV. My mom Lucy always had the neighbors in for coffee. I remember lots of birthday parties in that very often very crowded kitchen. Life was good!!! We had wonderful neighbors, too, Anna especially!

My younger sister Fran very often would have two meals for supper, one at our house, another at Anna's. Uncle Frank, Anna's husband owned a produce store and got in from work late. He adored Fran and got such a kick out of her convincing him that she hadn't eaten dinner yet. They also owned a TV before we did. So every Monday night we went into their apartment to watch the Milton Berle Show. Before the advent of TV, we watched Abbott and Costello movies on their movie projector, with her bedroom wall as the screen!

Mom and Dad decided to take a larger one-bedroom apartment on the side where Aunt Margaret and Uncle Eugene lived. Then eventually we moved to the "C" side to be close to my Grandfather who had moved into our building after Grandma died. It was quite a place – the Monroe – teeming with so many wonderful, lovable and quirky personalities, like one, whose apartment was simonized and covered in plastic covered from top to bottom. You had to remove your shoes before you went in! Another always had the Ink Spots' music playing on her record player. I tweezed her eyebrows. I tweezed every Saturday morning!

Ralphie and Anthony – whom I often hung out with, and who to-day, more than half a century later are still good friends of mine, very often would beat me at a somewhat barbaric card game of "Knuckles." If you lost, you got smacked on your knuckles with the deck of cards. Then there was Pippy who looked forward to the summer, when he would tend to his pigeon coop up on the roof. (See Arthur in chapter on Sports and Pastimes)

Some of my fondest memories at the building revolved around being on the roof in the summertime. There was nothing like getting a good tan on "Tar Beach" with Fran and my girlfriends. We would spread out our blankets and "roast" for a while. When it got too hot, we'd yell down to Mom to turn on the kitchen faucet. It had an extra-long hose with a shower nozzle attached and it ran up the fire escape over the roof ledge to give us quick relief. (At right, Donald Napoli on the roof, with St. Patrick's Cathedral in the background. Below left, older Sister Rosemary swinging Anne on another roof. Below right, Nicky Biletto hamming it up on a roof. We loved roofs.)

The roof had tarred walls up the side, which were not too high. But we knew enough not to get too close to the edge. The steam pipes all over the place were perfect for stringing clotheslines. Even hanging clothes was a social event! You were bound to meet someone up there to talk with. On a typical summer evening many of the neighbors would meet on the roof to escape the heat of the apartments. Occasionally you would see JuJu (real name Julius) shirtless with a white towel wrapped around his neck to catch any perspiration chasing after his son to get back downstairs to start his homework. I think it was Ralphie's dad who strung light bulbs up there so that everyone could enjoy the coveted card games late into the nights or the pizza parties on the weekends. On real

hot nights, after everyone had gone back down to their apartments, Mr. McClain (I never did know his first name) would whistle down to my dad to join him for a quiet game of checkers. We did have a lot fun up there on the roof!

On Sundays we ate one big meal at 2:00 p.m. So after church the aroma of frying meatballs would start to fill the hallways. My mom's were simply delicious! Uncle Dom would stop by every Sunday with my cousins Michael and Peter for a few "hot ones" before they were placed in the "gravy." There were lots of different recipes for the "gravy" (tomato sauce) depending on which town your relatives were from in Italy, but they all smelled fabulous! (Technically it was really gravy because there were meat juices in it. Ed.).

After dinner in the summertime, a few local musicians would congregate in the courtyard with mandolins and accordions and entertain us with Italian songs. Just about everyone would lean out their windows to listen. Then they would toss down coins that were carefully folded in pieces of paper in appreciation. My dad, Frankie, a real practical joker, would occasionally toss out a pot of water too. I wish that my children and grandchildren could have experienced the simplicity of life growing up as I did, during the late '40s and '50s.

As I look back now, living at the Monroe in Little Italy was truly a luxury, not measured in material things but by the wonderfully rich memories that were created there!

Friendships Forged in Little Italy

By Ralph Joseph Patete

In Memory of Two Friends, That Special Neighborhood,
That Way of Life
Friendship Loyalty Kinship Respect Family
Love Life Religion Culture

THE EARLY 1940S WERE A GOOD TIME FOR LITTLE ITALY. Many married couples were committed to family life and were having babies despite the dire events in Europe. It was a testimony of their faith and love for each other. It demonstrated their convictions and beliefs and that of their parents that all the sacrifices entailed with coming to America were well worth it. It was a hope for a better life not only for themselves but for their families and for the future generations that were to come.

A commitment to the world to make it better and that enduring friendship did just that for one and all.

This group of babies attended Old Saint Patrick Cathedral's Church and School. The Church was staffed by the Secular Priests of the Roman Catholic Church, the School by members of The Sisters of Charity, founded by Holy Mother Seton. These unselfish Catholic men and woman, who had no biological children of their own, indelibly imparted to their spiritual children a sense of pride, friendship, and loyalty, a respect for family, culture, church and country. They fostered a love of academic achievement coupled with love, respect, and friendship for one another. That has lasted over seventy years.

Through the guidance and living examples from their biological parents coupled with the guidance of these devoted spiritual parents, this group of young boys and girls growing up in THE NEIGHBORHOOD developed an enduring friendship and loyalty that still exists today. This bond of friendship was like a group marriage for richer or poorer; in sickness or in health; until death do us part. It mirrored the love our parents had for each other and for their fellow Italian-Americans who lived on the same floor, building, block, and neighborhood—Little Italy

With this analogy of marriage coming to mind and speaking of until *death do we part,* I recall and dedicate this short story on friendship  to two young friends of this group, who were taken away by GOD to HIMSELF during their teenage years. They were Louis Frezza and Charles Trentacosta (J. Guidetti, Louis and Charles in picture from L to R). We lost two wonderful and gifted friends. It was not until I became a parent, that I fully learned, and realized the sense of loss for their respected parents and families. We are consoled by our Roman Catholic Faith, taught to us by those secular priests and Sisters of Charity that both Louis and Charles are in a better place in front of the "Beatific Vision." For me and many of our group they are forever in our hearts, minds and souls as they were young friends, brothers, sons, and Catholic students of Little Italy. We love them both today as we did then.

Not only did this group share the common education of Old Saint Patrick's Elementary School, but also of Cardinal Hayes' High School, Xavier, La Salle or Regis High Schools. We furthered our education in the school of life and those of Fordham, Manhattan and other colleges.

I remember the entrance examination to many of these High Schools especially that to Cardinal Hayes. We were a group of a dozen or so guys including Louis and Charles walking North on the East side of the Grand Concourse. We were collectively asking and answering numerous questions we believed would be on the entrance examination. Three of this group from Little Italy scored or placed in the top ten of all those applicants taking the entrance exam that year for Cardinal Hayes. Another memory of those days was of Father Principe and the Altar Boy Society. And all the excursions we took in his red, crowded Chevrolet truck and all of the life teaching lessons we learned at the hands of this marvelous and generous cleric. To many of us he was our temporal spiritual father. We all owe him a lifetime of gratitude.

One last memory that is forever marked on my soul and spirit is that of the Bivona family, their love and friendship and sense of sharing. The entire extended Bivona family, beginning with the grandparents, their children and their children's children. Especially Vincent, Charles, Fay, and Jean. I especially want to mention the sacred memory of Vincent Bivona, when his son John and I visited him in the hospital. In his confident and fatherly manner he instructed and reminded us both that we had a wonderful, special, and unique gift of friendship among the group from Little Italy. He cautioned us and told us never to lose that friendship and to make it grow and mature. For Vincent recognized we all had and shared something unique, special, and of great value and strength. This is something that does not come to us that often in life, something that has endured the test of time.

We are friends, brothers and sisters all through this life and for all eternity. That is the friendship and bond that was forged in us all in our collective mother land of LITTLE ITALY. This I rejoice and celebrate here and in having reached my 70th birthday with all my Little Italy friends and family.

Editor's Note:

Ralph's wonderful sentiments remind me to highlight the family of women of the neighborhood. They were all sisters and sources of great support to one another, often through trials of great despair and sadness that cannot be described here. One memorable woman among my mother's friends was Josephine Granello, who shared her home and hearth with us so often, both in the city and in Greenwood Lake, N.Y. during the summer. And I will never forget her granddaughter and my childhood friend Joanne.

What wonderful memories of summer nights when many of these ladies would sit outside on folding chairs or benches to observe, comment, and chat about this or that. I joined my mother on a bench one night, and suddenly we were flung upward, as on a seesaw, when one of the heftier ladies took her place on the other side. It was a big laugh for all.

Needless to say, all of us males of the neighborhood were blessed with wonderful Italian-American women—as mothers, relatives, girlfriends, spouses, friends, or relatives. They were and are beautiful, passionate, compassionate, inspiring, and above all saintly in their patience with a different kind of meatball!

IT WAS QUITE A JOURNEY

By Catherine Miceli

WHENEVER ANYONE ASKS WHERE I CAME FROM, I'm proud to say that I was born and raised on the lower east side on Mulberry Street. It was the best neighborhood and the greatest group of friends. Everyone was like family.

Yes, I have memories, so many to mention. Just a little look back is my intention.

My family lived in a five-story apartment building on Mulberry Street. Since we did not have any heat, we had a belly stove that would heat our apartment by adding wood and paper to make the fire. In order to have a longer lasting fire, my dad would pick up coal and carry it up to our apartment on the fifth floor. My grandmother, Antonia Uricola, lived on the second floor with her son, my Uncle Johnny. They lived next door to Rose Tedesco Perrotta,

282 Mulberry St.

who was a fine dressmaker. She made all of my holiday clothes and also my wedding gown. My parents, Clara, Tony and I lived across the hall from my Uncle Sullivan, Aunt Anna and their four children, Annette, Michael, Robert and Salvatore. Unfortunately, grandma lost her youngest son, Michael, (also known as Bozo in the neighborhood) in World War II at Mount Marone, Italy in 1943. Those were the worst of times for our family. (See related story about him by Robert Uricola Ed.)

St. Patrick's Elementary School Graduation
June 1944

St. Patrick's Old Cathedral was on the corner of Mulberry and Prince Streets.

Tom and Virginia Datre,
Fr. Andrews,
Catherine and Whitey

The Rectory was also on Mulberry Street across from the back entrance to the church. St. Patrick's Elementary School was on Mott and Prince Streets. This was great for me as I could walk to grammar school just around the corner. The priests at St. Patrick's were always there when you needed them. Whether our questions were about religion or schoolwork, they took the time to help us. Thinking back, I remember Msgr. Rossi, our pastor, and Father McGuire (in my graduation picture). Later on, Msgr. Filitti was our pastor. Our other parish priests were Father Goodwine, Father Andrews, and Father Tomasso (who married us). Father Andrews later became a Msgr., but just wanted to be called Father.

Father Andrews christened both of our sons, Anthony and Joseph, even though we lived on Long Island at that time. The parishioners at St. Patrick's missed Fr. Andrews when he was transferred to St. Rita's Church on Staten Island. In 2010, a group of St. Rita's parishioners wrote a book about Msgr. Andrews. He would be 100 years old.

Sarah Lofaso, who is nine years younger than I, had similar experiences attending St. Patrick's school. My kindergarten teacher was also Miss Spera, and I skipped grade 3B and went on to 4B. I received Holy Communion and Confirmation a day apart. I loved my godmother, Susie Figliola, a beautiful person. She lived on the fourth floor, directly below us. She was a great friend of my mom's and our family. She had the voice of an angel, and I will always remember her singing her favorite song, "Maybe."

In June 1944, I graduated from St.

Godmother Susie Figliola

Patrick's Elementary School. I continued my education at St. Patrick's Cathedral High School (Archbishop Hughes Memorial) where I graduated in 1948. To this date I continue to meet with the alumnae every October. Together we attend Mass at the Cathedral and have lunch at Rosie O'Grady's.

At Cathedral High School I was a member of the choir. I also was a member of St. Patrick's Choir under the direction of Father Sansavarino, who was also the organist and great music teacher. We had a great group of young men and women from the neighborhood. There were also three young Italian men who had just moved to our neighborhood and joined our choir. Lucky for us, they had great voices, and we became a great choir. We sang most of our hymns in Latin at that time. For these were our roots and upbringing, where we learned, prayed, and did our choir singing.

The P.A.L. always was thoughtful of the neighborhood kids. They would close our street, put up tennis nets, and place ping-pong tables on the sidewalks. They taught us arts and crafts, and we all appreciated and loved learning all these new experiences. It was the best of times for all of us neighborhood kids. Yes, let's go back to Mulberry Street, where we played hide and seek, kick the can, and marbles in the streets. Another memorable and favorite street game, mainly played by the boys and is still being played in neighborhoods today, is stickball. The good thing about all these outdoor street games was that they made the kids go out and play and form better bonds with all their friends. It was a healthier way of growing up than to be glued to a television or a computer, like we have today. Being an only child, I looked forward to going out to play with my friends.

There are so many memories growing up on Mulberry Street. Grandma would take me shopping on Mulberry and Mott Streets to buy all the fresh fruits and vegetables from the push-carts (as they were called). They were lined up on the streets outside the stores. The chicken market was on the corner of Mulberry and Prince Streets. I can still

Uncle John Uricola,
Grandma Anthonia Uricola

see the owner running after the chicken to get him ready for the kill. I watched how they removed the feathers before selling the fresh chicken to cook. You couldn't buy anything fresher than those chickens. Grandma also had an icebox, no refrigerator in those days. She would need a huge block of ice to keep the food fresh. The iceman would put it on his shoulder and carry it up grandma's apartment on the second floor. The ice would melt into a pan under the icebox and after a few days repeated the process. We certainly have come a long way since then.

All the kids from the neighborhood loved when the rides came to our street. Similar to the ice cream trucks playing music on Long Island, these trucks also played music when they approached our street. The rides were in large trucks and only cost a nickel or dime. In the hot summer months, they would open the fire hydrants outside our building to cool off all the kids. We didn't have a car to go to the beaches. We traveled by train and bus. The train stations and bus stops were all in walking distance.

We spent lots of summer days and nights on our roof; we called it Tar Beach. We played games, listened to the radio and sat out in the sunshine. My Uncle Sullivan's hobby was to fly pigeons on the roof. We thought that was really neat, sending his homing pigeons with messages to his friends.

Top row: Dad, Charlie, Jeff
Bottom row: Rose LoFaso, me, Aunt

Catherine top right

On the roof: Catherine, Dad,
Mom, Uncle Johnny

Top row: Aunt, Mom, Rose LoFaso;
Bottom row: Dad, me, Jeff

All in all our parents really struggled through those years. We never questioned anything. We all made do with what we had. We didn't know that we were poor. That is how we kids grew up. This was good because it prepared us to cope with everything that we were to face in our future years ahead. Growing up in Little Italy on Mulberry Street with my loving parents, Clara and Tony Tuzzo, made me a better person. My parents set a fine example for me by the sacrifices they made. Attending St. Patrick's School and being so near the Old Cathedral also played such a big part in forming my character.

When Lily and Charles DeLeo moved to Mulberry Street with their three children, Virginia, Paschal and Lillian, I met my new best friend. Lillian and I started school together and remained friends for years. Her brother Paschal's death from an accident was a great loss. Lillian's dad worked as a caretaker on the church's cemetery grounds where we, believe it or not, would sometimes play and keep her father company.

Clara (Mom) Joe, Me on bottom. On top Lily DeLeo and Aunt Mary

In 1939, Lil and I joined the Brownie troop. So young and shy, we were a cute group. Virginia De Leo and Rose Guma were our Brownie and Girl Scout leaders at St. Patrick's. It was a fun time.

I was Lillian and Nat Marsala's maid of honor and godmother to their first daughter, Cynthia. When Whitey and I got married, we lived with my mom. We had our first son, Anthony. Lillian and Joe Catara, my best man, were Anthony's godparents.

When Anthony was two and a half years old, Whitey and I decided it was time to buy our first home. It wasn't easy leaving my mom alone, taking Anthony away from his Nana. She loved coming to visit on weekends, being with her grandson. She also was a big help to all of us. It was two years after we moved into our first home that we had our second son, Joseph, born in October of 1959.

We looked for a home with Lillian and Nat and their three daughters, Cynthia, Charlene, and Andrea. Later they had Jeneane and Paschal. We bought our homes next door to one another on Long Island. It was a great lasting friendship.

In 1946, St. Patrick's had dances for all the high school teenagers and their friends on Friday nights. While dancing the last dance, the Lindy, with one of the boys, Tangy, three young men walked in to check out the dance hall. They were Joe Miceli, Steve Riggio, and Joe Catara. Whitey, as he was introduced to me, knew Tangy and asked if he could cut in. I had never met him before, and I asked him where he lived. When he said Spring and Mulberry Streets, I couldn't believe that he lived just a block away. I suppose it was because

Catherine and Joe

he went to P.S. 21 elementary school on Mott and Spring Streets and I went to St. Patrick's. Whitey would then come to every Friday night's dance. He said that when he went home that night he told his father that he met the girl he was going to marry.

He was a great dancer and he loved the Lindy Hop (as it was called back then.) While we would dance the Lindy Hop he would do the split. The best Lindy recording by Glenn Miller was "In the Mood," and that seemed to be our dance song. When he asked me to be his girlfriend I told him that he was crazy. I was too young and my Dad would never allow it, as he was very strict. I was attending Cathedral High School at that time and was about fifteen years old. So that is how I met Joe Miceli.

It was at this time when Joe Miceli started to pursue a new life. He was a determined young man whose dream it was to become a fighter. I married Whitey knowing he was a boxer and that this was his life. What was he to do? He left school to work and support his family. This was to be his profession in life. He was born to be a fighter.

My life living with a fighter was interesting, amusing, exciting, and,

Whitey, Perry Como, Catherine

at times, not easy. I did go to the fights whenever they were local in New York, or in Philadelphia and Florida. I would sit holding rosary beads and pray that he and his opponent would not get hurt but that he would win.

We did meet many prominent people, movie stars, singers, comedians—too many to mention. We became friends with some of them. To name a few, I must mention Perry Como. We would go to all his Chesterfield Shows and speak to him after the show. He took the time to talk to you and find out about how Joe was doing. He was just a warm loving person.

Another great entertainer we met was Louis Prima. Everyone knows who he was and how great he was.

Harry James was another great guy. One time he treated us to the Astor Roof where

Catherine, Louis & Joe

Dick Haymes, Harry James, Helen Forrest, & Catherine

he and his band and Buddy Rich were performing. When we told Harry that we were getting married soon and going to California on our honeymoon, he gave us an invitation to Television City. There we saw the very first live television show in color with all the stars whose shows were being aired in black and white back in 1954.

Our invitation was also for us to go to the after party and see all these stars. One special guest was Mario Lanza. It was quite exciting walking through a parade of stars. Another great star we met in California at the racetrack was the impeccable George Raft, who told us how not to look at the camera when taking a picture.

Whitey & George Raft, 1954

Joe, Mary & Eddy Foy Jr., Catherine

Last but not least, we met Eddy Foy, Jr., one of the Seven Little Foys, a great show business family. Eddy Foy, Jr., who was starring in The Pajama Game on Broadway, invited us to see the show. After the show, my mom invited Eddy, Jr. and his son, Eddy 3rd, to dinner. Eddy 3rd was one of Joe's biggest fans. When Joe would fight in California, Eddy would assist in Joe's corner.

Well, our journey lasted almost 54

Sons Joseph and Anthony, Catherine and Whitey, 50th Anniversary

years. Although it was sad in July 2008 when Joe passed, our years together were the norm. Like all married couples we had the good times and the hard times. But since our first dance step, to the miracle birth of our latest grandson, Nicholas Joseph Miceli, born to my daughter-in-law Terri and son Joseph Miceli on January 23, 2007, we were surely blessed.

Nicholas Joseph Miceli

Joseph and Terri Miceli

THE UNIVERSITY OF MULBERRY STREET

By Salvatore Uricola

Adapted from an Email.

TONY WAS A BIG FAT GUY who owned a nightclub in the Village. Did you like the piece about Petrocino?[1] Boy he was tough. He used to call the  Mafioso rats. You know he lived in the neighborhood. I think on Lafayette Street. From what I was told by some old timers he was a tough man and he went after all the Mafioso. He formed the Italian squad, the first Italian to do so. The Mafioso were extorting money from Italian businesses. They even tried to extort the great Caruso and he was paying at first.

He went to Italy, and that's where he got killed. I asked my late grandmother who knew him vaguely, and she remembers the funeral that took place on the neighborhood and thousands of people showed up to pay their respects. That's the story about Petracino. There is a movie out called Pay or Die. Earnest Borgnine played him and if you get a chance watch it. I think you will enjoy it.

What happened to Jiles? You remember him I hope. He wasn't from the neighborhood but he loved to hang out there. Good kid.

You know Richard we were born right in the middle of it, we seen a lot. Like I told you before people wouldn't believe us.

---

[1] A park on Lafayette Street and Cleveland Place is now named after Petrocino. The editor and his wife attended the dedication in 2009, where the above plaque has been placed. Another highlight was the presence of descendants and relatives of the famous detective and a talk by Anthony Izzo (photo above), Chief Organized Crime Control Bureau, of the NYPD, who was inspired by Lt. Petrosino.

I miss my brother Mike (Second on right in picture from editor's collection. L to R, Louis Frezza, editor, Michael, and Nicky Biletto). He could have been a professor. He was a smart man. As for me I was in the demolition industry years ago and found bits and pieces of the past the people left behind. Sarah sent me an article on old St. Patrick's. I have a Catholic newspaper that I found at one of the job sites. The date is 1940 and shows all the old churches in New York, especially St. Patrick's. You know it burnt down one time and it was rebuilt. I have the article that goes back of  opening day and the fanfare that happened. At the time it was the first cathedral in NYC, and cardinals and bishops were pulling up with horse-drawn carriages to celebrate. I hate to part with the magazine. First I got to find it; you know I'm a pack rat. And when I find it, I will send you a copy of it. That's were Mother Seton started her order right on Mott St. to help the poor. That was called Sisters of Charity. There's much more in the article. Italian people used to go under the church for mass and the Irish on top. My grandmother used to tell me about the clashes. There was one Irish man left. His name was Phillip Manning. He lived where Faye had the candy store across the street from Buffa's restaurant. He was in a wheelchair, and I'm almost sure he was the last Irish man left. He told me a lot of stories.

I remember when they were building the Youth Center they hit graves and the job was stopped and they were putting bones in burlap bags. It's all hallowed ground in that area by the church. You remember Jersey Alley; it was called Jersey St. before the Friedman building went up that used to be a candy factory—the Holly and Hoops building. There were shanties there. My grandmother was born in one of them shanties on Jersey Street. It ran right into Lafayette and Crosby. The Puck building used to be the Italian Progresso newspaper. Richard, we lived different lives at a different time. I have good memories and bad, like I say. I think we were fortunate coming from a neighborhood like that. When people ask me where I was from or where I went to school. I tell them the University Of Mulberry St. What a neighborhood. Love to go back someday even if it were an hour. I may sound somber, but we will all meet again. Take care of yourself.

About Sally
From Richie

Sally "Ga Ga" was one of the neighborhood's loveable characters. A bunch of us would go to a summer camp upstate, which was empty in September. One of our classmates was a counselor there, and he had the keys. So we go up there and borrow 22 rifles and go hunting for woodchucks. Marty was with us, and he brought his mother's famous chicken recipe. First of all you had to boil the chicken. We had a fire going and a pot of water. We left the chicken, and we decided to take a nap in one of the cabins, and all of a sudden we heard gun shots "bang" "bang." We go outside and there is Sally at a distance shooting the 22 rifle at the pot and all the water is pouring out of it putting out the fire, and the chicken wasn't cooking anymore. So maybe he helped us prevent a forest fire. Anyway I think we went into the town to eat.

For us from the city a cow is a dangerous animal. We were going hunting for wood chucks and we wander into a pasture and all of sudden these cows come toward us, and these things are gigantic. We take off not paying attention to where we were running, and we wound up with a whole mess of cow dung on our shoes.

Sally's mother bought a rooster from the chicken market, and they kept it on the roof of their building. The rooster would crow early in the morning, waking up the entire neighborhood. Sally and his father decided that the rooster had to go. The rooster had other ideas and chased them whenever they approached him. Sally whacked the rooster with a bamboo pigeon pole and it fell off the roof, only to get wedged in a smoke stack on a nearby lower building. Now it really made a lot of noise for three days, and the neighbors were even more upset. Finally, shots were heard, and the rooster was never heard from again.

Family thoughts

By Richard. J. Rinaldo

I saw the film "Le Quattro Volte" (The Four Times), an extraordinary production with a Cannes award. It was shot in a town in the Calabria region of Italy. It appeared to have once been a fortress, and I was reminded of the origins of my father's parents in the Commune of Motta di San Giovanni in Calabria, which contains a Byzantine fortification, the Castel of San Niceto, shown in a picture here from Wikimedia commons. The film includes some portraits of life in the town, the sparse material possessions and living quarters of one of the inhabitants, for example. I could imagine the motivation for something better that compelled the immigration of my grandparents to America, especially at the turn of the 20th century when Calabria was the poorest region in Italy.

One of my relatives tell this amusing tale of his grandmother visiting a town in Calabria some years ago to see her ancestral home, touted by relatives as a villa with a balcony overlooking the sea. On arrival in the town no one wanted to talk with her. She contacted the Mayor, and after some inquiries he told her that they feared she might lay claim to the home. This piqued her high expectation even more. So she convinced the Mayor to intervene on her behalf, assuring him that she had no interest in claiming the home. He advised her that she could visit if she brought a gift, and they decided on a goat that they might roast for a party. With goat in hand they visited the home, which was a dilapidated old house with a small window and a tiny balcony, more of a window sill. It did, however, have a view of the sea. She returned to American exclaiming that she was glad they left, though she agreed that Italy was a beautiful place.

Not that America had streets paved of gold as the legend goes. My father grew up near Mulberry Bend. When he was born his crib was one drawer in a chest of drawers. When it snowed they protected their feet by wrapping them in newspapers with twine. Must have looked fun-

ny, but nobody got frost-bite. His father, my grand-father (at left with Grandma Victoria) had a pushcart selling vegetables on Mott Street. After a while he saved enough money to buy a house in East New York in a nice neighborhood. It stayed in the family a long time passed down to several families, and when it was sold everybody got a fair share. All the brothers and sisters of Fortunato and Victoria are gone along with too many of my first cousins, but nearly 200 descendants survive them. Tradition would have dictated my first name to be Fortunato, and I would have liked that, but my parents wanted me to be an American

My mother's family was Quaranta's (the Forties.) The boys were all musicians, and my Uncle Tommy led a group called Tommy Forty and his Orchestra. My grandfather John (shown at right) had one of those marching bands that we would see in the parades for various *festa*. They would also play in Chinese funerals. Charlie Panelli, a cousin on my grandmother's side of the family, was a trombonist with the *Loui-*

siana Five, an early and famous Dixieland jazz band. My father did not look favorably on music as a way to make a living, and though I took some drum lessons from my Uncle Jimmy and in the Sea Cadets, I did not pursue it further until recently, where I play some percussion in a church ensemble.

My Aunt Vera along with my mother, their siblings and parents lived at 217 Mott Street. (In the photo on left, L to R, are Aunt Vera, Grandma Theresa, Uncle Tommy, Aunt Adele, and my mother Rose, circa 1930s.) I had been several years ago to the Tenement Museum on Orchard Street, to the home of the Sicilian Baldizzi family that lived there in the 1930s. It had a lot of familiarity, bathroom in the hall, a sink and bathtub in the kitchen with the gas meter. The guide, a young woman told us about the lives of the inhabitants there and how it must have been hard for them. For example, maybe once a week the water was heated for a bath for the children. In three rooms, there were as many as ten people or more. When she played a taped interview with a member of that family, it brought tears to my eyes, as if I were listening to voices of my own family.

But, Aunt Vera, at 90, was still alive, and I wanted her to tell me about my grandmother's apartment in 217 Mott. What came through was not hardship but happiness—how much she loved that apartment and her family that lived there and the many holidays where all lingered for hours eating and drinking together.

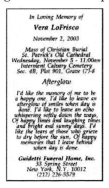

Aunt Vera was quite a character, lively and funny. (She is at right in the dancing girls photo). She passed away in 2003. The prayer card seen here has a very fitting reflection, "Afterglow," So, keeping "Afterglow" in mind, here's a happy memory of Aunt Vera.

It was her 80th surprise birthday party at a restaurant in the old neighborhood. She was overjoyed to see so many of her relatives and friends.

She said, as I recall, "This is wonderful. Everybody is here, just like a wake. In fact, this could be my wake. And everybody is so happy to be here, especially me!"

That was Aunt Vera.

Another family treasure, taken from us much too early, was my Aunt Lena, my Uncle Tommy's wife. Their wedding picture is in another section of the book. Aunt Vera had a place in Commack on Long Island, and we'd go out there for the summers, the women with the kids to get us out of the city. Aunt Lena was unforgettable, a Madonna in the flesh. Though her memory is about 60 years-old, her presence is as vivid as she might be just around the corner. Gentle, loving, and caring. Here she is with Aunt Vera on her right in the courtyard of St. Patrick's Old Cathedral, with the school in the background.

PART 3

NOBILITY

In the Introduction we mention the extraordinary nobility of the ordinary person, and the neighborhood was full of such people in its heyday. In looking at them we see also constancy. We include selective portraits and vignettes about some of them here—a barber, a butcher, a bookie, a bus driver, a family of restaurateurs, a newspaper vendor, a park worker, and several of our many doctors. The butcher is still there!

We stand on the backs of these people, among them our parents and grandparents, our uncles and aunts, older cousins and neighborhood priests and friends, which is why we include the collage on the facing page. They held our hands and held us high. They nurtured and protected us, gave us money for candy and clothes, school uniforms, egg creams, and spaldeens. They taught us how to tie our shoes or a Windsor knot. They gave us religion, lemon ice, and pride, and we loved them and miss them all.

They were our nobility, and to them we were their crowns and scepters.

Sal the Barber in the Make Believe Ballroom

By Jim Merlis

I NEEDED A BARBER NOT A STYL-IST, in a barbershop not a salon, owned and operated by one man, not a local franchise of a national chain, who would cut my hair, not tag my head like some graffiti artist. I wanted a barber.

"I know what you need," my friend Nick said as he interrupted the litany of haircutting demands I was making. He was smiling, sitting across from me at our regular restaurant. He's been going there for years, the food is good, but most importantly they let him smoke. Before telling me what I needed he slowly put his cigarette to his lips, puffed out a cloud of smoke and watched it rise before it gently broke apart into the air.

"You need to see Sal the Barber." My mind immediately leapt to Sal "The Barber" Maglie, former New York Giant and Brooklyn Dodger pitcher nicknamed "The Barber" because he often threw at batters' heads, giving them close shaves.

"His shop is on Mott between Prince and Spring," Nick continued. "They got two chairs there, but he does all the cutting. He doesn't have a phone, so just show up, and if you have to wait he's got these photo albums of pictures he took in Naples. Get a shave too, it's the closest thing to heaven. The whole thing will run ya twenty. That's without the tip." Then he leaned in and turned his head slowly to the left and then to the right, as if he were telling me a secret. His eyes were bright, his eyebrows raised as he said the words he knew would send me directly to Sal, the one thing I wanted from a barber, "Pal, he's even got one of them old fashion barber polls outside his joint." He moved back and took another drag on his cigarette, but instead of looking at the smoke or me he folded his arms and looked away giving me a moment to contemplate what he had just said. He knew what I wanted, I wanted the old school Barber, the old school haircut, one that was classic and timeless and nothing symbolized that more than the barber poll.

The next morning on my way to Sal's I was struck by how much Mott Street had changed. It used to be a neighborhood where men wearing untucked shirtsleeves would sit outside their homes and social clubs on folded chairs on nice days; talking, yelling, reading papers while other men passed and shook their hands and joked. Where gangs of boys would walk aimlessly with purposeful strides up and down the street all day, stopping only to gawk at pretty neighborhood girls. It was a neighborhood of juxtapositions being a hub of organized crime with no street crime, an ancient village in the most modern of cities replete with customs and shibboleths that separated its locals from outsiders.

These days the barriers have been broken down and the outsiders have opened up boutiques where you can be guaranteed that you're paying the highest price possible; young and beautiful men and women walk up and down the street in a certain these-are-the-good-old-days swagger, with a fearlessness that these good old days will last an eternity. These are halcyon times in the city, it's the safest big city in the country,

the only crime, one could say, are the prices at the Mott Street boutiques, but these new Mott Street pedestrians don't seem to mind.

Sal's barber poll seemed to be out of place in this space where it once fit so comfortablyWalking in I knew immediately that the shop was the last vestige of the old neighborhood and old village ways. I later learned that Sal's business hours were indicative of this. Like a mom and pop shop he keeps flexible hours. "Sometime I open at nine," I would hear him tell a customer in his thick Neapolitan accent on a subsequent visit. "Sometime I open later."

On the walls were three brilliant celebrity photos unlike any I had ever seen. There was the picture of Martin Scorsese with his parents (Scorsese grew up a few blocks away on Elizabeth Street. His autobiographical film *Mean Streets* takes place in Sal's neighborhood). Next to Scorsese was a picture of an actor, whose name I didn't recognize but underneath his name read the line, "The Robert DeNiro lookalike." The third picture was of the Robert DeNiro lookalike smiling that side of the mouth squinty eyed Robert DeNiro smile standing next to an uncomfortable and serious looking Robert DeNiro.

I asked for a haircut and shave.

"No shave, buddy," he said sharply, and then turning on his clippers asked, "you want it short?"

Two things I have learned about Sal: he calls everyone Buddy and he always wants to cut your hair short.

"Not too short," I said nervously. Sal chuckled and said under his breath, "Not too short," and put down the clippers and grabbed his scissors. "Buddy, I won't make it too short," he laughed as he began snipping furiously.

As the haircut proceeded, I tried to angle for the shave. I asked him if he knew my friend Nick, but he said he wasn't sure.

He asked me if I lived nearby, and I told him that I lived in Brooklyn. He stopped cutting and said, "I live in Brooklyn too, Borough Park, I started cutting fifty five years ago, right after the war." Before we could bond over Brooklyn, he turned on the clippers to shave the nape of my neck. When that was done I started to talk about Brooklyn, but he didn't seem interested.

I had given up. He was putting the finishing touches on my hair when he asked "You like this music?" The music was coming from a radio in the corner of the shop. It helped supply much of the old time ambiance, playing nostalgic big band music on an AM frequency. The DJ announced in an easy and dulcet tone that the station was from a small town I'd never heard of in New Jersey. He thanked us for being in  The Make Believe Ballroom. It was a great station, playing not only big band music, but also some of the more obscure songs by well-known artists. It was as if the Make Believe Ballroom was created and broadcast solely for Sal's Barbershop.

"Yes," I said.

"Really?" he chuckled skeptically.

"Oh sure, I like Louis Prima, Frank Sinatra, Benny Goodman."

"You really like Frank Sinatra?" He was still skeptical.

"I love Frank Sinatra," and I told him which albums I owned and how I went to see Frank the last time he ever played Madison Square Garden.

"Okay, I give you a shave." I had passed the ultimate test of the old school barber, the appreciation of Frank Sinatra.

It was incredible.

First there were the hot towels, and the warm shaving soap and the gentle brushing of the straight razor across my face. My eyelids grew heavy and I closed them. Occasionally, I opened them to see Sal's eyes behind his black framed glasses studying the small motions he was making as though he were sculpting my features. Then came the details. With his fingers he pulled my nostrils apart and cut my nose hair, he put his hand in my mouth so that it was smooth and he shave around its edges. When he was done my face was smoother than it had been since I hit puberty.

"So, you like your first Mott Street haircut and shave?"

I did, although I am a little miffed that he asks me that every time I see him. But then, we're all just Buddy to him.

That was how the story was going to end, but then I called my brother. On my recommendation, he'd started getting the short haircut I had turned down from Sal. After his first cut, he called me. "He's like an artist," he said.

"He's great," I said.

"He's better than great, he's an artist," he said.

"Like Van Gogh," I said.

"That's a bad choice of artist for a barber," he said.

"Sure, with the ear and all," I said.

"Michaelangelo works better, because he sculpted too and he's Italian and all."

"Michaelangelo," I said.

But just yesterday, my brother actually got a bad cut from Sal, one that he had to cut further when he got home, because Sal had missed a spot. And there were other things wrong too. *There's no Make-Believe Ballroom, anymore. The music is from a soft rock station, an FM* station, no

Sinatra, only contemporary classics. My brother learned that someone broke into his shop and stole his radio, and the new radio can't get AM that well. Maybe that's why Sal didn't seem quite himself.

"Poor Sal, did they take anything else?" I said.

"I don't know, I didn't ask," he said.

Who breaks into a barbershop? I wondered. Is there a big black market for scissors, clippers and AM radios? What kind of people would have done this? Was it vandalism or theft? Did Sal keep a secret stash of money in the shop, and how much could that have been? And, besides, I thought the city had rid itself of crime. Maybe the radio could be replaced, but where can one find a good AM radio these days?

Postscript by the Editor: This Salvatore Schettino, not to be confused with another Sal the Barber on Grand Street, left his barbershop reluctantly in 2001, a victim of the rising rents in Little Italy. Sal's retirement was featured in a New York Post piece, noting that the 89 year-old had been in business for more than 50 years. It tells us that he saw his wife Antoinette for the first time when she walked by the shop on her way to school. According to an article in The Villager in January 2005, some well-known places, like Paolucci's, experienced huge rent increases, in this case from $3500 to $20,000 a month. The owner closed the restaurant on Mulberry Street. The article also discusses how the old style handshake method of making rental agreements has been replaced by a more business-like approach.

Sal died in 2011 at age 97. Thomas Aiello let us know in this short tribute to Sal: Sal the barber died on Wednesday. He was hit by a car while crossing the parking lot at Eger Nursing Home on Staten Island where he resided. Sal touched all our lives in a profound way. His barbershop on Mott Street was a center of activity. Waiting to get your haircut on a Saturday was an education. Sal and his "magic touch" transformed the common man into a matinee idol. The conversation was mesmerizing as men from the neighborhood visited to prepare for their Saturday night revelries. If only the walls could talk. I became close with Sal in recent years. He visited my office with his son-in-law Bob for espresso and cannolis. I visited the nursing home bringing pizza and chianti. We spoke for hours. Sal knew everything. It was like being in the presence of a great teacher.

MEMORIES OF DOCTOR SPOSTA

By Theresa Bynum

ANYONE WHO WENT TO SEE Doctor Sposta can relate to these memories.

The waiting room was generally full of patients waiting to see the doctor. The room was also full of dust clinging to the most beautiful bookcases and chairs that weren't moved since the day they were first put there.

The doctor sat behind his desk in his office, while a cigarette burned down to his lips. It always amazed me how the ash never fell. While you explained your symptoms to him, he calmly opened his mail. Sometimes he took your temperature and I often wondered if the thermometer was cleaned after the last patient had used it. Anyway, the usual procedure was a dose of penicillin.

The needle came out and was tossed into the dish of a Bunsen burner to be sterilized.

You got your shot, and sometimes he asked for a payment of five dollars. No insurance, no fuss.

You were cured within a day or two.

In an emergency, the doctor made house calls. You could expect him to arrive at your apartment anytime from nine in the evening to midnight. Again, the procedure was the same. The needle was boiled in a pot, the cigarette ash burned down and you were cured.

Editor's note. Dr. Sposta was my family doctor and a legend to all of us. His plaque attests to the respect and love given to him in the neighborhood. His memory was old school and incomparable. At times he'd ask you if you were studying Latin and then recite in that language from Caesars's Gallic Wars.

Doctor Perrone

By Vivian Anselmo Beltempo

THE NEIGHBORHOOD WAS FORTUNATE to have had many fine doctors. Doctors Sposta, Testa, Cavallo, Contino and Perrone come to mind. All of those doctors practiced medicine the "old fashioned way," spending time to really get to know their patients and their problems. Their offices may have been small and far from fancy, but their skills were probably equal to those doctors who practiced medicine on Park Avenue.

I owe my life to Dr. Perrone. In early 1948, when I was about six weeks old, I came down with pneumonia. Fortunately for me, penicillin  was available to combat my pneumonia. It was a relatively new drug at the time—an antibiotic. Dr. Perrone, who had recently opened an office on Spring Street, near Guidetti's Funeral Home, came up to my apartment at 214 Mulberry Street several times a day to give me a shot of penicillin. His house visits would usually occur at 8 a.m., 4 p.m. and at around midnight. Years later, my mother would fondly recall how on one particular night, shortly after midnight, Dr. Perrone made a house call while dressed in a tuxedo, after apparently having attended an evening gala. I wonder what doctor today would have been so conscientious? (Photo: Dr. Perrone (right) with nephew Sonny (left). Photo courtesy S. Perrone).

My father was experienced in giving injections. He had injected his mother with insulin for many years, and as an Army medic during World War II, he had given many injections to GIs. However, he just couldn't bring himself to sticking a needle into his tiny infant daughter. With Dr. Perrone's encouragement and coaxing, my father eventually overcame his anxiety and was able to give me my morning and evening injections. Dr. Perrone continued to come up to my apartment, daily, to give me my afternoon injection, and when I no longer needed the penicillin, he would stop by to check on my condition every afternoon for a couple of weeks.

Thank God for Dr. Perrone!

Doctor Nicholas Testa and the Good Lord

By Donald Napoli

WE HAD THE GOOD FORTUNE of having many good doctors in our neighborhood—some of the ones I remember are Dr. Perrone, Dr. Mondelli (noted for assisting people with weight problems and dieting), Dr. Sposta and all the famous stories—stitching you up while the ashes was falling from his cigarette or after getting stitched he forgot to cut the thread and you walked home with a string hanging from your eye. He was a good doctor but what a trip. We in the Monroe Building (265 Lafayette Street) had Dr. Cirillo, Dr. Cavallo and Dr. Testa who lived there for a while but had his office on Spring Street. Dentists included Dr. Spota, Dr. Russo, Dr. Morelli (my favorite) and Dr. Sharig. Let's not forget that it was customary that doctors made house visits all the time.

Dr. Nicholas Testa was special to my family and I am sure generous with his services to many needy families in the neighborhood. I can remember as a 4-year-old one day, holding my mother's hand and walking down the one flight of stairs toward the door that leads to the garbage dump on the concrete yard below. My mother opens the door and flings the garbage over the railing. I spot a cat and in an instant I bolt free from my mother's grip and chase a cat up an adjacent fire escape stairway. I lose my balance half way up the stairs and fall head first a story and a half onto the concrete yard below.

While I do remember chasing the cat, I have no recollection of falling or what occurred afterwards. I was told my mother was screaming and several neighbors came to her assistance while I was on the ground bleeding and not moving—witnesses thought I was dead. Fortunately,

Dr. Testa had recently returned from the service and he was home in the apartment next to ours. He ran down in the yard carried me up in his arms, examined me and stitched me up in his apartment. I apparently landed on my chin and received only five stitches. I was then taken to the hospital for testing and everything showed okay.

The good Lord and Dr. Testa were certainly in my corner that day. During the time Dr. Testa was in the military, my mother would babysit for the two Testa children. Both Dr. Testa and his wife Bobbi were very appreciative and upon his return from the service promised free medical care for the Napoli family for as long as he practices medicine. Both he and his wife subsequently became godparents to my sister Marie. I always found him to be a competent, caring and compassionate physician.

BUFFA'S PRIDE

From Augie and John Buffa

EVERYBODY CALLED IT BUFFA'S, and we all were there more than once or twice for coffee or pastries or a sandwich. John Buffa tells us, "My family has been here all these years. The store we are in now started in 1928. There was a grocery store. And, then it became a luncheonette, a coffee shop and now it's a SoHo restaurant in Little Italy." (Deli) And we go there now after all these years for the same reasons and friendship.

John learned some business lessons at the store from his father. "My father used to run a tab for some customers. He would tell me, "See that guy there. You are not going to see that guy no more. I loaned him $20." This was part of the business. You know you loan people money and you tab up and some of them come back and some don't. But my father didn't care. He would sometimes say it was worth $20 not to see someone anymore.

Augie, John's brother relates some of the family history and its discipline: "My grandfather when he came here worked on the IRT subway. Then he owned a small Olive Oil company on Houston St. Finally we moved to 54 Prince. As a kid I

> ### Triangle Shirtwaist Factory Fire
>
> The Triangle Shirtwaist Factory fire in New York City on March 25, 1911, was the deadliest industrial disaster in the history of the city of New York and resulted in the fourth highest loss of life from an industrial accident in U.S. history. It was also the second deadliest disaster in New York City...The fire caused the deaths of 146 garment workers, who died from the fire, smoke inhalation, or falling to their deaths. Most of the victims were recent Jewish and Italian immigrant women aged sixteen to twenty-three; youngest were two fourteen-year-old girls.
>
> *~from Wikipedia, the free encyclopedia*

felt I lived in this place and on this street because I was always here working. My father was a tough, tough cookie. I remember one day I must have done something wrong. He hit it me on my head with a wooden spoon left a big bump. I guess I deserved it."

Last August Augie attended a Memorial Mass on the 100th Anniversary of the Triangle Shirtwaist Factory. In that tragic fire many immigrant women were killed, some from the neighborhood, but John's aunt, Josephine Nicolas was a survivor. He had with him that day pictures of his aunt.

John tells us, "My father told me a story years ago about how the Italians when they came to this neighborhood had to go underneath the church because they weren't good enough for the top where all the Irish people were. My father said the Irish kids used to throw eggs at the Italians as they would come out of there. Everybody was on the bottom of the ladder and one time we were there. Everybody gets out of the bottom and eventually rises to the top I think. Who ever thought that we would have Italian governors, and we had some Italian mayors, and God knows we will probably have an Italian President one day. I mean we came along way and I think we are going to realize the Italians are just as good as anybody in this country, if everybody would forget about the Sopranos and all the other things they think the Italian-Americans are all about. We are not that way at all. We have a lot of Italian history and culture and good values that we brought to this country, and we are proud that a lot of that is still in the old country still."

Editor's note: Further memories and reflections about the neighborhood by Augie and John are in various parts of this book.

CELEBRATION OF CHARLIE

By Camille Morano

ELIZABETH SAT IN THE KITCHEN impatiently waiting for her grandfather to wake, up. She looked toward the bedroom door hoping it would soon open. It was a month since Grandpa had come to live with us, she thought. Today he was going to teach her how to play poker. It was so much fun having Grandpa living with them. He told her stories and he made her laugh. She loved it best when he spoke of his being a little boy.

The story she liked best was the one about how he started to sell newspapers. He was eight years old and his father shined shoes on this New York street corner. After school, he used to sell papers on the same corner. She couldn't believe that he sold papers for the rest of his life until he had come to live with them. One day he

NOVEMBER 23, 1959

Charlie Morano doing what he's been doing every day for 62 years—selling newspapers at Broadway and 8th St.

Never Missed a Day
Newsdealer Serves As Live Landmark
By GEORGE N. ALLEN.

showed her a copy of a paper that had a picture of him, at his newsstand. He had a cap on, and he looked old. He told her he was seventy-one years old at the time. There was also a story all about him. She thought that her grandfather must be a famous person.

The bedroom door opened and she ran to greet the old man with the tousled white hair and crinkly face. His suspenders were hanging off his shoulders, and he carried yesterday's papers under his arm.

"Grandpa, Grandpa, you promised to leach me how to play poker today, "she said. Slowly, a smile began to cover his face, eyes gleaming, cheeks wrinkling and a perfect set of false teeth shining. It was a smile that sent a message of love. 'Hey! Queen Elizabeth, let me wash up and eat my breakfast first. That's the main thing."

'You promised, you promised, Grandpa." His smile took on sound and his body moved with his laughter. He did what he had done every morning since he came to live there; he took out, his false teeth. Elizabeth loved it. Do it again, Grandpa!" He did, and then he made his way to the bathroom.

Camille called out to him "Charlie do you want ham and eggs?" "That's the way to go," answered Charlie.

Snagglepuss, the parakeet, perched high on his cage whistled his approval of Charlie's answer.

When Charlie came out of the bathroom, Snagglepuss flew on top of his head. "What's that a mosquito?" said Charlie. Elizabeth rolled on the floor in laughter. "Grandpa! You're funny."

The bird flew back to his cage satisfied that he had said good morning to the-newest member of the family.

Elizabeth liked that her mommy and daddy called her grandpa "Charlie." She sometimes wished she could call him Charlie too.

Charlie sat down to eat his breakfast. He thought aloud, "I am eighty years old and until a month ago, I lived a lifetime on Mott Street in Manhattan. I am here in this country place of Staten Is laud for a month; what I thought I could not get used to I am beginning to love.

My youngest son Carmine, his wife Camille, this home and most of all this little five year old, Queen Elizabeth, are my new life. Camille quietly listened, smiling.

He told the family once about the seventy-two years he had sold newspapers on a Greenwich Village street. There was noise, the smells, the crowds, all the people he had known during those years, and the hustle and bustle. He felt he could not live without it all. Now he was nourished by the quiet care of the three of us. "I'm a lucky old man, and that's the main thing."

Maybe he was thinking about that now, but Elizabeth brought him out of his reverie, "Grandpa, here's the cards. How do we play poker?"

Charlie knew it was time to keep his promise. "Okay Queen Elizabeth. First, you shuffle the cards. "Shuffle, what's shuffle?" He grinned again "it means you mix up the cards like this." The cards slowly intertwined into each other as Charlie moved them around in his hands. "That's funny Grandpa." "You think so Queen," he said.

"Then you deal two cards face down. After that you deal one card face up, then you 'Ante.'" "What's that?" she asked. "Queen Elizabeth, you want to know everything." You ask more questions than a dog has fleas." This time his smile was tender. "Ante means you bet. You look at the two cards that are face down and see how much you want to bet. We are playing for pennies. We will play for one cent or two cents. You can only bet two cents when you have a pair."

"What's poker, Grandpa? When will I know if I have poker?' "Hold it up: I'll show you. You get seven cards but you only use five of them." "That's silly; I want to use all of them."

"Pay attention Queen! The highest hand in poker is a straight flush." Elizabeth was lost now. Charlie laughed when he saw her puzzled expression. "Okay we'll begin with, a pair; a pair is two of a kind. You folla? The highest card is an ace, then comes the king, queen, jack, ten and you go down to the two. Folla?" She shook her head yes.

"The lowest hand in poker is a pair of twos." "Can I win with two twos, Grandpa?" "Yeah, if the other people playing have no pairs or nothing else. After the pairs comes three of a kind. Three of a kind beats one pair or two pairs. Folla?" What comes after three of a kind?" "A straight which is two, three, four, five and six or seven, eight, nine ten and jack," he replied" "Do they have to he the same color," asked Elizabeth? "Nah that would be a flush. Folla?'"

"No Grandpa, what s a flush?" He said, "The cards have four suits. There are spades, which are black, clubs, which are black and look like flowers. The diamonds are red and the hearts are red and look like hearts. If you have five flowers or five hearts or five spades or five diamonds you have a flush. Folla?"

"Grandpa, you're making me dizzy. Why can't we just play poker?" Charlie said "I'm making myself dizzy. Let's go Queen."

He dealt out two cards face down and one card face up. Elizabeth had an ace, and he had a queen. Charlie said, "Hey, you bet because you have the highest card." She bet a penny and Charlie dealt her a two, his card was a king. She bet another penny. Her third card was an ace and his was a ten. Elizabeth screamed with delight, "I have a pair, I have a pair Grampa. I bet two cents." Charlie loved watching her excitement. He then dealt her a three and himself a queen. "You have a pair too." "Yeah but your aces beat my queens."

The last card for Elizabeth was a two and Charlie's was a seven. "Grandpa! Gramps! I have two pairs." She jumped off the chair and ran around the kitchen. "Do I have poker?" "Hold it Queen; we have to see what we have in the hole." Elizabeth had an ace and a five; Charlie had a queen and a ten. "I have three aces and two twos! What's that Grandpa?" "Queen, you have a full house. You win."

"Do I have poker, do I have poker?" "Yeah! You do; you win the pot!"

"Grandpa, can we play tomorrow, she asked?" Charlie winked at her knowing that he had fixed the cards for her to win. "Queen Elizabeth, that's a rumor!"

THE LASTING BUTCHER

By Richard. J. Rinaldo

AT **87** YEARS OLD, Moe Albanese can be expected to be comfortable in his own skin. And he is, but he also makes you comfortable when you talk to him, even over the phone. He is straightforward and engaging, and gentle even when critical.

With numerous articles about him and his family, a You Tube video, and a National Italian American Foundation sponsored short film, "The Last Butcher," under his belt as well as a Robert De Niro commercial for American Express, in which the shop is included, one would think that Moe might be full of himself, but he is not. He is well, just Moe-the-Butcher, a family man, (at left with brother Vincent) a grandfather to seven and a great grandfather to five. Like most old-timers whose lives were intimately linked to the neighborhood, Moe reminisces fondly of the old days, when the neighborhood was like an Italian village in which everyone knew one another—like a family. He mentions that you could sleep with your door open, how neighborhood folks looked out for one another and all the children, and the lack of gates on storefronts. He reminisces about the numerous feasts that were celebrated such as San Gondolfo on Elizabeth Street. He remembers the EL (elevator train) on the Bowery, the Sunshine Theater on Houston street and very cheap rents.

Today, he reminds us that, there are few of the old-timers left. Business is not that brisk either as the current inhabitants of the neighborhood, who are mostly professionals and well-healed "don't cook or know how to cook," but rather eat out in the numerous restaurants in the neighborhood.

A graduate of Manhattan College, LaSalle High School, and Public School 21, Moe has been working as a butcher since 1947. According to its website, "The Albanese Meats and Poultry Market had its humble beginning in New York City's famous 'Little Italy' in 1923. Started by Moe-the-Butcher's father and mother, Vincenzo and Mariannina (Mary), the Albanese Family has been serving the very finest meats and poultry for nearly 85 years." Moe learned his butchering skills from his father, but those skills seem to be a family thing, with another Moe Albanese having a butcher store almost directly across the street.

According to the website for the shop, Moe's father Vincenzo passed away in 1954 (Bless his soul). Moe and his mother then ran the store together and his Moe's location became known in the neighborhood as Mary and Moe's to distinguish it from the other Moe's butcher shop. Mary (Bless her soul) passed away at the age of 97 in 2002. But Moe remains. When asked, "How long?" he answers, "Until they kick me out!"

The following, reprinted by permission from their website at Moethe-butcher.com, expands on the above:

Mary, "Moe-the-Butcher", and "Albanese Meats and Poultry" have appeared in movies, documentaries and TV commercials over the years. They've been written-up in many newspapers and magazines, including, The New Yorker, The Village Voice, The New York Times, and Mary even appeared in the 1992 Fall Catalog of J. Crew. Both the shop and the family have been an inspiration to artists, restaurateurs and film makers, including directing giants like, Martin Scorsese and Francis Ford Coppola.

Moe, Mary (and her younger son Vincent) were featured in an American Express TV commercial starring Robert De Niro, which reflected on his "New York" and showcased the Tribeca Film Festival, which Mr. De Niro co-founded to help revive the city after the tragedy on 9/11. Mary Albanese, the matriarch of the family, can be seen in a still picture shot sitting in her familiar chair outside the butcher shop she so loved. This shot of Mary was the same one that was used in a short film featured at the "9/11 Tribute Concert" hosted by Paul McCartney and other celebrities at Madison Square Garden.

A Bus Driver

By J.J. Anselmo

MY FATHER, JOHN "JOHNNY DALE" ANSELMO, drove a bus in Manhattan for 30 years—and he hated the first 29 years of that job! He would often come home from work steaming after a hard day behind the wheel—somewhat like Ralph Kramden, but at 5'-11" and 180 pounds, his bus drivers' uniform fit him a heck of a lot better than Ralph's did.

As a pre-teen, I would occasionally ride on his bus for the last run of the day. Of course, I didn't pay the fare. I simply cut a piece of newspaper into the shape of a bus transfer, and handed it to him. I soon realized that maneuvering a big bus through the First and Second Avenue traffic was, indeed, difficult and dealing with the passengers and making change only added to the difficulty. In fact, his first two years on the job had been even more difficult because the buses had manual transmissions, thus requiring a lot of gear shifting in heavy traffic.

One cannot drive a bus in the City for 30 years without being involved in a few fender- benders. He had his fair share—the most embarrassing one being the time that he smashed into his boss' double-parked car as he was pulling his bus into the 126th St. bus garage. It took him years to get back on his boss' good side after that accident.

Like most bus drivers, he had many "encounters" with dangerous or irate passengers. On two occasions, he had a knife flashed in his face. On more than several occasions, he had to use his "Eastside" fighting skills, including using the bus' fire extinguisher as a weapon, to protect himself from unruly passengers. On the funnier side, there was the time when a woman, upon realizing that she was on the wrong bus, swiped his hat off his head and ran down the subway with it after he had refused to give her back her fare—which was standard Transit Authority procedure at the time.

Ironically, he was once accused by a female passenger of being a Nazi SS man. The distraught woman, who had apparently spent some time in a German concentration camp, was absolutely sure that he was a Nazi who had managed to escape to America after the war. His blue eyes and light complexion, coupled with his well-fitted uniform and hat, had probably triggered bad memories. The more he exclaimed, "I'm an Italian…a Sicilian!" the louder she yelled, "Nazi bastard!"

After 29 years behind the wheel, his seniority at the bus depot finally allowed him to get his "dream job"—moving buses within the garage onto various lines (maintenance, washing, etc.). No more dealing with passengers for him! But, after two weeks, he was bored silly, missing the interaction with the public. As they say: be careful what you wish for. After three more months of working in the garage, he was able to get back to driving on the streets, which made him happy as can be and made him realize that the first 29 years on the job had not been that bad after all.

Parks Man

By Richard J. Rinaldo

MY FATHER WORKED FOR THE NEW YORK CITY Department of Parks for 41 years. He passed away at 78, and his earlier days are somewhat murky. Sometimes he mentioned the Forty Thieves, but I can't remember the context. He was involved in politics for a while with Al Marinelli, a local leader. And he had a job in advertising of same kind as well. He was born in 1903 on Mulberry Bend, and his crib was a bedroom drawer. He was one of seven brothers and sisters, and between them they began a clan that now numbers more than 200 or so.

He was a studious and rather quiet person. My earliest memories include sitting on the floor beside him reading the comics while he read the rest of the evening paper. He studied hard for Park Department examinations and rose through the ranks, starting out as an attendant picking paper and leaves with one of those sticks with a long spearlike piece of metal on the end. He finished his long and dedicated career as a Superintendent of Parks, a position that earned him a chauffeur. But he didn't really enjoy those days, I think. He liked the earlier times as a General Foreman, where he personally knew all the people that worked under him.

The one thing I always remember is that even as a General Foreman in charge of a district, his office was always near the toilets and smelled badly. The department did not have many structures in the smaller parks to accommodate offices. He was well-respected and liked in the department, which allowed him to get me out of trouble when I worked in a park one summer. The folks that came to the park loved me as I took my recreation leader role seriously, but I was also a bit of a goof off. Not a proud moment for me as he struggled with his sense of duty and love for me. I remember too my errant youthful bragging about stealing a bar of candy from somewhere. My reward was a big smack on my behind with a warning never to do that again.

While he worked at Washington Square Park, they discovered that the famous Arch was hollow, since a helicopter flying over saw one of those hippies sunbathing. Seems he had found a way into the Arch and was squatting there for some time. Dad had to deal with all kinds of problems, like people wanting to memorialize the tree their dog peed on after the dog died. Only in New York. Right?

He was also a very honest person, and I remember vividly how he chased a pickpocket off a bus, after observing him trying to steal from a lady.

He taught me how dry socks in five minutes or so, without a microwave or drier and how to break a cord, without a scissor or knife. He taught me that it's important to make sure you don't have a Broadway front and a Bowery back in everything in your life.

He loved to travel in his later years and was in his glory in Europe. But his greatest joy was seeing a grandson, and he was truly proud of my service in the military. He knew Italian but never taught me. He wanted me to be as American as possible. All of our parents felt the same way.

He also enjoyed the company of many friends in the various senior citizen facilities in or near the neighborhood after my mother passed on. He knew how to make

homemade wine and even anisette, and he always shared everything with friends and family.

THE BOOKIE

By Richard J. Rinaldo

THE BOOKIE SLIPPED INTO THE HALLWAY QUICKLY, muttering about the surveillance team. He breathed a sigh of relief as the car full of plains clothes police continued on its way, barely hesitating in his territory.

It is uncanny how he knows that they police rather than lawyers on their way to lunch or an athletic club. But after all, it's part of his job. He is someone who collects illegal bets on the numbers.

He says, "I can smell a cop. Look at the car. No white wall tires. Antenna on the trunk. Six guys in it and they're wearing cheap clothes. It's a lousy color and dirty. They are not neighborhood people." This is not readily apparent to everybody. But he knows, and after all he has been arrested or "pinched," as he would put it, only once in 30 years on the street.

He was the oldest of seven children of a hardworking bricklayer, and a premium was placed on earning a living. Legitimate work was hard to find. "When I started in this business there was nothing better. A lot of guys were doing worse things," he says. He adds, "I don't even have a big car. My kids go to college, but they have to help." They know that his work is illegal, but it is an accepted feature of their environment and they would say, "People who live in glass houses should not throw stones." Most of the neighbors are his customers. To him the "numbers" are a quasi-legitimate business; giving his customers a service they want. When no plains clothes police are around he is as much a feature of the block as the local barber.

He announces the numbers in a crude code, which changes constantly. For example, he will loudly proclaim to his butcher, "Hey. I see you have beef for $1.95 a pound today. Or to the grocer, "Is that coffee only $1.95 a pound?"

His customers have a lot of affection for him. Their attitude is comfortable, warm and close, almost matter-of-fact. This is not the dealings of sharpies and hard-core criminals, but rather the commerce of everyday life, the unexciting goings-on of neighbors and townsfolk. "How's your brother, I heard he had a heart attack. Give him my regards. I hope he feels better soon."

To his customers he is part of the fabric of their lives and a rub of affection on the ache of life's aloneness. He represents a hope of easy reward in a world where one must struggle merely to survive. And he delivers just enough to keep that hope alive.

More importantly though, he is a personal link with the winning, in contrast to the windows and televisions of off-track betting or the impersonal newspaper announcements of state lottery results.

He will make his "hits" a local grand event. "Did you hear who hit the number? Yeah, he almost fainted." And of course, his business enjoys the advertisement. He is a part of the world of the village, family, and extended family in an impersonal society where a wave of unknown and powerful forces snares lives and tosses them like rowboats in a gale.

He was on television once. A network team did an expose on bookmaking. In fact, they followed home and talked to his neighbors. The inconclusive legal battle lasted a long time. He claimed they violated his privacy. Yet, he beams a proud but sheepish grin as he tells about it. "They could've made me an offer at least before they did it. I don't like this sneaky stuff."

He has few regrets or misgivings about his life. He sauntered off down the street, a happy, prideful sway in his gait. He glanced quickly at a passing car. Seeing no threat, he looked ahead to his customers.

Donald Napoli tells us more:

The other thing that you learned pretty early in life you learned how to play numbers. They weren't discreet about it. Tony had a strip of papers three-fourth of an inch long. When he rolled it out, it might have been three feet long.

And Joseph Graziano:

On Mulberry Street at a certain building there a little place there and there was some paper sticking out. So I'm waiting for someone and I started pulling these papers out and there were numbers written over all over these papers. Somebody came, almost ready to beat the crap out of me because these numbers were waiting to be picked up.

PART 4

A SAINT, A PSYCHIC,
AND A SCULPTRESS

DOROTHY DAY

Compiled by Richard J. Rinaldo

 *Dorothy Day has been designated as "A Servant of God," one of the steps to canonization in the Catholic Church. While she became known for her revolutionary views about war and other matters, she was known to us as a person who helped the poor no matter their ideology or the cause of their condition. Although she did not live in our neighborhood, we visited her Catholic Worker mission on nearby Chrystie Street with Father Principe. There we saw the homeless men receive food*

According to Jim Forrest, once a managing editor of The Catholic Work-er, the publication Day founded with journalist Peter Maurin, "The Catholic Worker attitude toward those who were welcomed wasn't always appreciated. These weren't the 'deserving poor,' it was sometimes objected, but drunkards and good-for-nothings. A visiting social worker asked Day how long the 'cli-ents' were permitted to stay. 'We let them stay forever,' Day answered with a fierce look in her eye....They are our brothers and sisters in Christ."

Dorothy Day speaks for herself here, although I have titled the pieces and added the pictures:

ON LITTLE ITALY

We love our neighborhood. There is not a beauty par-lor in it and not a news stand for blocks. Each street is like a little Italian village, and on these hot nights there is music and dancing in the street and everybody stays up until after twelve, because the houses are so hot and airless. The babies are sleeping in carriages and two-  year-olds toddle around the curbstones; the playground keeps open till late and there is plenty of fresh air all around. It's a good walk to the river, North River, or East River, and sometimes we walk down to the Battery and rest our eyes, short-sighted with living in canyons of tenements and rested by the long fresh view over the Bay.

In the daytime, markets are the most beautiful places in the world. Glorious color strikes the eye and the appeal to sight and taste makes one forget the offense to smell. There are fish markets with their eels, snails, blue-black mussels with the seaweed clinging to them, little clams and octopuses and all kinds of fish.

There are fresh figs, fresh almonds, melons, peaches and plums-- every king of fruit is heaped on the push carts, even Concord grapes with their first hint of the autumn to come.

Housewives go by with their shopping bags, hucksters sing their wares, music stores blare with song, children dodge to and fro between the stands, beggars edge through the crowd with hat outstretched and leisurely storekeepers sit by their wares enjoying the sun. There are even some good smells in the air,--smells of spaghetti, ravioli, olive oil and roasts, coming from the little restaurants on all sides.

And two streets away is the Bowery with its stark hunger and color-less misery.

This text is reprinted from "Dorothy Day Library on the Web" at URL: http:// www.catholicworker.org/dorothyday/ and is not copyrighted. It is from Day, Dorothy. "House Sounder, Paper Smaller, Line The Same". The Catholic Worker, August 1937, 1, 2. The Catholic Worker Movement. http://www. catholicworker.org/dorothyday/Reprint2.cfm?TextID=324.

ON BREAD

 Bread keeps coming in from the Divine Providence temporary shelter for children, and Al Gallion, who does all the driving now, picks it up daily. But the food bill has mounted perilously. Tony de Falco called up this morning. He has the corner grocery at Hester and Mott Streets and we have traded with him and his family since 1936. He always has let us charge our groceries and comparing prices, he's been as reasonable as most wholesalers. When we were getting our new headquarters here five years ago, he let the bill go up into the thousands and we never really caught up again. Right now the bill is five thousand dollars, a heavy, heavy load for him to carry and for us to owe him. Am-

mon's fast of ten days did a little to lower it! Guess we'd all better do a little more fasting. Trouble is, even going on that principle, "everybody take a little less, and there'll be enough to feed more," more and more always are arriving. Our guests start arriving at five, lining up for coffee and bread; two hundred or so then. The house, about fifty-five of us, eat at seven thirty; the house eats again at eleven thirty. There are pancakes today, and Smokey Joe, who was in the marines, is reminded of tug boats and calls them collision mats. The line comes again at one o'clock, two to three hundred servings of soup and bread; then there is a lull until supper time at five thirty, and last night there were seventy-five sitting down to table. The extra at night are mostly women who live at the Salvation army or in the neighborhood who earn enough to pay for their lodging, but not quite enough to eat on. There's the woman who sells pencils and chewing gum, who has the deaf and dumb son. There is the old Jewish woman with the scarf around her head who gets feebler, day by day. She is clean and well cared for, but we don't know where she lives or who her people are. She just comes in and sits down and eats, and when she leaves she puts a half dozen slices of bread in her pocket book.

Old Joe Davin was not happy on Welfare Island and now he is home again. He thought he would like it having worked there once, but he was lonely and now he is home again in the bosom of the family with everyone dropping in and out and offering him cold drinks, hot drinks, meals and between meal snacks. Surely there is a deep significance in that phrase, "they knew Him in the breaking of bread of bread." When people share food together they are communing, they are comforting one another. That's why our grocery bills are so high, there is so much of it done around here.

When I was a little girl my mother used to impress on us all that it was a terrible thing to hint. I remember one occasion especially of a visit we paid and I kept hinting that I liked the doll my little friend had. I got it when I got home, but not the doll.

During the summer we received three statues of St. Joseph, all of them works of art, which surely should be a sign that our good friend is watching over us. St. Teresa of Avila said that she never asked anything of St. Joseph that it was not granted. So we ask him to impel you to help. Paying the grocery bills is casting bread on the waters. It will return a hundred fold.

This text is extracted from Day, Dorothy. "St. Joseph's House (Christie St.)." The Catholic Worker, September 1955, 7, 8. The Catholic Worker Movement. http://www.catholicworker.org/dorothyday/Reprint2.cfm?TextID=692.

THE PSYCHIC FRANK ANDREWS

By Richard J. Rinaldo

I FIRST MET FRANK SEVERAL YEARS AGO when
he graciously agreed to allow Ciao, Little
Italy to place our plaque about Play Street
on his building on Mulberry Street. He
just as graciously accepted our change of
heart, when we explained that we would be
concerned that his building might eventually be sold or demolished in the future,
whereas the location of the Parish House
for the Basilica of St. Patrick's, next door,
would be of a more permanent nature.

His full name is Frank Andrews Iacuzzo. Like our own parents (he
is one of us, both his mother and father being of Italian origin, Sicilians), Frank's family wanted him to become fully American and did not
teach him Italian, though they spoke it themselves. Also it was his father
that suggested he skip the Italian last name, as it was too often mispro-
nounced and misspelled. I suspect, though I did not ask, that officially his
surname remains Iacuzzo. Regardless, we should be proud that someone
of his stature lived in the neighborhood since 1967 and loves it still, as
most of us do. His sister lives there too. As for his career, *New York* magazine wrote him up as "Best in New York" in 1995, and he got 5000 phone
calls in one week. (He could not answer them all.) While he does not talk
about his current clients, except in the most general terms, he has read for
Princess Grace, John Lennon, Yoko Ono, Perry Ellis, whom he advised to
become a designer, Franceso Scavullo, and Jason Alexander. Not a Beatles
fan, on meeting Yoko Ono he asked if John came from Russia and was
related to Vladimir Lenin! Notwithstanding his lack of popular musical
taste, the *New York Post*, (Jan 12, 2012) reported that he "...is so revered
in otherworldly circles that Andy Warhol once painted his portrait." It is
easy to see why. He is engaging, humorous, and according to an interview

in *The New Yorker*, "Hanging out with Andrews is fun. While he's slight in stature, he's a big personality, talking quickly and getting excited when he 'hits' on something." Exactly, and you don't have to get a palm reading to see that. As we talked in his parlor in December 2011, he would often jump and say, "You'll get a kick out of this story." I did, and I hope you do too, as we proceed. For Frank is as Italian as one can be— generous, ebullient, and forthcoming at the same time he is discreet. According to one interviewer it was Marion Tanner, reputed to be the real Auntie Mame who suggested he become a psychic; "You have big eyes, you see things," he recalled, according to *The New Yorker*. Again, on the money.

Frank lives at 261 Mulberry Street in a Federal Town House built in 1827, next door to the recently renovated Parish House of the Basilica of St. Patrick's Old Cathedral. Many homes in this style were in the neighborhood before being destroyed to accommodate the building of tenements. The house needed a lot of repair when he bought it. As carpenters, painters and others began work a number of friendly residents warned him that city "master builder" Robert Moses had designs to drive a highway right through the neighborhood. Frank demurred—"Ain't gonna happen," he told them, and thankfully, he was right.

Frank's choice of his new home had an interesting epilogue involving Gian Carlo Menotti's opera, "The Saint of Bleecker Street," which apparently had the original title of "The Saint of Mulberry Street," which was rejected for some reason. His cousin Gabrielle sang the title role in the opera and the staging depicted all the physical characteristics of his house—next to an empty lot, across

Frank's building during a stickball game in 1991

from a church, on the street where the feast of San Gennaro was celebrated, near tenements, and having a side window which allowed light to enter. Frank only learned this much later when the libretto fell out of a book on his bookshelf.

His early days on Mulberry Street were also interesting and funny. Since he was an unmarried adult, some of "the boys," as Frank calls them, approached him and welcomed him to the neighborhood, but firmly warned that "we don't put up with anyone touching our women or children." He said, "Ok, don't worry," and that was that!

Apparently he also got wind that some of them thought he had a touch of "malocchio," the dreaded "evil eye," discussed more later in this book. As such he often received gifts of pasta, meatballs, and hero sandwiches to appease him.

The location of Frank's house next to what was then the Rectory of St. Patrick's Old Cathedral was also interesting. One day he heard a gentle  knock on the door. He opened it and was flabbergasted to see Mother Theresa, with a bevy of nuns behind her on the steps, seeking the rectory of the church. Similarly, one early morning knock turned out to be a lady in a shawl with a young sheepish looking man behind her, asking if Frank could do a confession. Frank says, "I should have done it. I would have given him one hundred thousand Hail Mary's as penance." We should be happy that he did not seek his otherworldly vocation as a Catholic priest, though he likes his next door neighbors in the Parish House. "They try to get me to mass," he says, and he does goes over there sometimes, but fears that when he dies he would not be among too many friends, if he went to heaven. He wants to be where they go.

Back in the old days, being down the block from the renowned Ravenite Social Club, where John Gotti often hung his hat, had advantages for at least one of his well-to-do looking clients, who being early for an appointment decided that she needed a cappuccino and some Italian pastries. So she went there and took a seat, feeling a little strange being the only women in a room full of men smoking cigars and playing cards. One of them, however, rose and came to her table asking if he could help her. She asked for a cappuccino and a pastry. The cappuccino was promptly served and the "waiter" then left to return with a cannoli for her. There was no charge. She asked, "Why?" Mr Gotti replied, "You're a friend of Frankies." "How did you know?" she asked, and he replied, "You're one of those uptown dames."

Frank read for some of "the boys," and their wives as well, apparently before Tony Soprano and others turned to psychiatrists and Prozac rather than psychics for their problems. He told one lady that her husband would soon go to Kansas, not knowing that he was currently in the New York State prison in Ossining. Her husband was later transferred to the federal prison at Fort Leavenworth, Kansas. Frank predicted that the husband would be released from jail and that they should be careful. The husband was later killed. He warned another to keep her son home, but she failed, and her good boy was arrested for stealing a car.

Frank also knew Louise Nevelson, the sculptress, whom we discuss also in this chapter. He was disappointed that she did not leave her spacious home on Spring and Mott Street as a museum to display some of her work. He recalls her visit for dinner accompanied by her longstanding companion, Diana MacKown. Louise shared the fact that they had never had sex, despite their years together, and one of his other guests, a very sophisticated lady remarked, "What a pity!" Louise liked Frank's rocking chair so much that he gave it to her. On a reciprocal visit he did not see it, but during a tour of the studio recognized some of its parts in one of her works! Nevelson, he noted, loved to scrounge for wood throughout the neighborhood, even from friends!

Frank's father used to tell him that his house on Mulberry Street was a lucky charm, and as the years have gone by, he could not agree more. He sees living there as a blessing and is thankful for spending so much of his life among the company of so many wonderful Italian and Italian-American people. He finds sadness too as so many of the old timers pass away, and as we parted he mentioned that he had to go across the street for a wake at the Basilica. And Frank's neighbors were right to bring him gifts in deference to his powers. He probably does have the eye, but the good eye, the one that sees and helps people.

Thank you Frank, for being a good neighbor.

Further information about Frank: Frank is a Tarot and Palm Reader, lecturer, teacher, consultant, and columnist of the *New York Post* and *Mode Magazine*. In addition, having many celebrities as friends and clients made him a popular guest on television and radio talk shows. With over 30 years' experience in matters of the occult, Mr. Andrews is known as the "Rolls Royce of Psychics" (N.Y. Daily News), "Psychic to the Stars" (CBS-TV News) and "Best Psychic in New York" (*New York Magazine* 1995). He has lectured for the New York Advertising Club, the Museum of American Folk Art, the Philosophical Research Center, Unity Fellowship, Mystery Writer's Club of America, SS Canaberra Cruise Line, Amerikanus Cruise Line, and the Spiritual and Ethical Society of N.Y. He has been the subject of feature articles in the *New York Post, New York Times, the Village Voice, Vogue, Harper's Bazaar, the N.Y. Daily New, Mademoiselle, the New York Observer* and many other publications both national and international. He was also featured in many books about his clients. He has contributed to numerous fund raisers for a variety of cultural, medical, and children's causes. His phone number is (212)226-2194.

THE SCULPTOR

By Richard J. Rinaldo

WE NEVER REALLY KNEW WHO
SHE WAS when she first entered our consciousness with
her long, flowing garments,
crazy hats, beads, sandals,
and eccentric makeup. (Photo at right with granddaughter Neith Nevelson, from
Wikimedia Commons.) She
roamed the neighborhood

for wood and other objects lying in the street or on the sidewalks next to
tenements, factories, and even a funeral parlor. She picked up crates, pal-
lets, two by fours, and even a discarded embalming board from the funeral home, according to Joseph Guidetti, then owner of Paul A. Guidetti
& Son Funeral Home. She apparently used it in one of her works. After
she died at age 88 in 1988, more than 250 people attended a service for
her, according to the *New York Times* obituary story, "Friends of Louise
Nevelson Gather In a Memorial for the Late Artist," by Grace Glueck
(Oct 18, 1988). Among them were "stellar figures from the worlds of art,
fashion and the movies," wrote Glueck.

The famous sculptor lived on Spring Street in a sprawling three-
story apartment complex. According to Joseph Guidetti, who had been
there, it was very dark looking with walls painted black, reflecting her
penchant for the dark colors in her art. She used black spray sometimes
on objects she found for use in her art, and neighbors complained because
the spray drifted onto their clothes hanging to dry outdoors on their
clotheslines. Nevelson loved to eat at the original Lombardi's restaurant
when it was located on Spring Street between Mulberry and Lafayette
streets. She also visited the Café Primavera on Spring and Mulberry almost daily with her companion Diane McKown. They often joined one

of the local power brokers with whom they remained friendly.

Nevelson showed a keen interest in historic preservation of the neighborhood. She apparently joined Jacqueline Kennedy in a fruitless effort to have the Beaux-Arts former Police Headquarters on Centre Street restored and used as some type of museum or cultural center, but the developers won out, and it is now a luxury condominium, though it is a New York City Landmark.

I remember Ms. Nevelson. The entrance to her apartment was on Mott Street next to Sal the Barber's. (See separate story about Sal.) Sometimes on cold winter nights we'd try to huddle in the enclosed entrance, and she would come down to throw us out. I never really liked her, but I was kind of a street urchin as a youngster and probably deserved the hostile stares she seemed to fling my way. When they were looking into the design for the Vietnam Memorial, and I was still in the Army, I wrote her suggesting we might collaborate, at least conceptually on my part, for a design. I never heard from her. However, she seemed to like my mother and would stop and talk to her. My mother (above left) dressed up and even wore gloves and hats, long after they were fashionable in the neighborhood. Maybe Nevelson saw in her a devil-may-care form of style similar to her own, and admired it in my mother.

I guess her legacy as far as the neighborhood goes was that bits and pieces of it live on, transformed by her work into art. The neighborhood's contribution was the tolerance, if not respect, it afforded her, some measure of companionship, security, and neighborliness, and affordable space for her work, I'm sure, at least in her early days there. Budding artists would likely find the rents insurmountable today.

Pen on Paper © Ron Crawford

Ron is a New York artist living in Little Italy. He is also an actor on stage and screen. His favorite art challenge is to sketch quickly and try to capture a moment. He also enjoys finding a subject for his oil painting and taking days to finish. His neighborhood, of course, offers much to an artist. Go to roncrawfordart.com for more of Ron's work. He loves to cook Italian. To see Ron on film get "Arthur and the Invisibles" from Netflix and sit the family down to watch. He plays Arthur's grampa.

PART 5

RELIGIOSITY

In Memory of
my Beloved Niece Cathy
from Serafina Viglietta

134

St. Patrick's Church and School

By Richard J. Rinaldo

On March 17, 2010, the feast of its patron, St. Patrick's Old Cathedral was officially declared a basilica by Pope Benedict XVI, fulfilling a promise by Archbishop Dolan at the celebration of the bicentennial of the cathedral on June 7, 2009 to seek such a designation. As such it became the first basilica in the New York Archdiocese. The hand embroidered-ombrellino (umbrella), depicted here is a symbol of this new basilica signifying its heritage to protect the Pope from inclement weather and might be interpreted as the mandate

of the Church as protector of its flock from all manner of harm. As Monsignor Donald Sakano, pastor of the cathedral pointed out so clearly at the dedication of the cathedral as a basilica on December 5, 2010 at a vespers ceremony there, "If these wall could talk they would tell of struggle, injustice, poverty, prejudice, but they'd also tell you about success, close community, family, good times."

St. Patrick's Old Cathedral and its school was an integral part of "the neighborhood" and our lives as many discuss in this book. It was our path to faith and education, even if we strayed at times. For Catholics, Baptism, Confirmation and Holy Orders (for the priesthood) leave an indelible mark on the soul, and most of us were baptized and confirmed in the cathedral.

In the early years of Italian immigration into "Little Italy," the newcomers did not participate in services in the main part of the Cathedral, where mostly Irish Americans attended. Instead, they went to a chapel in the basement. This was later interpreted by some to mean that the church was not immune to the all too typical cycle of immigration to America, which involved rejection of outsiders.

Just as the Nativists rejected the Irish Catholics, who defended the church with Bishop Hughes in the 1850s "... the Irish were not always welcoming to other Catholic immigrants -- the Italians, Germans, French...," according to Patricia Lefevere writing in *The National Catholic Reporter* last year. In turn, some Italian-Americans gave Puerto Ricans a hard time as they came to the neighborhood.

In any case, many Italian Americans supported the church and eventually became central to its vibrant life. They donated and refurbished nearly all its stained glass windows. They also built the Youth Center on Mulberry Street with their generous contributions and fund raising efforts by beloved pastor, Rt. Rev. Msgr. Bonaventure Filitti. Boy and Girl Scout troops, active Holy Name and St. Ann's Societies and a well-attended and highly successful elementary school marked the high point of the Italian American experience at Old St. Patrick's Cathedral.

Moreover, whatever truth might lie in Lefeverer's assessment, attending services in the basement of the church was probably not a rejection of Italians, but more likely one of a variety of ministerial approaches adapted by the Catholic Church in New York to accommodate the wave of Italian immigrants at the turn of the 20th century. In some places there were national churches, entirely staffed by Italian speaking priests, which catered to the immigrant population. The Church of the Most Precious Blood in the lower Mulberry Street area was one such church, established by Vatican decree in 1888. A 1900 baptism certificate of one of my aunts came from that church. At right is one from 1917 of my uncle from St. Patrick's Cathedral. Another such church in the neighborhood was The Church of the Most Holy Crucifix on Broome Street, built in 1922,

but in consideration of changing demographics of the city and neighborhood, discontinued as such in in 2005, when the building became the

Roman Catholic Chapel of San Lorenzo Ruiz. It was declared the official "Church of the Filipinos" and attached to the Philippine Pastoral Center of the Filipino Apostolate. Likewise, Our Lady of Loreto on Elizabeth Street was a mission organized by the Jesuits in 1891, to serve the large Sicilian Italian population that resided east and west of the Bowery and north of Broome Street. It was closed and after becoming a Holy Name Center for homeless men, it has received a new mission to become The Archbishop Fulton J. Sheen Center for Thought and Culture. Archbishop Dolan appointed Fr. Michael Hull as its founding Director and is calling on Fr. Jonathan Morris and Monsignor Sakano to assist him in getting it going. As Monsignor Sakano pointed out in a Basilica bulletin in July 2010, "In this era of seeming retrenchment, it is wonderful to be called to develop the vision of a Catholic center for thought and culture. This will take time."

Many of us can remember our college days when in the evenings we repaired to Dave's Corner or one of the local coffee shops to debate those topics and philosophies we studied, ranging from Aristotle to Aquinas, or articles from *Commonweal* and *America* magazines. Some still subscribe, and we include two pieces from the former later in this chapter. We were privileged as well to hear from the likes of Dorothy Day, a candidate for sainthood. And who could be more interesting to listen to on such topics than our local parish priests, whose education made them both articulate and erudite. We were richly endowed by our church on such matters! Those blessings and memories are priceless, and we applaud the new center as a place where such experiences will continue in a new form.

Returning to Italian immigrants, in many cases there was another approach to serving them, that of having a single Italian speaking priest attached to an English parish. Finally, there was the approach that St. Patrick's employed at one point, the "annex congregation" or "duplex church," according to a Cardinal Hayes High School 1959 text, *Outline History of the Church in the United States.* The rationale behind this approach was that "the Italians could not support their own establishment."

Rev. Bernard Lynch, pastor of the Church of the Transfiguration, another neighborhood "duplex church" in the earlier years if Italian immigration, when the neighborhood

extended further south into what is now Chinatown, saw part of the solution in getting the children into Catholic schools, and that was precisely what happened with St. Patrick's Old Cathedral School, staffed, by the way with mostly Irish-Catholic nuns of the Sisters of Charity, the religious order founded by St. Elizabeth Ann Seton. The school was established in 1886, and it is New York's first and oldest parochial school. It closed in 2010 as the parish and diocese confronted changing needs and a new demographic.

The following "Memories" of the Cathedral were part of a "Remembrance of the Solemn Rededication of the Old Cathedral by His Eminence Terrence Cardinal Cook on Sunday May 21, 1972." This was, of course, before Elizabeth Ann Seton became a saint and before our cathedral became a basilica. Images have been added. For more on the history of the Basilica see *http://www.oldcathedral/history.php*

But before leaving the Basilica we should mention Saint Michael's Russian Catholic Chapel located at 266 Mulberry Street, between the Basilica and the Youth Center, which was founded to minister to Russian Catholics wishing to follow the Byzantine rite in New York City. We remember Father Andrew Rogash, its pastor. Sometimes we attended services there, and they were a testament to the catholicity of our Catholicism. The Chapel is still active. See *http://stmichaelruscath.org*

MEMORIES

To historic St. Peter's Church, located on Barclay Street in lower Manhattan goes the distinction of being New York's oldest Catholic Church. Less than a mile northeast, on the corner of Mott and Prince Streets, stands the city's

first Cathedral Church—St. Patrick's. Although only the shell of St. Patrick's remains intact, after the Church was completely gutted by fire in 1886, this cathedral is one of the earliest examples of Gothic Revival architecture in this city.

When the cornerstone of Old St. Patrick's was laid on June 8, 1809, the city's population was about 90,000 and the cathedral was considered to be out of town, at the end of winding lanes. Its site had been a cemetery maintained by St. Peter's Church, for the 13,000 Catholic residents of the city. Progress in building the cathedral was retarded by lack of funds, the death of the first bishop, Luke Concanen, and the hard times brought about by the War of 1812. Despite all the setbacks the edifice was sufficiently completed to be dedicated on May 14, 1815, and on that day the New York Gazette described the cathedral as "a grand and beautiful church, which may justly be considered one of the greatest ornaments of our city...." Formal and severely plain in its appearance, it has great dignity and character in its restrained simplicity. Its side walls rise to a height of 75 feet, and the inner vault is 85 feet high. It is over 120 feet long and 80 feet wide, with six clustered columns on either side dividing the interior into three naves crowned by Gothic arches forming a *coup d'oeil*. Near the west wall stands the huge marble altar surrounded by an ornately carved, gold leaf reredos. At the opposite end of the church in the choir loft is to be found a most historic organ, an Erben 3-41, in unaltered condition. This organ was built in 1852 by an organ maker of superior craftsmanship, the famous Henry Erben, and is one of less than a dozen such great instruments still to be found in New York City. Beneath the church lies a labyrinth of well-kept mortuary vaults and outside, to the north and south is a cemetery containing many old graves and tombstones. Most famous is that of Pierre Toussaint, a Black New Yorker, born a slave in Haiti, whose cause for canonization is being considered by Rome. By 1817 the grand structure was finally completed under Bishop John Connolly, at the final cost of $90,000.

During the next two decades some of the most violent exhibitions of religious bigotry ever seen in the United States, were directed at Old St. Patrick's. In 1835, an attempt was made to burn and destroy the cathedral and in 1842, a mob broke all the windows in the church and rectory on Mulberry Street, where the third bishop of New York, John Dubois had his residence. In 1844 the so-called "Native American" disturbances reached a new peak of violence when a torchlight parade, formed in City Hall Park, marched up the Bowery with the avowed intention of burning down the cathedral. The first Archbishop of New York, John Hughes was now heading the diocese, and he rallied the parishioners to the defense of their church. Armed men took up defense positions inside the cathedral and behind the wall of the graveyard. Learning of the forces which had been mobilized to oppose it, the anti-Catholic mob abandoned its attempt to destroy the cathedral and ran off.

As time went on, Old St. Patrick's was the center for many historical happenings in New York. Within its walls

-in 1820, the first priest was ordained, the Rev. Richard Bulger

-in 1826, a concert of classic music was given starring Madame Malibran of the Garcia Company, the first operatic troupe in the United States

-in 1838, the first bishop was consecrated, the Most Rev. John Hughes

-in 1842, the first Diocesan Synod and in 1854 the first Provincial Council of New York were held here

-and finally, on April 27, 1875, the crowning glory, the greatest event in the history of the Old Cathedral was the investiture of the first American Cardinal. In rich and colorful rites attended by members of the hierarchy, clergy and laity, both Catholic and non-Catholic, Archbishop Bayley of Baltimore, placed the red biretta on the head of the fifth bishop of New York, John Cardinal McCloskey.

As the years went by and wave upon wave of immigrants from Europe came to settle in New York- St. Patrick's Old Cathedral became the church of generation after generation of people who helped to build America. This venerable church cradled the Germans and French, then the Irish and the Italians who built the roads and dams, and worked in the plants and factories- that helped to build this city and this nation. These hard working new Americans were deeply interested in seeing that their children received a good education, and most were sent to St. Patrick's parochial school across from the church on Prince Street. Here the school and convent of the Sisters of Charity is housed in one of the largest and finest examples of Federal style architecture in this city. It was originally the first Catholic orphan asylum established by the foundress of the Sisters of Charity, whose cause is now up for canonization, Mother Elizabeth Bailey Seton. When this occurs, she will have the distinction of being the first American-born saint. From 1817 on, a grammar school has been operated in connection with the Old Cathedral, and so today St. Patrick's School can boast of being the oldest, continuously operating school in the archdiocese. The Old Cathedral reached a milestone when on May 25, 1879 it ceased to be the seat of the archdiocese and became a parish church. The change in status was the result of the completion of the new and present Cathedral of St. Patrick at 50th Street and Fifth Avenue, whose cornerstone had been laid in 1858.

The Bowery, Mulberry Street, Mott Street and much of this part of little old New York was once a fashionable area- but time has taken its toll. The old immigrants have moved away, and the new Spanish-speaking and Chinese people are joining the third generation Italians who still remain. But the churches, like this landmark cathedral, still continue to serve and to minister to the people of God. If this ancient church has had a rich and inspiring history, it is due in large measure to the great love that has surrounded her, and if like all old buildings, she has her share of ghosts, they are happy, benevolent spirits!

Pastors Past and Present

More Memories and Reflections

On a recent visit to the Basilica I joined this group of ladies, all lifelong Italian-American residents of the parish, at an afternoon mass and adoration service. Following the services, I also joined them for their customary get together in the Parish House. They talked about a variety of topics related to the Basilica, their love of the neighborhood and their faith,  fond memories of their participation in religious observances, feasts, and loved ones. They accept that the neighborhood has changed a lot, but its church remains their anchor in this sea of change.

Donald "Red" Napoli provides a few vignettes about our church. Blame me for the titles:

Heavenly Sundays in Little Italy

By Donald Napoli

Easter Sunday 1963, everyone dressed to the nines, guys with their sharkskin or silk and mohair suits, the girls not to be outdone, with their Easter bonnets, fancy dress and pocketbooks. After the 9 A.M. mass at St. Patrick's, the guys all made a stop at John the bootblack on Prince Street for the best shoeshine in the neighborhood and when the customary trip to Piccolo's Pastry shop on Spring Street for donuts and pastry. Right near Piccolo's we usually bought the Italian bread on Sunday's, from either Bocci's or Parisi's. Our job was to bring home the bread and the various mixed donuts, jelly or cream etc., right after mass. Punctuality, unfortunately, was not one of our strengths in our younger days. By the time we arrived home, usually an hour later or more after all the horsing around, half the Italian bread and donuts were gone. Walking in the front door, I could hear my mother screaming between slaps "Where were you, the mass was over two hours ago?" It was all worth it. How could you possibly carry around that bag of goodies for an hour or two and not eat anything? It was amazing that we went home with something left in the bag.

When we finally got home, there was always the meatballs frying in the oil and what tastes better than just meatballs with fresh Italian bread (fortunately, we still had some) dipped in a pot of hot sauce. You truly believe you died and went to heaven.

Photos:
Easter Sunday 1963 (Top to bottom):
on Mulberry St., Elizabeth St., Mott St., and Prince St.

Vito Gentile adds this poem to our Sunday thoughts:

SUNDAY MORNING

I am awakened by my mother's voice
She is down in the kitchen below
Sweetly singing the prelude melody from La Traviata
She is cooking
I can tell
There is only her serenade
And that sense of Sunday's quietness all around me
I thank God for all these pleasures
The sun is still opening its eyes
It must be before seven in the morning
And the aroma of thick black coffee tickles my nose
It is cold but my window is open
I snuggle in a half daze under my warm blankets
The breeze blows the curtains
They keep cadence with the hiss of the steam pipe –
Keep cadence with the patter of my wooden Venetian
blinds
Their vertical shadows swing back and forth
Like two silent metronomes they give me pause to day-
dream
Ssss!
Oh, the sound of beef as it hits hot oil
She is already preparing dinner?
Pots and pans rattle
Spoons fall
What comforting sounds
Someone is playing with the radio
My father must be awake
Italian radio commercials softly blend with my mother's
singing
And I hear his slippers slurping across the floor
He is gathering and dragging chairs around the kitchen
table
My uncles should be arriving any minute

They'll join him in a cup of coffee
And have their traditional Sunday morning argument
Where are my aunts?
Home of course, cooking Sunday dinner
Ssss!
Onions, mmm
Garlic, parsley, oregano, mmm
Fresh tomatoes, mmm
Basil, salt, pepper – a dash of sugar – what a smell!
She probably made meatballs too
I think I'll have a meatball sandwich when I get up
Well, maybe after Mass
Who wants to hear her screaming about not receiving?
I believe I smell almond cookies
When did she bake them?
I hope my uncles don't finish them all
Oh, tomato sauce!
Your smell –
It smothers me with kisses
I am at your mercy
What a life I have
Who has it better than me?
The burdens of the world
Let them blow with the curtains
I'll never miss them
Not today
I must be in paradise
If heaven could only be like this!
God bless me
God bless my mother's cooking
God bless all Neapolitan cooks
What a magnificent Sunday morning!
I feel so relaxed
So –
Not since the womb have I felt so secure

Praying for Tips!

by Donald Napoli

WHILE MANY OF US KIDS PLAYED ALL THE SPORTS activities in Little Italy, we also prayed. With the guidance and spiritual direction of Father Francis J. Principe, some of my friends and me became altar boys at St. Patrick's Old Cathedral. Since the entire Mass was said in Latin it was a challenge to learn a new language. Controlling the incense vessel that was suspended by chains was another difficulty. On a few occasions, I can recall being assigned to an early Mass— waking up a little late, quick shower, rushing to get dressed, out the door and running down Prince Street past Buffa's Delicatessen to Mulberry Street. Then up the sacristy steps a quick change into my black cassock and white starched surplice and ready to go on the altar for Mass just before old man John was ready to pull on the rope ringing the church bells. I can remember spending many hours at Church and serving at various hourly Masses including weddings, funerals, benedictions and major feast days. A wedding assignment was special because you always received a tip from a gracious groom or best man after the ceremony. I can recall receiving as much as $10, quite a sum in 1956 for a 13 year-old.

Editor's note: Old man John was the sacristan of the church. He was in charge of the sacristy, where the vestments were kept along with sacred vessels. He was also in charge of the church building itself and its contents. And, you'd better not cross him, not so much because of his position in the church's hierarchy, which was not too high, but because he smoked an Italian manufactured cigarillo tobacco product, which smelled just awful to a young person. He would blow the smoke in your face, if you offended him in any way, and sometimes just because he wanted to see you choke and cough! Then your mother or father would accuse you of smoking on the sneak, saying "and you an altar boy, you hypocrite." This was sometimes the price of being an altar boy.

Red also mentions "hot sauce." This is not the tabasco type of "hot sauce," but rather the sauce that was cooking in a pot on your mother's stove, usually with the meatballs and other meats simmering therein. In fact, most of us called it "gravy," and technically that was correct because gravy is a substance made from the juices that ran from meat during cooking, and there was a lot of that in the pot.

How Little Italy Made Me a Saint

By Richard J. Rinaldo

WELL, NOT EXACTLY, and anyone who knows me knows that I never was a saint. Far from it. Still something wonderful began with visits to the neighborhood whenever possible during trips to New York. It seemed that these visits confirmed my love of the place time and time again. With the encouragement of some friends and several priests from the parish I began collecting pictures from friends about the neighborhood. We placed them on a site called Schwup.com with a link at the cathedral's website. We also set up a Facebook page and a website. Having learned about all of this Msgr. Sakano asked me to attend some meeting to plan the Bicentennial Celebration of the Cathedral. Living in Virginia made me less than an ideal participant and my cousin's sister, Virginia Dell'Olio took up the slack and developed a wonderful set of pictures, which would be looped into a slide show with music for use during the Bicentennial at the Youth Center on Mulberry Street.

So naturally I wanted to go back to the neighborhood to attend the bicentennial celebration, and it fit right in with a visit of my wife's brother and his daughter from Germany. They came along as did my son Brian. As luck would have it, the bicentennial of the cathedral was on a Sunday and the preceding day was the 50th Anniversary of my 1959 Cardinal Hayes High School class.

Everything was set. I would meet a fellow classmate, close friend, and cousin, Ralph Patete and other classmates at St Patrick's Cathedral on Fifth Avenue. On Sunday we would got to mass at Old Saint Patrick's Cathedral, view a the celebratory parade, visit the school and youth center and later go to dinner arranged my friend Vinny LaBarbera at an Italian restaurant with lifelong friends from Kindergarten.

But something was missing. Something was wrong. For about 50 years I was a lapsed Catholic! It nagged and nagged at me, but I did nothing about it. Moreover, even as a youth I was surrounded by good Catholics, it seemed, wherever I went—relatives family, friends old and new, people and priests I admired and respected.

On Friday we went to Times Square from our hotel on 31st Street. There was a church on the street as we headed west. We saw it again on our return, the Church of St. Francis of Assisi. On Sunday, very early in the morning, I left the hotel, intending to head east to Fifth Avenue, on my way to St. Patrick's Cathedral on 50th Street.

Instead I headed west. When I reached the church of St. Francis of Assisi, there was a Franciscan priest in his traditional brown habit with hood. I asked him if there were confessions today, and he said, "Sure, here's the schedule," pointing to the sign posted behind us on the church wall with the schedule of services. I replied, "Well, I might be occupied then, but it's been about 50 years." He said, "Come here," and drew off to the side where he gave me general absolution immediately. Thus began my re-membering process to the Catholic Church and a return to the Communion of Saints.* The neighborhood was there for me, and a priest was there for me at the right time and place.

*According to the Catholic Encyclopedia, "The communion of saints is the spiritual solidarity which binds together the faithful on earth, the souls in purgatory, and the saints in heaven in the organic unity of the same mystical body under Christ its head, and in a constant interchange of supernatural offices. The participants in that solidarity are called saints by reason of their destination and of their partaking of the fruits of the Redemption."

PHYLISS
MEATBALLS ON THE STOVE

By Virginia Dell'Olio

SHE KNEW HER MOTHER WOULD NOT BE HOME FOR A WHILE. It was Sunday morning and as the solemn bell of the old church tolled, it meant to everyone in the Italian American community that it was the Offertory at Old St Patrick's Cathedral. After the Offertory came Communion and then after Communion came the final blessing. So the child knew she still had plenty of time. After all, her mother still had to go to the local bakery "Piccolo"; that other Sunday ritual to buy drop cakes and doughnuts bursting with sweet custard or raspberry jelly and those crumb cakes! The Piccolo counter would be four deep giving the child extra time to carry out her mission.

Italian American families in Little Italy attended mass every Sunday. That's why the child was left alone that morning. She had a slight fever but that would not stop her mother, Phyllis, from going to church. Like clockwork at 9 o'clock on Sunday morning Phyllis' sister Nettie would open Phyllis' door which was never locked, peek in and tell Phyllis she was "making the 10." That was code for "she was going to attend the 10 o'clock mass." Like most Italian American women, she "started her gravy" before she left for mass and left the slowly bubbling mass on the stove to gather flavor.

Most of Phyllis's life was motivated by food and feeding her family. She was taught by her Neapolitan mother who expected her to teach her children the recipes that kept the family eternally bonded together. Phyllis was the keeper of the torch and the child wanted to be just like her mother. The child watched skillfully. She was motivated by hunger and a sense of duty so she eagerly paid attention to everything her mother prepared and how she prepared it. Even though she was so young, the child understood the importance of her role in the family. She would one day be the nurturer, the provider, and the keeper of the torch for her own family.

So while her mother was busy receiving Communion, the child dragged the wrought iron chair across the kitchen making sure not to scratch the linoleum floor. It was heavy and difficult to move, but the child knew exactly how to do it. She pulled it across the kitchen to the front of the stove so that she could stand on the chair and see exactly what was on top of the stove. Like most children who were left alone often out of necessity, she had a maturity way beyond her five years. She was taught early the important survival skills she needed to know. The child knew the parts of the stove and what they were used for. Consequently, the child never got burned.

She stared at the dish in anticipation. There they were! The beautiful round morsels were piled high like boulders forming a pyramid. This is what she smelled that morning while she lay in bed through a hazy feverish sleep. Although during the week, there was just barely enough food, on Sunday you could feast and never felt sad. Sunday was happy.

So she carefully picked up the prize between her thumb and index finger and slowly savored every single bite. It was worth the struggle. It was worth waiting for all week. She was triumphant. She had a fried meatball on the stove!

Little would the child know that thirty years later, her own children would come for Sunday dinner and the first thing they did when they arrived was look for the fried meatballs on the stove. This would please her tremendously because this was a validation of who she wanted to become…the nurturer, the provider and the keeper of the torch. She would know then that her mother was smiling down at her. This was the ultimate accomplishment. She was able to span the generations and keep her children firmly vested in their heritage and appreciation of family by keeping that one tradition alive…meatballs on the stove!

THE RULERS

Augie Buffa and Joseph Morale about the Sisters of Charity

Augie Buffa:

I REMEMBER GETTING HIT ON MY KNUCKLES with an iron ruler. I remember why. They asked me a question like "Who was God"? And in the 2nd grade as a child I just froze. So they hit me. Blood came out of my hands, and back home I told mom and dad. They said, "Those are the breaks kid."

Joseph Morale:

My earliest memory of the neighborhood was of the first day of school at St. Patrick's, crying hysterically. Woman in black. Terrified. But made friends for life there. St. Patrick's was at that time the mecca—if you went to public school you were looked down upon like you did something wrong. We went to this Catholic school with the Sisters of Charity and they sometimes showed us no charity with their rulers, but they did a good job.

Editor: As if to prove a point, I remember some of our lay teachers. Apparently they did not share the Sister's methods, and they quickly lost control of the class.

Holy Name Society and Mother Cabrini Guild 1959

The Choir in the '50s.
Top center
Fr. Sansaverino,
Music Director.
Middle right
Mr. Campbell,
Boys Choir.

St. Patrick's School

Memories of St. Patrick's Old Cathedral

By Sarah Ann LoFaso

I WOULD LIKE TO SHARE WITH YOU some of my earliest memories of growing up in Little Italy and the influence that St. Patrick's Old Cathedral parish had on my life. Like most seniors today, I like to think back to the 1940's and 1950's as the "Golden Years."

I was a grandchild of Italian immigrants who came to the United States in the early 1900's in order to find work and to raise a family. Their work ethic was superb. It had to be so hard for them at such a young age to leave their families in Naples and Sicily and to sail across the Atlantic Ocean. They arrived in a land that was strange to them, and they could not speak the language of their new country. However, St. Patrick's Old Cathedral, a Catholic church, strengthened their faith and gave them an extended family. The church and the Sisters of Charity at the school educated their children to make them feel welcome in their new country. To them we are all so grateful.

In 1945, when I started school at St. Patrick's, World War II had just ended in June. My classmates and I were all suffering from the effects of the war. Two of my uncles were in the war, and one did not return. Our families were anxious about the return of the boys from the war and they were working hard to make ends meet. All of the women in my family worked. That is the kind of household most students grew up in at that

One of Sarah's birthdays with her family

time. My loving maternal grandmother Jenny cooked for the restaurant that she and my hard-working grandfather Ciro owned on Mulberry Street. My mother Phyllis and her sisters Frances, Eva, Jean, and Geraldine all helped in the restaurant. They worked hard at a young age first in my grandfather's bakery and then in the restaurant. They would deliver the bread from the bakery to the local restaurants.

My paternal kind grandmother Cira sewed in the factories when she was young. At the time I was at St. Patrick's she was sewing police uniforms at home. With her petite Sicilian hands, she sewed and knitted beautifully. She crocheted beautiful scarves for the furniture. My compassionate paternal grandfather Dominick came to America to work on the railroads. They had five children, Charles, Carmine, Salvatore, Frank and Rose. Aunt Rose sewed and she went to school to learn designing. I can remember her sketching models with beautiful suits and dresses. My admiration for quality fabrics began at that time.

My grandmother taught me to knit and sew when I was eight years old. It was in both my grandmothers' kitchens that I learned the art of cooking. They knew how to cook the delicious meals from Italy. During that time, I remember my grandmothers packing clothes and other goods to send to their poor relatives in Italy.

My first thought about St. Patrick's School on Mott and Prince Streets in lower Manhattan takes me back to my kindergarten days. My teacher was Miss Spera, a diligent and organized teacher. She was short but full of energy. One of the things that I remember most about kindergarten was the large Dick and Jane book that she had up on the blackboard. She would point to the pages with a large pointer and teach us how to read.

The day in June that I completed my kindergarten year, I was told that I would not be going into first grade. I was to skip first grade and go on to second grade in September because I could read. I can remember being sad about this because my friends would be going to first grade and everyone loved the first grade nun.

In September, when I began second grade I can remember the nun being very serious. She made sure that we perfected our reading and writing. At St. Patrick's, no matter what subject we were studying we were always corrected for grammar and

spelling. About this time, I believe we may have started to wear our uniforms. Girls wore a white blouse with a Peter Pan collar and a small navy bow under the collar. We had navy blue skirts and oxford shoes. The boys wore navy pants, white shirts and a navy tie.

In our classrooms at St. Patrick's there was a crucifix hanging high over the blackboard and a statue of the Blessed Mother in the corner near the window. An American flag would be hanging on the wall close by. Each morning we said our morning prayers, and we saluted the American flag. The nuns would open the windows wide and have us do exercises to wake us up. In May, the month of Our Lady, we would crown the Blessed Mother with a wreath of fresh flowers and have a vase of freshflowers in front of the Statue each day. We would sing lovely songs when crowning Our Lady and offer the Rosary for Her intentions.

Once a week, our music teacher, Mr. Campbell, would come to St. Patrick's to teach us music. I learned how to play the Bells at that time and how to read music. We never had a gym at St. Patrick's that I can remember. Our gym was the playground behind the school at lunchtime if the weather permitted. Growing up in the city the children experienced lots of exercise walking the streets near their homes. I can remember running around the playground with my classmates and playing hopscotch, jumping rope, and bouncing a ball to the alphabet. My mother didn't like it when some of the boys would teasingly pull the braids in my hair on the playground.

We sang and danced frequently in the 1940's and 1950's. Who can forget the beautiful Big Band music? To celebrate the end of World War II there was a block party on Mulberry Street in Little Italy where both my grandparents lived. Everyone was happy that the war was over because so many of our boys were killed or wounded in the war. My Uncle Salvatore, a Sergeant in the Army Air Corps, returned home safely but his brother, my Uncle Frank, (on right with me) who was in the Army Infantry, was killed in Anzio, Italy in 1944. (See Patriotism chapter.) In 1946, my mother Phyllis was diagnosed with leukemia. With all the pain and sadness that was going on in my personal life at that time, the nuns at the school always offered me a certain sense of security.

Most of all when I think back at my grammar school days, I can remember how kind the nuns always were to me. They would try to take the place of my mother by keeping me close to them. Once I can remember having the lead in a school play. Our yearly plays were usually held in the auditorium beneath St. Patrick's Old Cathedral on Mulberry Street or at Our Lady of Loreto auditorium a few blocks away. (Sarah in play at St. Loreto in picture above). So much preparation went into the production of the plays. Aside from all the acting and music rehearsals, there was the costume designing. The nuns made all the costumes. They would take me with them to Orchard Street in the Jewish section of lower Manhattan where we would shop for the fabrics. I learned how to bargain by shopping with the nuns. They would constantly get the salesperson to lower the price of the fabric and we had fun doing it.

The plays were always a success. Everyone in the neighborhood looked forward to them. There were songs from the theater and one year we even performed a Minstrel Show. These were happy days for the students and a great motivation for all.

We would have processions at St. Patrick's Old Cathedral on Corpus Christi Sunday or in May for the Blessed Mother. The boys wore navy blue suits and a white shirt and the girls would wear white dresses. I can remember carrying a basket of flower petals and dropping the petals as I walked down the church aisle. The Blessed Sacrament was in the procession up and down the aisles under a canopy.

One May, the nuns asked my mother, who was very ill, if I could crown the Blessed Mother during a ceremony at Mass. The left altar at St. Patrick's was dedicated to the Blessed Mother. On a Saturday in May, I climbed a ladder and placed a beautiful fresh flowered crown on the statue of Our Lady. It was such an honor for my family  and me that day. In the 1970's, that altar was used to film the Baptism in "The Godfather."(In picture above procession with Sarah on right and Madeline LoFaro on left)

My mother's friend, Rose Tedesco Perrotta, who was a local dressmaker, made all my white organdy dresses and they were beautiful. She made my First Communion and Confirmation dresses. When I was seven years old, I received First Communion on a Saturday in May and Confirmation the next day, Sunday.

Confirmation Day 1947- Sarah with Aunt Frances

Our leisure time was spent with our families. In the city streets, the boys played stickball and stoopball, while the girls played ball, hopscotch, rope jumping, marbles, or walked their doll carriages. On Saturdays, there would be Western movies in the auditorium of the church. I can remember Hopalong Cassidy, Gene Autry, and Roy Rogers in the films. When the Youth Center was completed, the boys played basketball and the girls played table tennis. In the 1950's television was introduced into our homes and we were able to enjoy listening to the wisdom of Bishop Fulton Sheen, to hear Perry Como sing his favorite songs, and to watch Jackie Gleason in the Honeymooners. My parents also had an RCA Victrola when I was young. We always had music in our home as my parents and I enjoyed singing.

I also remember the air raids in New York during those days. The mortuary vaults under the church were used as a bomb shelter. The children at St. Patrick's school were taken below the church to the tombs for protection and safety.

Archbishop John J. Maguire performed the wedding ceremony for my parents, Charles and Phyllis Lofaso in September 1938. He baptized me in April 1940. He was the Very Rev. Msgr. at St. Patrick's at that time.

In the 1948 St. Patrick's PARISHIONER Bulletin, the Very Rev. Msgr. Bonaventure J. Filitti was Pastor and it lists Msgr. Maguire, Rev. Paul M. Andrews, Rev. Joseph G. Goodwine and Rev. Ernest C. Broglio as the parish priests. In my later school years, I also remember Fr. Joseph T. Dimino, Fr. Francis Massarone and Fr. Francis Principe. Fr. Dimino went on to Washington, D.C. to head the U.S. Military Archdiocese. They were all dedicated priests who were always there for the parishioners.

St. Patrick's Masses were said in Latin and the children sang in English and Latin at the Mass or services. I remember an active Knights of Columbus with the men of the Parish at that time. The December 1948 PARISHIONER mentions a Mother Cabrini Club, and a Girl Scout

Troop No. 254. My mother, Phyllis, was a member of the club and the women were always kind to her during her illness. The talented Dolores Silece supervised the Girl Scout Troop in which I was a member. Frances Scuesa and I looked forward to the Girl Scout meetings in the auditorium and the trip that we took to Alley Pond Park. Years later, I would join Dolores in the Editorial Department of McCall's Magazine. She was Assistant to the Art Director Otto Storch, and thanks to Dolores I was secretary to the Editor and Publisher, Otis Wiese.

Bishop John DuBois is buried to the right of the main entrance to the Old Cathedral on Mott Street. The Bishop founded Mt. Saint Mary's Seminary in Emmitsburg, Maryland. A few years ago, I was at a retreat at the Seminary with the John Carroll Society of Washington, D.C. It was during one of the seminars at the retreat when a priest who was presiding over the seminar, mentioned that they would like to move the Bishop's remains to Emmitsburg so that he could be among all the Seminarians who study at the beautiful Seminary that he founded. The St. Elizabeth Ann Seton's Shrine is close to the Seminary.

As Catholic schoolchildren we were taught love, obedience, and respect for others at all times. Our classes were quiet. The nuns controlled the class not the students. Any student that could not keep up with the others or had bad behavior problems usually were sent to Public School No. 21 at the other end of Mott Street.

My brother Frank at Confirmation

St. Patrick's did not have special classes for students at that time. Most of the children at the school were grandchildren or children of Italian immigrants who came to America in the early 1900's. They settled in the Little Italy section. During that time, at St. Patrick's School there were a few Irish left as most of them started to migrate to Brooklyn and Queens.

On the Wednesday before Thanksgiving 1948, I went to school and I was looking forward to our class party. My third grade teacher, Sr. Gertrude, came to see me and she told me we had to

My family shortly before my mother's passing

go home because my mother was very ill. When we arrived at my apartment on Cleveland Place I ran into the bedroom looking for my mother, but she was gone. Sr. Gertrude called me to her and she sat me on her lap and told me that while I was at school earlier that day the Angels came to take my mother to Heaven. The reality that at eight years old my beautiful, loving mother was gone and that I would never see her again stayed with me for a long time. Sr. Gertrude was at my side to guide me all the time after that day.

After the wake at Guidetti's Funeral Home on Spring Street, my Mother's Funeral Mass was at St. Patrick's Old Cathedral. My friend, Kathleen Mahoney's father who was a Tenor in the Church choir, sang the Ave Maria for Mommy. He had the most beautiful voice, and I can still hear him singing it today.

The priest and nuns at St. Patrick's were praying to Mother Elizabeth Seton (at right) and to Mother Frances Cabrini (at left) for a miracle cure for my mother. The two are Saints today. Saint Frances

Cabrini statute is on my mother's tombstone at 2nd Calvary Cemetery.

As time went on, the nuns showered me with affection and love. I was a good student and I appreciated school. I liked to read and write and enjoyed history-my favorite subject. Our religion classes were Catechism classes preparing us for the Sacraments and teaching us the history of the Catholic religion.

My loving, caring father Charles, who was devoted to his children, believed that our mother was always there watching over us even though we couldn't see her. It brought us all closer together and much closer

to God. In 1950, my father purchased a summer home for us in Greenwood Lake, N.J. As city kids, Frank and I enjoyed spending our summers in the mountains and learning how to fish, swim, row a boat and paddle a canoe. Dad bought the house because his close friends Jim and Tess Rinaldo and John and Lil Masi had homes in Greenwood Lake, N.Y. He thought it would be good for our family to get away from the city after the loss of my mother.

I have so many fond memories of the nuns and the priests at St. Patrick's. However, the only time I can remember crying was when my Uncle Sam got tickets for a special Yankee game at Yankee Stadium. On Thursdays, we would be dismissed from school early as the public school children would come to St. Patrick's for Religious Education. Uncle Sam and I would go to the Yankee Stadium to see the Yankees play whenever they played home games. I loved the games. They were always so exciting. Growing up in the city the Yankee Stadium and Central Park was where I could see green grass.

One day I played hooky from school as Uncle Sam wanted to take me to an important game. At the Yankee Stadium, Uncle Sam bought me a large Mickey Mantle button to wear on my jacket. I was in the fifth grade at the time and my teacher was an old stern nun named Sr. Anita. When I went to school the next day, she asked me why I missed school the day before. I told her I was at home sick. I lied and she knew it. She looked at my Mickey Mantle button and she said, "No, you weren't, you went to the ball game." The next thing I knew she slapped me hard across my face and the inside of my mouth began to bleed. The lesson was never to lie. Aunt Rose went to school to complain to the Principal about the cruelty of the nun. That was the only time in all my twelve years of Catholic education that a nun ever struck me. Not long after that happened the nun died. All the children were lined up in the halls of St. Patrick's school as we were getting ready for a Holy Thursday service at the Church. I was standing near the staircase and I saw the nun go down the steps and trip on her gown. She fell down the flight of stairs and hit her head and died. The poor old nun must have been suffering in her own way all the time.

Since St. Patrick's was a poor parish – many old nuns came to teach there. Much sadness was present at St. Patrick's after that Holy Thursday.

The Irish immigrants built St. Patrick's Church and the red brick schoolhouse. The cornerstone of Old St. Patrick's was laid on June 8, 1809. It is listed on the National Registry of Historic Landmarks. Designed by architect John Francois Mangin it was dedicated on May 14, 1815. It is one of the earliest examples of Gothic Revival Architecture in New York City. In the choir loft is a historic organ, built by Henry Erben in 1852. The organ is one of less than a dozen such great instruments surviving in the city and it is still used in liturgies today.

In the late 1990's a beautiful Memorial Mass was held at St. Patrick's Church for John Kennedy, Jr. who lived not far from St. Patrick's in Tribeca. An Irish organization, the Emerald Isle Immigration Center, offered the Mass for young John who like his father, President John Kennedy, died too young.

Film producer Martin Scorsese went to St. Patrick's School. He is a couple of years younger than I am; therefore, we were not in the same grade. Most of the young boys that went to St. Patrick's were good students. They  usually became Altar Boys as my brother did. We were all preparing for Catholic High Schools. The girls usually went to Cathedral High, and the boys to Cardinal Hayes, Power Memorial, or Lasalle Academy where my brother Frank attended. After I graduated in June 1953, I went on to Cathedral High across from the Waldorf Astoria Hotel and near the new St. Patrick's Cathedral on Fifth Avenue and 51st Street.

Everyone who knew them held the priests and nuns at St. Patrick's Old Cathedral in great respect. They devoted their lives to the children at the school. They were always humble and kind to the parishioners. I can remember Msgr. Filitti tapping us on the shoulder, nodding his head, and smiling down at us. To me he appeared to be a large man with a warm, smiling face. Little did we know it at the time, but our characters were being formed for the future. Our love of God and His Mother was taught to us by the good example of the nuns and the priests at St. Patrick's. We will never experience such love and humility again and for that we are forever grateful to them. The friendships that were built among the children of that generation will last forever.

Sarah Ann LoFaso may be contacted at Salofaso@yahoo.com

THE SIN OF SLUMS
By John Stanley

"The slum is a great weight that must be carried,
an affliction like a running sore or a collapsed lung"

GENERALLY SPEAKING, slums are unlighted, unclean, unfragrant, uncapacious, unbeautiful and frightening. They are a social capital sin, producing ills that cripple and pervert human lives.

When Father Vincent McNabb was urging men to go back to the land, he called the city a proximate occasion of sin, and counseled men to take their families and settle in rural areas. Father McNabb is now dead, and cities continue to grow in size and density.

The slum is a symbol of injustice and lack of fraternity among men. "Am I my brother's keeper?" Greed keeps slums in being. There are, it is true, "economic forces" at work, but they don't work in a vacuum, unattached to flesh and blood suffering or to avaricious men. Some men make money from the slums. In the process they mutilate their brothers and, of course, themselves.

Concretely, one form this greed takes is trying to get as many human beings as possible to occupy X cubic yards of air enclosed by masonry and set on X square feet of earth, and get them to pay as many dollars as possible for this occupation. Generally speaking, men will not be taken advantage of in this way unless they are helpless to remedy their own situation. So in order for a slum to exist there must be a large number of relatively helpless people available. Slums exist all over the country, of course, but in New York slums traditionally involve people who have just arrived in large numbers from outside the city, from Europe, from the South and now, of course, from Puerto Rico. Frequently they lack a marketable trade and are illiterate, either absolutely or in the English language. They arrive in an impoverished condition from an impoverished area, attracted to New York because of its wealth and opportunity, well advertised and dramatized. They can easily be taken advantage of because they have no resources.

New York is probably the epitome of the "city" today for most people. It is the biggest in the world; UN headquarters; Radio City; theater; most spectacular waterfront, and so forth. And too many of its people live in some of the grimmest physical and spiritual conditions imaginable. A few live in shining towers surrounded by sun and music and warmth. Too many exist in rooms entirely lacking in clean air and sunlight, and to describe them in such words as "squalid" or "dreary" or "wretched" is pedestrian understatement. Their burdens are cruel.

Consider, for example, a woman I met a couple of years ago. She had four children under the age of ten, and she lived in a fifth floor walk-up on Elizabeth Street in lower Manhattan Island, an area predominantly Italian-American. The streets are dark and narrow and choked with cars and trucks. There are in the neighborhood not only tenement houses, but small factories and warehouses and machine shops. The pavements are broken and uneven; the walks are always littered, and the gutters ·are never clear of garbage and refuse.

This woman's apartment consisted of four small rooms, with a toilet in the hall which is shared by other families. Her apartment is five flights up; every time the children are to go outside she has to take them down five dark flights of iron stairs, then remain with them on the sidewalk while they play so that they won't run out into the traffic. Before she goes back upstairs she does the marketing, taking the children with her. That done, she goes back up to the four small rooms. Once in the morning and once in the afternoon she climbs the five flights, even while she is pregnant, and when she shops she has to carry up provisions for six people. There is no central heating, of course, so coal must be hauled up by the hundred-weight-at much greater expense than having it delivered by the ton into a basement bin.

Even at that, this sketch does not represent the worst of all possible situations. This woman has a husband who earns "good money" in a nearby factory. There are always food and shoes. She does not have to go out to work. She is a superior person and in good health; she can be strenuous in her care for her children. She is the heroic type, and her story is a sort of idyl. When one has recounted it one has recounted the best possible. A story like hers is the bright side of the medal.

On the darker side consider an old house near Cooper Union-a handsome old house, in point of fact. It is decayed now, and probably marked for demolition, but it has better lines than those great brick fortresses over on First Avenue below Bellevue that form a "project." This old house is a rooming-house now, and a scowling mulatto in sun-tans lets you in and directs you up a short, quite wide flight of stairs. You make your way past a derelict in a semi-comatose condition with the fly of his pants open and sores and slobber and dirt all over his face. A fat little blonde girl is sitting on the landing and some old men and women in greasy looking clothes stare at you from a doorway. You can see the lathing through the gaps in the plaster walls, and it has been a long while since the floor was swept. A gray cat looks at you with a kitten in her mouth. You ask, and an old woman, very thin and wrinkled, points down an almost entirely darkened hallway. You make for a dimly lighted doorway at the end of the hall and find yourself looking at the artifacts of some one's family life.

Two double beds, pushed together, sagging in the middle and covered with brown army blankets dominate the room. There is a shredded shade at the win dow which looks out at a brick wall. What appears to be about a forty-watt bulb hangs by a cord from the ceiling, and the color of the walls is beyond recall. Lengths of cord have been strung across the room in several directions for drying clothes. A large dresser, a cardboard closet and a three-burner gas-stove have been wedged in somehow. A boy of perhaps thirteen or fourteen years sits on the bed completely idle, melancholy sag to his shoulders. He is thin and dark with heavy, well-shaped lips and curly hair. You ask him and he answers with a Spanish accent that you must knock on the door opposite. There you find a woman, heavy, in her fifties, with gray hair falling around her shoulders, and wearing a cotton wrapper and felt slippers. You state your business and an angry voice answers, "No, no, come back after." You ask her a question; she does not understand, and she calls to the boy to translate. At the end of a short, three way conversation it comes out that you've got to re turn at five and see the agent, and that a room in this place costs sixteen dollars a week.

This is a slum dwelling. A whole family exists in that room, eating, sleeping, talking, punishing, loving, everything. This has all been told before, yet people do not seem to believe it, feel it. This family is not the only one living this way. All over the city the same thing is going on. Harlem, of course, is a byword. It is like a fire in a forest, burning here with a lot of smoke and flame, then sometimes leaping over to another area, or occasionally creeping underground almost unseen, except that the ground is hot; holocausts everywhere, leaving only the smoke and ashes of vanished hopes and brutality and the denial in action of all credos.

A slum area is an area in which things are out of order. There is an absence of what there should be for the proper development of the human person. Each person needs a certain minimum of air and space and sunlight. At different ages requirements for these things vary. An infant of one month needs little space. At five he needs more space. At eight still more. Between ten and sixteen he needs tremendous amounts of it. Not long after that the amounts required begin to decrease. At sixty he has to have not very much. But go up to streets people look down on from Morningside Heights, or walk around Mulberry Street or Mott or over in the Village, say along Perry Street, and you see how acute is the space shortage.

Boys have the hardest time of it. They may be able to play a little stickball, stopping every two minutes to let a car pass. During the summer they play cards by the hour, boys of eight, ten, twelve years old. They toss pennies and get chased by angry-voiced trades men. They smoke cigarettes in the doorways, and just hang around. They have enormous energies, and lack the intellectual and spiritual development to profit from the terrible asceticism imposed on them. So things happen. There is no need to re-count the daily contents of the police records and the tabloids. But not only these obvious things happen, but deeper things, quieter things; time-bombs are ignited that explode ten or twenty years later.

Nor is it an answer to say these things also happen in leafy Westchester or sunny Long Island. It is no solution to confuse the prob-lem of the former with the problem of the latter; the one is not the an-swer to the other.

A slum is not just a railroad flat on Second Avenue. I know one rail-road flat uptown between First and Second Avenue that is luxurious, and there must be more. After you climb two flights of stairs that warn you to expect wretchedness, you step into room laid with Chinese silk rugs and hung with antique velvet and brocade. There are shiny automatic things in the kitchen, and every year the family take the Ile de France and spend the summer at their place in Brittany. For them living where they do is not slum-living. But as you go out the little girls on the stoop of crumbling brownstone are pale from lack of sun and air, and too much penny-candy. It is hard to state the problem neatly and find easy solutions.

Every once in a while in Greenwich Village people start talking about building a new playground. Then there is a great outcry from other people about the sacrilege of tearing down some "fine old place," and The Villager announces meetings and writes editorials about the proposed infamy. Usually it is pointed out that in this particular "mews" or "court" some writer wrote the final lines to some deathless prose or other. And so the children continue to dart in and out in front of transcontinental trailer trucks and read endless comic books indoors. All of which is not to suggest that the provision of one more concrete playground would be achieving the millennium.

Nor is the millenium reached by building a platoon of sixteen-story cliffs; if you marched them up and down the five boroughs it would not then make this the best of all possible cities. Some of the very old houses, three stories high and with a back yard that takes up half the property, are perfectly satisfactory urban dwellings-if they are occupied by a single family, with a couple of roomers taken in, possibly, as was the original intention for these places. After all, not everyone can, or would want to, live on acreage. But most of the people in the area do not live in such buildings; most live in six- or seven-story walk-ups built fifty years ago for profit. And these buildings occupy almost all the land. This is not to mention the twenty-story places, complete with door men, which occupy all the land and vast cubic yard ages of sun and air. These were hardly conceived as places in which the family unit could best fulfill its function of nurturing the individual person physically and spiritually; they are simply investment opportunities.

So in such neighborhoods everyone within miles around must pay tribute to history and ignorance and the profit motive, and they pay in coinage of sun and air and space and quiet and beauty. This last is important. Every day countless persons must be af flicted aesthetically, spiritually, by ugliness, and so we beget people with coarsened sensibili-ties, people made sad by they know not what.

The slum is a great weight that must be carried about on the back of the individual and the community; it is an affliction like a broken hip or a running sore or a collapsed lung. For those who live int he suburbs outside, slums are atmosphere that surrounds a funny little spaghetti joint that you went to years ago with somebody's classmate, and afterwards you went to Sammy's Bowery Follies and drank beer and some bum... But for the native, the slum is a place where dreams turn into nightmares and mothers put their babies into wire cages to protect them from the rats. A place where you wage a constant war against bedbugs—cockroaches you accept. This is, of course, New York City, U.S.A., 1955.

The slum is the place where fertile young wives of virile young men restrict their families to one or two children and stay away from the Sacraments for years because they are doing something they cannot get absolution for; or if there is sufficient social pressure they may approach the Communion rail anyhow, rationalizing that it isn't wrong. They are products of the same bleak tenements, with many brothers and sisters, and they are not going to go through what their mothers went through, nor force their offspring to go through what they went through.

The continuation of the slum is contingent on the strength of a variety of vested interests. For example, the merchants who have their shops in the area may be absolutely dependent for survival on the continuation of the existing situation. They would be ruined by any radical change. In some instances, the area has been marked for clearance for years, but opposition is too strong to bring it about. And the inhabitants have a vested interest in the very real community that flourishes there; they don't want to be set adrift. And often there are parishes which have built churches and schools and convents at enormous expense and sacrifice. The problem is too complex to admit easy solutions and too urgent to be kept from solution.

It is the easiest thing in the world to hire house wreckers and bulldozers, but it is less easy to decide what is to be put in the place of what has been pulled down. It would be folly indeed to rid the house of a devil, to sweep it clean, only to admit seven more devils more terrible than the first to take his place. Why are they building now the way they are building? To enable people to fulfill their capacities of body and spirit and to help each other carry burdens, or to achieve a maximum density of population and in sure a ready labor market?

What effect will a generation of living in a highly regulated "project" have on an inhabitant? You live in three rooms frequently inspected, get up to an alarm-clock radio, go down to the street fifteen stories by elevator, push onto the subway, punch a clock, punch it again going out to lunch and coming back and leaving for home, jump on the subway, up in the elevator, defrost three "TV meals," turn the radio down at eleven, and so to bed. Maybe it's good. It's different. Maybe it will develop the virtue of docility; that's a good virtue. But it all has to be thought about still.

This has all been said before, of course. But it must be emphasized that angelism is not admissible; we are not disembodied spirits. Matter helps form the man; matter is important and powerful. Men build houses and houses build men.

It has been a generation now since Virginia Woolf spoke of the necessity of a room with a latch-key and five hundred pounds a year. She was principally interested in women and why they hadn't produced the art men had, and she was concerned with the ma terial reasons for this. But every man needs five hundred a year and a room, not to write fiction, but to build a life. And he shouldn't have to make getting to some green fields or white fields and clean air a day's excursion.

This society, this system, imposes on a man an asceticism he is spiritually unprepared for; to be fruit ful, supererogatory penances must be freely chosen. Poverty is holy only when it is freely chosen. Maybe you have to be rich before you can be poor; St. Francis was, and St. Bernard, and St. Benedict, and St. Therese and St. Teresa. And not as many works of art and literature and music come out of frozen garrets as the romantics who call themselves rugged individualists would have us believe.

The deprivations and sufferings in the slums of cities like New York are unnecessary and wasteful of human energy. There was a lot of talk about these things in the thirties when people were going to see "Dead End," and it is true that a lot of those terrible places have since been torn down. But a lot of other bad places have grown up in the meantime.

We spend quantities of our treasure and time and energy on H-bombs and aircraft carriers. But you cannot blame the slums on war; they are not father and son, they are two hideous fellow-travelers. Many slum dwellings came into being during the prosperity that followed the war. Slums continue to exist as concretized, incarnated greed, sloth, ignorance. Here is the core of the problem. If we could face this, the rest would be comparatively easy.

Mr. Stanley, a frequent contributor to The Commonweal, is a freelance writer who lives in New York.

PRIEST OF THE SLUMS

EAST SIDE SLUMS ARE NEVER PRETTY, but in summer the crowded tenements look more forbidding than at any other time of year. Their occupants fill the narrow, hot, crowded streets looking for coolness. Every block has its "social clubs," in front of which men stripped to the waist listen to the ball game and play poker, while their wives keep an eye on the children. Despite the attempts of the police to close them, the fire hydrants run continually all day and well into the night, while the youngsters dart in and out of the stream, or direct the water at some unfortunate motorist driving past with his car window open. A good number of the older boys and girls crowd into the subways of the city and head towards some out-lying swimming pool, so flooding it on particularly hot days that it takes on the appearance of a huge neighborhood bath tub. Boys who don't have the money to go to the Island sit around playing cards or play stick-ball in the truck-crowded streets, while the girls just watch or walk around aimlessly.

At night the streets come alive with people, and are so congested that it is difficult to walk. The rock 'n roll records of the juke boxes, the blare of portable radios and the constant din of talking and shouting make it impossible to sleep before midnight. It is here that I have lived for several years as a curate in an Italian-American parish.

Because of the great number of national parishes built during the tides of Italian immigration, my parish church is one of many situated in this very compact area. The farthest one would have to walk to church in this section would be about three short blocks. Yet the attendance at Mass is so small that it never ceases to shock those who come from the outside. So often you are asked, "Why?" Why is it that there are so few, relatively speaking, going to Mass when the entire section is supposedly Catholic? Why doesn't the Church have more influence on the lives of these people, so many of whom have been trained in the parish school? One cannot give a simple answer to such questions. He can only give observations he has made.

ONE OF THE ILLUSIONS many have is that it is possible for someone, merely by living in a slum area or even by devoting himself to helping its inhabitants, to come to understand their ways of thinking. I have often met people who choose to live here for the sole purpose of sharing the poverty and misery of the people. For the most part they are sincere and earnest, especially those who help Dorothy Day at the "Catholic Worker" on Chrystie Street. Some, however, are merely feeding their pride and relish the "prestige" which their Mott St. address gives them among their less self-sacrificing friends. These people soon weary of the whole thing and go off looking for new "experiences." But it is hard even for the sincere ones to be mentally like those they live among.

First of all, many who live in slums are very well-off financially, but choose to live there for reasons ranging from national loyalty to the fact that their livelihood depends upon it. Some are so involved in the neighborhood rackets that they could not leave even if they wished to, while still others will not leave because here they are "somebody" while elsewhere they would be unknown and perhaps unacceptable.

It is even more difficult to grasp the state of mind of those who wish to leave but cannot because they have no "out." They are trapped in social quicksand, which drags them down deeper and deeper into the depths of poverty and despair. There is no choice for them; they must accept a situation that is bearable only as long as they know no other life. However as they especially the young white-collar workers-come in contact with others, life in a slum becomes a curse and their Mulberry St. address a stigma. It is this feeling of despair, this sense of frustration that is so hard to grasp fully. No matter who he is, or what his motives, a person who lives in a slum area but also knows that he can terminate that stay at the moment he wishes, can never grasp the hopelessness of one caught there. Physical presence is not sufficient to obtain the outlook on life which those people have who live there of necessity.

Further, the priest and the dedicated layman who try to serve Christ in His poor have some realization of the virtue and value of poverty. They understand that it is possible for a Christian to elevate his physical destitution into a source of spiritual riches. Such a state of mind is rarely found among the poor themselves, even among the more devout. In all fairness, it must be admitted that the virtue of poverty is much more easily grasped by those who take that state freely than by those who have it thrust upon them. I do not wish to give the impression that it is a state people should accept impassively and stoically without any attempt to improve it. Every means possible should be used to remove those conditions that hold so many in economic slavery. But so often, the priest often finds that poverty so hardens a man's soul that he is led to reject God, Who is looked upon as the cause of a situation that is the result, not of the Divine Will, but man's greed. Because, paradoxically, so few of the poor have any concept of the value of poverty the task of the priest is greatly complicated.

ALTHOUGH THE GREAT WAVE OF ITALIAN MIGRATION into this area has passed, the traditional prejudices of the Latin mentality still find here one of their last strongholds. The great majority of men do not at tend Mass, but leave such things to the women of the family. Morning Masses are for the most part attended by the older women, joined in the autumn by some of the school children. It is very depressing to realize that despite all one's efforts the majority of boys will cease to go to church with any regularity once they leave the parochial school. The girls continue to go, but no parish can prosper spiritually without the men of the family attending to their religious obligations. The one consolation is that more and more boys are going to Catholic high schools and, as a result, the number going to Mass is increasing. Even they, however, are not completely free of their environment, for many of them go to Confession at least once a month, yet do not go to Communion because they do not want to be seen doing so by the "boys."

Another basic problem is the lack of adequate living space. Two rooms are often the only quarters for families of from four to eight people. Because boys and girls are thrown into such close proximity, sex ceases to be a mystery for them at an early age. For many, if not for most, married couples, birth control seems the only answer to their problems. The Church's teaching on this practice is either ignored or attacked as an "old-fashioned law" that makes an already difficult situation impossible.

A crowded tenement apartment destroys any attempt at family life. Husbands spend hours in the "clubs" while the wives gossip on the comer. The older boys form into gangs, each one in a sense controlling a definite section of the neighborhood, and many of the girls become more or less attached to them.

Numerous rackets flourish in this atmosphere. Gambling begins among the very young. It is difficult to walk a block without seeing eight-year-old boys playing cards for money. Dice games that go on for an entire weekend are not rare, and a few men have deserted their families and fled the neighborhood because they couldn't pay their losses and knew the penalty for "welching." The loan shark thrives in this water, and is found even among teenagers who, like their elders, lend money at exorbitant interest to those of their own age-group. Although there is little addiction among the members of this parish, many are involved in narcotics, and justify this by saying they don't sell the "stuff" to "their own," but only to "outsiders."

THE PRIEST CAN FIND NO EASY ANSWER to these problems. Few wish to speak to him of their difficulties. One reason for this is common among all Catholics. When one speaks to a priest of a personal moral problem he realizes that a definite-and often difficult-course of action will be demanded of him. For this reason, Catholics often prefer to tell their troubles to a bartender than to a priest. A priest by his very vocation cannot be a mere sympathetic listener. His duty is to instruct, advise and, when necessary, even forbid under severe penalties. Knowing this, many prefer the status quo to the advice of the priest who will demand radical changes in it. There is, further, the natural reluctance to be seen talking to anyone who even resembles authority. One of the first lessons a youngster learns is that "talking" is the most serious violation of the code the "boys" live by.

Another obstacle facing the priest is an utter lack of appreciation of the finer things in life. The supernatural is built upon the natural, yet the intellectual atmosphere breathed in a slum is poisonous to the mind. The inability to grasp the natural virtues make it difficult to understand the supernatural ones. The D. A. haircut, the pegged pants and loose belt, the pointed suede shoes, the wide-brimmed hats among the boys; the clash of colors, the poorly applied makeup, the tight toreador pants and leather jackets among the girls, show not only bad taste but a lack of that sensitivity of soul so important if one is to grasp the deeper and more fruitful doctrines of the Faith. Since this is so, the priest finds that he most frequently emphasizes the negative aspects of the Faith-sin, death, judgment and Hell.

However, the strongest link in the chain that binds people to their slum mentality is human respect. "What will people say?" The men stay away from Mass be cause, if they went, they would fear "what the boys will say." Women practice birth control because, if they got "caught," they know "what the neighbors will say." Boys fight, gamble, cheat because if they don't they are afraid of "what the fellows will say." Every life in a tenement building is an open book for all living there to read. Human respect shapes their lives.

In the slums as elsewhere the priest is often a lonely figure. He is looked upon as a salesman for a product that people don't want to buy. He is a constant reminder to his people of a way of life that they secretly admire but often lack the moral courage to follow. He sees his young following in the footsteps of the tawdry idols of the slum. He finds his kids rolling drunks on the Bowery, or armed with clubs and knives looking for Puerto Ricans. For a priest these are not just "anti social" actions; they are sins and these are souls which he is asked by God to help save. This is the motive if you wish, the fear-that drives the priest on despite discouragement.

The priest further realizes the slums are the result of forces that are complex and varied. He has little or no control over them and so is powerless to change the physical aspect of the slum. His fight is primarily against the spiritual wounds the slum inflicts on its inhabitants. They are deep and are often fatal, but the priest tries to heal them despite the tremendous odds against him. The work is, from a human point of view, so often marked with failure that it seems to achieve few visible results.

Despite this, the "slum" priest is for the most part a dedicated follower of Christ who loves his people with great love. They are, it is true, the cause of his discouragement and weariness, but they are also the cause of his joy. He realizes that he must never stop trying to bring these souls closer to God, because it is only by so doing that his own soul will find Him.

The author is a parish priest who, for obvious reasons, wishes to remain anonymous.

RIDING SHOTGUN:
FATHER FRANCIS J. PRINCIPE

by Richard J. Rinaldo and Friends

DAVID GONZALEZ, A *NEW YORK TIMES* REPORT-
ER and Cardinal Hayes High School graduate gave us a great story that surely resonates
with those of us who know Father Principe.
David wrote about his experience of being boxed in for an hour in the Bronx by a
double-parker in "Don't Box Me In Double
Parker." (Sep 10, 2008). David confronted the
double-parker, who responded, "Everybody
does it." Feeling that this excuse was mor-
ally indefensible, David wanted to confirm

his judgment. So he called Father Principe, his former religion teacher at
Hayes, explaining to us that, "This would make perfect sense to anyone
who attended Cardinal Hayes or Cardinal Spellman high schools in the
Bronx any time over the last half century." David continues, "The Rev.
Francis Principe has to be one of the sharpest minds we ever encoun-
tered, a teacher who introduced us to Pierre Teilhard de Chardin, St.
Paul, Bob Dylan and Martin Scorsese." Concerning Marty, he recounts,
Father Principe, once suggested that he take some business courses in
college "just in case the whole movie thing didn't work out."

Vincent LoBrutto, writing in his book, *Martin Scorsese, a biography*,
tells us: "When Marty and his classmate Joe Morale, went to see Frank
Sinatra in the musical *Pal Joey*, Principe dismissed the story of a girl-
chasing dancer, and dressed down his students by suggesting that they
would been better served by playing basketball on such a beautiful day."
Returning to David's ethical question, Father Principe provided an answer: "You can't say 'everybody does it' because if that was the case, we'd
still have slavery. People have to judge if something is fundamentally

right or wrong. You know, the concept of majority rule can often be tyrannical, especially in moral and legal matters." David concludes: "Next time, Father Principe rides shotgun."

David's conclusion is truly apt, and we thank him for suggesting the touchstone of Father Principe's time as a parish priest at St. Patrick's Old Cathedral. Father Principe arrived there in 1953, his first assignment after ordination.

Father Principe rode shotgun for our spiritual, ethical, intellectual, social, and cultural lives. He was there for us, as he was for David. And more so. This is not to diminish the influence and good graces of our Sisters of Charity teachers, our pastors, school administrators, and other parish priests and lay teachers in so many ways, especially in the context of the challenges we faced growing up in the neighborhood. (See related pieces "The Sin of the Slums" and "Priest of the Slums.") Names like Rose Parella, the school secretary, Trixie Spera the kindergarten teacher of multiple generations, Father Massarone, Msgr Tommaso, Sisters Cecilia and Rose Marietta and others who are mentioned elsewhere in this book, will forever be remembered. But Father Principe was and still is special.

When he came to Little Italy he was fresh, bright, articulate, and athletic, as well as being physically tough, a virtue strongly admired, especially by the guys of the neighborhood. I would guess that he weighed about 150 pounds (and probably still does),  and he blamed it on the lousy institutional food of the seminary, though he never criticized the cooking of the rectory. Despite his size, he played football at Cardinal Hayes as a lineman. (He is also a class of 1945 Hall of Famer and at right several of us with him at induction in 2005.) He would tell is how he broke most of his fingers playing against much larger opponents. He also took a group of us to the seminary at Dunwoodie, where we played some basketball against him and the seminarians. Our arms ached for days after their constant hard, hacking. With a referee, the game would have been one of foul shooting on our side!

 I was in the sixth grade when Father Principe came to our class to read to us Myles Connolly's book, *Mr. Blue,* described by a John Murphy review at catholic fiction.net as a "a little gem of a book." Murphy tellingly notes that "Blue discovers his vocation: to live among the poor and downtrodden as one of them, bringing to them the story of Christ...." They would become "Spies of God, he decided. Their unselfishness, their patience, their courage, their amiability, their fine wholesome lives would be living sermons to those

who read only the newspapers and disdain the preacher... And such, briefly, was his great dream of a Secret Service for God." Or maybe just people "Riding Shotgun" for the rest of us. Today Father Principe is spiritual director at Cardinal Spellman H.S. God has His ways! (Photo at right: Father Principe with two of the gang in front of the school in 2001.)

Editor's Note: Here are some more reminiscences (with titles from me) about Father Principe's time with us by several neighborhood guys:

OLD IRONSIDES
Joseph Morale

I was an altar boy and that's probably how I met father Principe who was a big influence in my life, because he was the first one who would take us out of the neighborhood to different places. Being an altar boy was like being elite of St. Patrick's School, like a football player or jock in high school. One time we went in his Chevy van, which I called "Old Ironsides" to an exclusive boarding school in Westchester maybe, where there were young ladies from South America. Their fathers may have been wealthy businessmen or politicians. Father Principe was doing a midnight Mass, and he needed altar boys. I was one of them. Another was my good friend

Anthony Viglietta. Also Jimmy Bynum. We had a great time after Mass. They fed us and gave us ice cream, which was kind of a big deal too. He also took us to Rockaway Beach in the summer and taught us to body surf. And swim. We really had a great time. We used the Belt parkway and we all were screaming and yelling all the time. What patience he had. We were sometimes 10-12 guys, and we probably broke every regulation. On one trip Father was driving a bit fast, and we got stopped by a cop, who on seeing the Roman collar let us go with a warning. The seat of honor in the van was in the front—riding shotgun, so to speak.

SPARKS ON THE FREEWAY
Richard J. Rinaldo

One time we were going upstate in "Old Ironsides" and the van was so full of us because father Principe hated to leave anybody behind. But the bottom of the van was making sparks on the road and this time the state trooper had us turn around to go home.

He brought us all out of the neighborhood, to restaurants, operas like Madam Butterfly, plays like Graham Greene's *Our Man in Havana*, as I recall. He introduced us to Dorothy Day, a saint in the making, and Dwight Macdonald, one of America's finest writers. For me Father Principe was the reference point of a learned person. He talked to us about Christ and Christianity, about theology and philosophy and still does, when we see him. We heard classical music for the first time in the rectory (except for opera at the Feast of San Gennaro). He took us ice-skating and body-surfing.

BARTENDING
John Buffa

Another thing about this neighborhood for me was being an altar boy. (His older brother Augie tells us that he had to take a test to be an altar boy, but failed the test!) One of the perks being an altar boy was being part of Father Principe's group that he took to Rockaway Beach and other places. This may have been his way to recruit us. We also got into his van and we used to go and then maybe sometimes we would go off to his father's bar up in Harlem and we would wait outside while he used to give his father an hour or two of relief, by tending bar.

Easter Sunday
Martin Scorsese

In a letter in America *magazine concerning Rev. Robert E. Lauder's article* "His Catholic Conscience: Sin and Grace in the work of Martin Scorsese "(2/27/2012), *which attributed a remark about his film* "Taxi Driver" *to his teacher at New York University, Haig Manoogian.*

"I would... like to point out one inaccuracy in the article. It concerns the remark, "too much Good Friday, not enough Easter Sunday." It was made by our parish priest, the Rev. Francis Principe.... It was after a small screening of my movie "Taxi Driver" in 1976. My then publicist had invited a small group of friends to the Plaza Hotel afterward, including Father Principe. His response to the movie after the screening was, 'I'm glad you ended it on Easter Sunday and not on Good Friday.'"

At a get together in 2001.
P.S. A lot of eyes moved as a beautiful woman just came into the restaurant!
Italians!

OLD ST. PATRICK'S CATHEDRAL SCHOOL OF JUNE 1950

By Patrick. J. Montana

IN 1950, NEARLY HALF OF THE MORE THAN 10,000 NEW YORKERS living in the heart of Little Italy identified as Italian-Americans according to the *New York Times* article published on February 21, 2011. My memories of my grammar school graduating class in 1950 substantiate that fact – but more like 100 percent were Italian-American.

OLD ST. PATRICKS CATHEDRAL SCHOOL
JUNE 1950

In looking at this photograph of my graduating class from Old St. Patrick's Cathedral School of June 1950, I remember every name. Everyone was an Italian-American whose name ended in a vowel – even Monsignor Bonaventure J. Felitti, our Pastor (pictured) and Father Paul Andrews who I believe changed his name from Andreacci. Almost everyone resided on Mulberry, Mott or Elizabeth Streets. A few classmates lived on Lafayette Street and a couple of the ladies came from as far as Second Avenue.

My original of this photograph hangs on the wall in Ray's Restaurant on Prince Street between Mott and Elizabeth Streets. I suggested to the owner, Ralph Cuomo (now deceased) that it deserved a place of honor there since he was a graduating member of the class and thus in the photo and also because the restaurant is diagonally across the street from the school.

Our basic values in the Catholic tradition were instilled by the Sisters of Charity as well as discipline. I can even remember all of my teachers. Miss Spera in kindergarten, Miss Parella in the first grade. Then came the nuns – Sister Elizabeth, second grade; Sister Carmela, third grade; Sister Elizabeth (again), fourth grade; Sister Cecilia, fifth grade, Sister Patricia, sixth grade; Sister Cecilia (again), seventh grade and Sister Joseph in the eighth grade.

Most of us attended St. Patrick's Old Cathedral which was across street from the school and religion, therefore, played a large role in our education. In fact, I was one of the few altar boys in my class who served at Mass on a regular basis mainly because I lived at 247 Mulberry Street which was about 100 yards from the Sacristy of the Church and thus it was easy to reach me.

My best friend in this class (on left in picture) was James Carosella (former President of the New York City Parks and Recreations union and now deceased). Jimmy the Count (as we called him) lived in the Monroe Building (265 Lafayette Street) and our buildings were back-to-back. One day in 1948, there was a severe snow storm and blizzard. Some truck got stuck on Prince Street between Mulberry and Lafayette and was abandoned. Jimmy and I decided to steal the contents of the truck thinking they were probably valuable only to learn that the truck was filled with cartons of toilet paper. We, and our neighbors, had enough toilet paper to last a year! Jimmy and I are pictured on the church walk wall on graduation day.

Another classmate of mine was Joseph Cesoli (pictured at the far right in class graduation picture). We called him Slugger. He lived on Mott Street but always came around Mulberry and Prince to play stickball, stoop ball or punch ball during those days. Many times we played handball in Houston Street Park. In fact, several of the ladies in our class competed against us at times. One day after graduation Slugger got a toothache and had the dentist pull out all of his teeth. Some years later, he invited me to Jones Diner on Lafayette and Great Jones Street for coffee. He was a practical joker and told Otto, the owner, to give me whatever I wanted. He said he was treating me to dinner. He proceeded to order a full dinner and so did I. When the bill came he told me he was broke and smiled without his teeth. I laughed so hard that I paid the bill and kept paying it every time we went to Jones Diner because he made me laugh so much. What a character.

As I view this photograph, the only classmate still living in the neighborhood is Marie Caterina, better known as Marie Cats. You see, most of us had nicknames which still stick even in the later years.

Go back another decade to 1940 and I am pictured with the vest at three years old standing in front of Sister Caroline at our Lady of Loreto Day Nursery. I remember very few of the kids in that class but I do remember Sister Caroline. She was pretty, soft-spoken and liked me.

Our Lady of Loreto Day Nursery.

I guess I was the teacher's pet at that time. Most of our parents during the 40s and 50s were hard-working Italian-Americans with young children. The Day Nursery at Our Lady of Loreto Church was the only way they could afford to work and not worry about the safety and care of their toddlers. Many years later we played basketball in Our Lady of Loreto's gym before the St. Patrick's Youth Center was built. Guys like Eddie Morano, Ali Zito, Carmine Lofaso, Andy Tuzzino and me made up a team. In fact, they named me Bevo after the Rio Grande College basketball player, Bevo Francis, because I had a set-shot like him. These were fine and lasting memories during the early school years.

Feast of San Gennaro

By Patrick J. Montana

LITTLE IS KNOWN ABOUT SAINT GENNARO except that he was the Bishop of Benevento, an historic city in south-central Italy, where he died a martyr in 305 A.D. During the persecution spearheaded by the Emperor Diocletian, the bishop was beheaded and his severed head and body while still dripping blood were gathered up by an old man who wrapped them in a cloth. A woman of Naples, named Eusebia, dried up the blood with a sponge and filled a small bottle with the precious red liquid.

Saint Gennaro's body is preserved in Naples where he is honored as the principal patron saint of that city on September 19 of each year.

The blood of the Saint is contained in two small glass bottles which are sealed and enclosed in a metal case which is designed to expose the blood for viewing. The blood, which is normally solidified and dark in color, occasionally becomes liquid and reddish, sometimes bubbling up and increasing in volume. This wonder occurs usually on September 19, the anniversary of his martyrdom, and on the first Sunday of May, the feast of the transfer of the Saint's relics to the catacombs of Naples.

Of course, the miracle of the blood has sparked a great deal of controversy over the years, but to date no one has really been able to explain the liquifying of the Saint's blood.

The recurrence of this miracle through the centuries and even in our time, guarantees the popularity, particularly among Neapolitans, of this famous Saint to whom they pray for protection and for all kinds of favors they need or desire.

WARNING: DON'T TRY THIS AT HOME

Editor's Note: Below is an extract by permission of **Anthony Mancini** *from his novel,* **Minnie Santangelo and the Evil Eye.** *It is about "The Fascination," a product of the evil eye, the dreaded* malocchio. *You may be wondering why we include this in the chapter on Religiosity, since the Catechism of the Catholic Church says: "Superstition is the deviation of religious feeling and of the practices this feeling imposes."*

There are several reasons. First, this was part of our experience in Little Italy. Almost everyone I know has had the ritual performed on their behalf, usually by some elderly woman, a friend of the family, family member, or neighbor. Secondly, we all believe in evil in the world, and we seek help against that evil. As Catholics we also know or believe that prayer is important. As you will read here, praying plays an important role in fighting the evil eye. Additionally, according the Catholic Encyclopedia "…many superstitions of our own day have been acts of genuine piety at other times, and may be so still in the hearts of simple folk." And many of us are that. Finally, it is from a book of fiction!

This fictional work deals with the ritual used to cure someone from being overlooked. This is the malady that might occur if someone looks upon you with envy, or even just with some compliment, where they forget to say, "and God bless you." But, there are many other facets of religiosity layered onto our experiences in Little Italy. Among them is devotion to saints, whose intercession was sought in many ways. For example, Saint Pantaleon, the patron saint of the numbers, who supposedly could give lottery numbers in dreams, or as we learn in Mancini's book, St. Anthony, who could protect you against the "evil eye." There was also St. Blaise for throat ailments, and we looked forward to getting our throats blessed with two crossed candles on his feast day. Also St. Lucy for eyesight and many others.

So, here is the fictional account of the cure for being overlooked:

Again. Warning: don't try this at home. Even though it spills the beans on the process, you are supposed to get the power only on Christmas Eve from somebody who already has it.

Excerpted from Minnie Santangelo and the Evil Eye
by Anthony Mancini

DRIVEN BY FEAR AND DETERMINATION, she went into the kitchen to collect the necessary articles for the first ritual: a deep dish, olive oil, and a teaspoon.

Back in the bedroom, she set the dish on a night table near her feverish son and filled it with water from a pitcher. She scrutinized his waxy features and felt certain he had been overlooked. The ceremony would tell the tale.

Trembling slightly, she poured a teaspoonful of olive oil. With the medal in her right hand, she thrice formed the sign of the cross over Remo, each time repeating the Lord's Prayer. Keeping the medal in hand, she repeated this process first over the oil, then over the water.

Minnie's hazel eyes gleamed like burnished copper throughout the ritual. Her cheeks were flushed, her hair straggled in damp ringlets.

She dipped the medal into the teaspoon of oil and let the soaked charm drip into the water until seven globules fell, forming round rafts on the surface. Calming herself, she waited.

Before long, the seven drops merged into a single, large oval form, an ogling sign. *Fascination.* Just as she had feared. She took another grip on herself, determined not to be intimidated by this new evil visitation. She would have faith in her own powers.

The battle had begun in earnest.

She strode to her son's bedside and crossed his brow seven times with the oiled medal, repeating the Lord's Prayer each time. He stirred, frowned, and mumbled in coherently. There was nothing to do now but wait.

She had considered then decided against calling Doctor Bevilaqua. She knew in her heart he could do nothing for Remo. She saw with burning clarity that her own powers of healing were being put to the test. She prayed she was making the right decision. Two hours passed. Remo's bed was a furnace. The Fascination was very strong. Again Minnie went into action.

In the refrigerator she found a three-sided clove of garlic which she placed in the small cloth bag that had contained her wedding-ring box. She tied the bag of garlic around her son's neck. Again she waited.

Another hour passed with no improvement. Minnie noticed to her surprise that as time went by she gained energy. Yet her confidence sagged. Nothing was working. Stronger medicine was called for.

Minnie returned to her reference books and learned something that dismayed her greatly. It was said that if the overlooked person slept after being Fascinated, it would be more difficult to cure him. Remo had recently been escaping into sleep too often, unnaturally. No wonder her job was so hard.

She shut the book, rushed into the bedroom, and shook her son gently, then roughly, trying to awaken him. He groaned, but didn't gain consciousness. After a while, she gave up. She would have to try more antidotes.

Minnie frowned at the distempered walls of the bed room, and then spat on her fingertips. She applied the spittle to her son's purple eyelids.

With an effort, she removed Remo's sweat shirt and returned with it to the kitchen. From the cupboard she produced her largest spaghetti pot, filled it with water, and set it on the stove to boil. In a few minutes, she placed the sweat shirt in the bubbling water to condense away the evil, poking at the garment with a long fork and chanting, "May the Lord heal his suffering and return the curse of the evil eye to the source."

She repeated the chant three more times, swirling the shirt in the boiling water, perspiring from her struggle.

Still another hour passed, but nothing seemed to be working. If anything, Ray's condition was deteriorating. He kept mumbling deliriously. Minnie decided to go on to an even stronger antidote. She collected a salt shaker and kitchen knife and went back into the bedroom.

Now she crossed herself three times, carefully omitting to say amen. She made the sign of the cross three times over the dish of water, saying an Our Father, a Hail Mary, and a Gloria. She put a pinch of salt in the water, and then doused her index finger with olive oil.

She let three drops fall and quickly picked up the knife. With the knife, she cut through the drops of oil, moving vertically from top to bottom and horizontally from left to right.

She chanted:

"Due occhi fha toccato,
Tre santi fha aiutato:
Padre, Figlio, e Spirito Santo. Stu malocchio se ne va via
E non piu avanti."
"Two eyes have touched you,.
Three saints have helped you:

Father, Son, and Holy Ghost.
May this malocchio depart
And proceed no farther."

She took the mixture of oil, salt, and water to the kitchen window overlooking Hester Street and Little Italy. She poured the liquid over the rusted fire escape into the street. *"Aqua e sale,"* she chanted. "Water and salt. Whatever the envious witch has invented, let it fail. Let it fail."

She shut the window against the chill October air.

PART 6

SPORTS AND PASTIMES

"Street Games Little Italy" by Vincent Scilla
Oil on canvas

VINCENT SCILLA lives in New York City and resided in Little Italy for a time. He has been exhibited at Maxwell Davidson Gallery, had two successful solo exhibits at Union Square Gallery and a solo exhibit at Turnstile Gallery, featuring work from his book BASEBALL published by MQ Publications of London. Mr. Scilla's work has also been included in group

shows at Baseball Hall of Fame and Gallery 53 in Cooperstown, New York, Yogi Berra Museum at Montclair State University, Hofstra University, Fairfield University (solo show), Sports and Entertainment Gallery, Venice, California, Rizzoli Gallery and Safeco Corporation in Seattle. **vincentscilla.com**

Marciano & Jersey Joe

His painting recollects some of his memories of "The Neighborhood"

FROM MEAN STREET TO PLAY STREET

By Richard I. Rinaldo and Friends

The recollection and power of another era was a reminder that our sports, as a part of and a companion to history, are a way to give context to our lives and to our collective past, present and future. ~Kostya Kennedy in *Sports Illustrated*.

My memories of growing up in New York in the late '50s early '60s revolved around sports. I especially remember my Uncle Nick who had sports relationships with some colleges. He coached men's basketball, and when he did they won almost every tournament they played. He also coached at St. Patrick's and helped us win games. ~Anthony Viglietta

Our sports have become more and more about money.... But to most of us they're still about the stories we tell one another, the transcendent moments that lift us—the very way we define ourselves. ~Terry McDonell in *Sports Illustrated*

DURING OUR TIME, from the late 1940s to the 1980s, Mulberry Street from Prince to Houston was used as a "Play Street," mostly by guys and gals from the neighborhood. Sometimes the city provided a traffic stanchion with a sign "Play Street" to block vehicular traffic from entering the street. Vincent Scilla's painting on the opposite page depicts some of the many games that we played there.

The street was also known as "Church Walk," as most of it on the east side of the street comprised the back of St. Patrick's Old Cathedral and its cemetery and St. Michaels Chapel of the Russian Catholic Church. Or maybe it was because the rear entrances to the church were there and involved a rather long walk to the actual entrance to the worship center. (As a kid it seemed really long and then you knew that you would enter in the front of the church on display to everybody already present. You better have your Sunday best in order and not come too late.) The street was a perfect one for playing because of the small number of tenements compared to most streets in the neighborhood.

Just north of St Michael's there is a Youth Center, built by the Cathedral under the leadership of Msgr. Filitti, discussed earlier. Father Principe once invited Dorothy Day to speak there. What she said is long gone from my memory, but the aura of calm and other worldliness of her presence remains, as if to confirm, for me at least, her inevitable sainthood.

I recall a passage from Thomas Merton's, *The Seven Story Mountain*, where he describes from his boyhood a church in St Antonin, France. He said, "The church had been fitted into the landscape in such a way as to become the keystone of its intelligibility. Its presence imparted a special form, a particular significance to everything else that the eye beheld ...." For us, by the grace of its presence, our church provided a great boon, binding a secular intelligibility to its sacred presence. A saint was even buried in the cemetery. So, we played and lived among holiness, sometimes risking some kind of sacrilege by climbing the cemetery wall to tread ever so lightly around the gravesites.

The Youth Center also served as conference and sports center, dance hall, and theater. How I shook on its stage while attempting to sing a song from *South Pacific*. The Holy Name Society used it often for their meetings and special breakfasts since it had a small kitchen. And we called it a gym, not a health club or a wellness and fitness center. In the cold winter evenings we congregated at the entrance, pounding on the steel doors and howling, "Open up the gym and let the hoodlums in." Our minder was Joe Christi, a former boxer with all the standard physical accoutrements— a smashed nose, scarified eyelids, and a paunchy gut. In my memory he resides in the kind, caring people category. He would go to bat for any neighborhood kid that got into trouble. He worked for the N.Y.C. P.A.L (Police Athletic League). I guess the church couldn't afford to pay him or had some kind of cost-sharing deal with the P.A.L.

When I visit Mulberry Street, the special acrid, dusty scent of the place, the feel of the wind and sun, the grit of the sidewalk, the aged staunchness of buildings and frame of sky between short one in the foreground and tall ones in the background, even that of one of the most famous in the world, the Empire State Building, awakens fond memories

of religion, play, and neighborhood.

This was our arena, our coliseum. And you were in the center of it facing other gladiators or lions. General MacArthur talked of fields of friendly strife, which sowed the seeds of future victory. Our field was Play Street, where there was stickball, football with stuffed milk containers, stoopball, kings, handball, picture card flipping, hockey on roller skates, spinning tops, marble shooting, and card games

Here are the seeds of life itself. To jump and leap, climb over a wall, swoosh a basketball into a net, hit a little ball with a broom, and catch one on a fly. Pitch marbles or play skelsie.

John Buffa tells us more:

I mean I wasn't the type of guy that would play stick games. I watched all the games, but I watched guys Eddie Morano and Vinnie Head. I was one of the spectators, and I enjoyed it as much as anybody. But the things I remember were the cigar boxes when you put the holes in it and you had to roll the marbles

> Play is where life lives, where the game is the game. At its borders, we slip into heresy, become serious, lose our sense of humor, fail to see the incongruities of everything we hold to be important. Right and wrong become problematical. Money, power, position become ends. The game becomes winning. And we lose the good life and the good things that play provides.
>
> *~Excerpt from Dr. Sheehan on Running (1975)*

out. Marbles—that was my sport. I remember playing skelsie. We played by drawing the boxes for this street game on the sidewalk and then shooting a soda cap of cork, maybe filled with melted crayon, at the targets of someone else's cork or the numbered box. You remember the Pepsi cola box or orange crate that we put on top of a 2x4 and the old roller skate halves that we put on the bottom on each end of the 2x4. That was our scooters.

We sometimes ran the scooters down a steeply inclined hill next to Transfiguration Church on Mott Street in Chinatown. We called it machine gun alley because it was one of those streets with cobblestones, and the skates sounded like a machine gum when used either with a scooter or on your feet. Free massage. Every part of your body vibrated and tingled for a half hour after that ride. After a while the wheels on the skates began to lose the metal and you really had a rough time on them unless you got replacements. How did we survive that daredevil ride?

An additional rough game we played is described here by J.J. Anselmo

Johnny on the Pony is a rough "street game" which is rarely played anymore. The underlying, but usually unstated objective of the game, is to physically punish the opposing team to the greatest extent possible. Teams usually consist of four individuals – almost always-teenage boys or young men. A coin flip decides which team will be the "pony." The smallest team member – known as "the pillow" – puts his back against the wall. The second team member bends over at the waist at about 90 degrees and plants his head into the stomach of the first team member, whose stomach serves as a cushion or pillow – hence the name given to the first team member. The third team member bends over close to 90 degrees and wraps his arms around the torso of the second team member. The fourth does likewise with the third team member, forming, in effect, a "pony" – albeit a six-legged pony.

The opposing team members, one at a time, run towards the pony from a distance of at least 20 feet, and just before reaching the pony, jump as high into the air as possible, and land on the back of one member of the pony. If the pony should cave-in before all four of the opponents have landed on it, they get to do the whole thing over again. The opposing team also gets to go again if the pony cannot hold the entire team for ten seconds after the fourth team member has landed on the pony. If the pony holds the load through the ten-count, the opposing team then becomes the pony. It is obvious that if the teams are mismatched in terms of weight and/or strength, one team could wind up taking most of the punishment while the opposing team would be dishing out most of the punishment.

Excerpted from the novel, The Newsstand, © 2011, by J.J. Anselmo, printed at McNally Jackson Books.

We played a lot of the games in the street with a little pink rubber ball called a spaldeen, made by the Spalding Co., available in local "candy stores" for about a quarter. It was allegedly made from the rejected insides of a tennis ball, and the bounce was pretty erratic sometimes. We hit it on a stoop for stoopball, which involved running three bases, or another version where a missed grounder was a double and a missed fly a home run. Eddie Morano and Allie Zito were really good at hitting fast and low ground balls—tough to catch. Anthony Viglietta and I gave

The Stoop

them a run for their money, but more often than not we would lose two of three games and go home less fifty cents. We always bet, even if just token amounts. Sometimes we hit the spaldeen with a bat made from a broomstick you had to find. Then you had to figure out a way to get rid of

The Stoopball Field

the whisks. Sometimes we broke or burned them off, but maybe you found someone who had a saw. We also played punch ball with the spaldeen.

We also played Bounces and Handball, both discussed here by Vinny LaBarbera in an Email:

BOUNCES

Game was played inside the school yard fence PS 21--Located at Elizabeth St---Between Prince & Spring St---Objective was a Stickball Bat (Broom Stick)---And a Ball (Spaldeen) & Two high concrete walls--Hitting the ball against the wall----As many times as it bounced (1) Single (2) Double (3) Triple (4) Home Run----If you hit (3) Walls it was an Automatic Home Run---Usually played with 3 players on each team---My Teammates were Nunzie BonViso & My Brother-in-law Joey Carmello--As a team we were the best in the school yard--We rarely lost. The best player to ever play the game of bounces--Was Jimmy (Twins) aka Tips) Contino--He was something

HANDBALL

Also Hand Ball was played in the school yard---My partner was Nunizio BonViso--He was terrific---Among the best hand ball players were Jimmy Contino and Vincent (Spin) Spinelli--Also his brother Matt (Spin) As a team Vincent & Matt (Spin) were great---

The best handball (black ball) player that ever played the game from " Little Italy " was Joseph LaMalfa---Joey was born on Elizabeth St.—Went to PS 21 & PS 130------Cardinal Hayes HS---City College—Became a Civil Engineer----Won 2 tournaments-- sponser—New York Daily Mirror newspaper---1961—62

There was also the game of bocce, played by older residents. This this game was actually played in a park outside the neighborhood, on Houston Street east of the Bowery. (Picture from Wikipedia Commons-Theoria/Vorbis.)

Many more details of all these games, common to many neighborhoods of New York City, are well-documented elsewhere, including stickball. But, stickball was special, the mother of all street games in Little Italy and deserves special treatment here.

Pen on Paper © Ron Crawford

STICKBALL

By Richard Rinaldo and Friends

THE FAMOUS STREET GAME STICKBALL is still played in Little Italy on occasion and in many neighborhoods of the city. Columnist Pete Hamill called it "the finest game ever invented by human beings." Stickball often pitted rival teams from other parts of the city, including Spanish Harlem, against the Italian-Americans in intense and exciting weekend games, involving no small measure of betting amongst the numerous onlookers. Hamill points out, "the biggest ever was for $28,000 down on Mott Street in the '50s." That's about $240,000 in today's dollars.

> The rules come from baseball and are modified to fit the situation, i.e. manhole covers for bases or buildings for foul lines. The game is a variation of stick and ball games dating back to at least the 1750s.
>
> *~Wikipedia*

Stickball was like religion in that it manifested itself especially on Sundays on Church Walk. Spectators often wore their Sunday best and the offerings were the bets. Umpiring was a difficult task, but there is no record of rancor, bedlam, or mayhem between the many ethnic groups represented--Whites, Blacks, and Hispanics. Rivalry and competition was balanced with courtesy, good sportsmanship, and the camaraderie of sport. The game displayed qualities of friendship and friendliness, tolerance of other ethnic groups, pride in youth, the joy of life exhibited by players and spectators, and feats of athleticism and daring. And a lot of hollering and excitement, especially on close calls!

It was played with a bat, which was usually made from a broom stick, discussed earlier in this chapter along with the spaldeen ball. After a while the balls disappeared from the market, but Spalding is making them again today along with stickball bats. Rules varied in different parts of the city but generally mimicked that of baseball. A homerun here was automatic if the ball hit the water tank of the Puck Building on the other side of Jersey

Street or stayed on its roof. A fair ball bounced off a wall into the cemetery was an automatic double, unless a member of the defending team managed to get over the wall quickly, retrieve it and get it back over the wall to tag out the runner. This sometimes happened, despite the formidable odds and athletic skill required. I remember "Blackie" Marsella running and leaping up, hitting the wall with one foot and gaining height. Then he placed one hand on the top of the wall, continuing higher, seemingly suspending himself there for a split second to look over the wall for the ball and then dropping down to get the ball and return it into play, all before the runner could get to second base! The wall is about ten feet tall!

On Mulberry Street, there was no pitching during the games played on the street with bases. Instead, the batter bounced or tossed the ball in front of him and swung at it, being allowed one or two swings. A separate game involving pitching into a chalk marked square on the cemetery wall was also played, in the vicinity of the current Mulberry Street library. J.J. Anselmo provides another excerpt from his book *The Newsstand* to tell us about that game:

Let's play some stickball John-John! Me and Vinnie against you and Danny," challenged Frankie.

"Okay," said Danny, "A dollar a man."

John-John balked, "Let's play for fun."

"Nah, a buck a man, you cheap bastard!" yelled Vinnie.

John-John reluctantly agreed to play for money. He never liked the idea of playing for money. He felt that sports should be played simply for fun. Unfortunately, it was an unwritten rule in the neighborhood that once you became a teenager; you *had* to play for money. It was part of the betting mentality that pervaded the neighborhood.

They walked down Lafayette Street to the parking lot on Kenmare Street. There were very few cars parked in the lot, and fortunately, none of the cars were blocking the "home plate" painted on one of the brick walls that bounded the parking lot.

The game was quite simple. Balls and strikes were determined by whether or not the pitched ball hit the painted home plate. Each team was allotted two outs per inning. If a ground ball, line drive or fly ball was fielded cleanly, the batter was out. There was no base running in the game. A ground ball that got past a fielder was a single. A ball hit less than 20 feet above the building wall behind the pitcher was a double; above that level, it was a triple. If the ball rebounded far enough off the wall to hit the building wall by the batter, it was a home run. To make the game more interesting, a ball caught off the wall on a fly was an out.

Excerpted from the novel, The Newsstand, © 2011, by J.J. Anselmo, printed at McNally Jackson Books.

Eddie "Eyes" Morano was an icon of stickball and of sports in general in Little Italy. He organized the stickball games, which was no mean feat, as it involved players from many parts of the city, required a trustworthy money handler for the frequent betting that would occur, and at least one umpire, who would be willing to risk life and limb, it seems, in deciding close calls. He also organized basketball and softball games and entered us in various tournaments with the myriad of administrative, scheduling, and logistical matters that involved. His description of the game and other sports here:

RULES OF THE GAME OF STICKBALL:

"Home teams supplied the balls. Most of the time we played one swing. Hit the ball and run the bases from home plate. Eight men on our team mostly. Puerto Ricans for short time played with gloves. Play street signs were needed by younger players. Older group were allowed

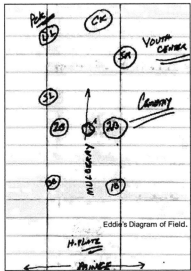

Eddie's Diagram of Field.

to play without the sign and got the OK from the police. They also removed any cars that were on the field.

I started playing stickball at 10 years-old and with the older group at 14. I played until I was 30 and then began playing softball not the same.

In the 1930s there was a paper called the New York Graphic. It ran a punch ball tournament throughout the city. Our area was represented by the Mottville All Stars. They played the game with a "Pimple Ball"  and that was lively. They were the older guys and wore orange and black shirts. The pitcher threw the ball on one bounce to the puncher (batter). Punch the ball and run the bases. Our home field was Mott Street between Houston and Bleecker. After the war punch ball was over and stickball came in strong.

We started playing stickball on Mott Street between Houston and Bleecker in late 1940s. We moved to Mulberry Street in the early 1950s. We started to play for big money, $500 to $3000 mostly against the Puerto Ricans and the Italians from Pleasant Avenue. We played all over the city.

In 1957 the dodgers and the Giants moved to California. On Sundays in NYC there was no sports in town. So *Daily News* reporter Robert Sylvester wrote us up in that paper. His column was called "Dream Street." We played for money with each player putting in whatever he could afford and spectators also bet (big money). The home team had to cover the bets. Some of the guys I played with were Vinnie Head, Frank Tiger, Al Zito, Sylvie Tripani, Jimmie Tips, George the Cop. Also older guys Whitey Marsh, Mickey and J.R. Reini, and Anthony Bonomi. Editor: At left above, players Vinny "Blackie" Marsello, Nunzio "Ned Sparks" Consalvo, Allie Zito, Eddie). The late Gary Lipani (at right) was another great player, especially at third base.

Stickball was great but we also played touch tackle. How about Saturday morning in the park. We would choose up and play for three hours in the band box."

(Editor's Note: This was a very narrow and small park on Houston Street between Mott and Elizabeth, basically concrete, called a band box by Eddie because that's what they called small baseball parks, like Ebbets Field.)

Here's also an extract from one of Eddie's 1967 "Sport's Highlights to the gang."

SPORTS HIGHLIGHTS

AT THE GYM:

THE ST. PATRICK'S INVITATIONAL TOURNAMENT WILL START ON SATURDAY, MARCH 10 AND END ON SUNDAY, APRIL 1. FOUR GAMES WILL BE PLAYED EVERY SATURDAY AND SUNDAY STARTING AT FIVE O'CLOCK. TEAMS FROM ALL OVER THE CITY HAVE ACCEPTED INVITATIONS. OUR CYO JUNIOR TEAM AGE 15-17 IS IN CONTENTION FOR THE CITY PLAYOFFS. THE TEAM WILL TAKE PART IN THE ST. FRANCIS DE SALES TOURNAMENT AND ALSO PLAY AS THE HOST TEAM IN OUR OWN TOURNAMENT. THE ST. PATRICK'S HOUSE LEAGUE ENTERTAINS 40 BOYS AGE 15-25 ALL OF WHOM BELONG TO THE PARISH. THE LEAGUE IS COMPOSED OF FOUR TEAMS AND GAMES ARE PLAYED EVERY WEDNESDAY AND SATURDAY.

Here is Eddie's list for the starting lineup and fielding in stickball:

STARTING LINEUP MOST OF THE TIME

EDDIE	2B
TIPS	OF
TIGER	CF/SF
HEAD	3B
GARY	OF
NUNZIE B.	OF
SYLVIE	OF
BLACKIE	1B

JOE BLACK WHEN AROUND

Vinny LaBarbera comments about Vinny Head: The Best Ball Player-"
Little Italy---Was Vinny "Head" Curatola-/ Hester St.--He excelled at
:-----Stickball--Baseball--Basketball--

Eddie was also a great player and competitor in every sport we played.
But another great player deserves special
mention and though he was not from the
neighborhood, he was highly respected and
admired—Louie Russo (at right) from Pleasant Avenue uptown—Holy Rosary and Our
Lady of Mount Carmel parishes. Louie was
one of those few players who found the holy
grail of stickball on Mulberry Street, hitting
the water tank on the Puck Building during
a game. I consulted with a physicist friend to

determine how
far the spaldeen might go if the tank was
not there to be hit. The result was about
520 feet, meaning that the ball would travel
to Jersey Street (what we called Jersey Alley) at 260 feet and about 260 more feet to
Houston Street. Joe "Black" Russo, who also

hit the tank
says that he hit
it with the ball
on a downward
arc, so it couldn't be that far. By whatever
measure, this was a mighty shot reverber-
ating with the sweet sound of a *phwock,* as
Hamill might describe it. The picture on the
left of Bobby DeLeo at bat gives some perspective of longitudinal distance, while that
on the right shows the vertical.

Vinny LaBarbera gives us his staccato take on Louie:
Louie Russo--Short Bio---Holy Rosary-Our Lady of Mount
Carmel-Stick Ball & Soft Ball Legend------Member of the
Stickball Hall of Fame-2000--Also one of the Greatest Soft Ball

Players of all time--Born--Italian Harlem--Played 116st Pleasant Ave.---Only player according to Eddie Morano --To hit the "Tank-"Puck Building on --Mulberry St--During a big game--Ball hit the Tank w/ such force --Ball Traveled--To ---Next Block --Broadway--Lafayette St.--And he was Left-Handed--" Quite a Feat "----Eddie also said that he was the most feared hitter he had ever played against---Currently lives in ----Mahopac NY---With his Wife Mary-----

Eddie Morano tells us about Vinny Head getting married and another tale about stickball:

I have a story I wanted to share with you that struck me very funny when it happened. It was the early 60's and our gang was invited to Vinny Head's wedding on the Sunday of Labor Day weekend. The next day (Monday) he would leave for his honeymoon – this was a problem. On that Monday we were supposed to play stickball against the Holy Rosary Club guys. These guys were at Vinny Head's wedding and they were busting our chops that we couldn't beat them without Vinny Head playing. They even said they would play on Mulberry Street, so we wouldn't have to go to their neighborhood without Vinny, they didn't want to crush us and then have us travel. Without the Holy Rosary guys knowing, Vinny Head planned to leave for his honeymoon later on Monday, so he could play the game first.

Monday morning comes and Danny Black went to wake up Vinny Head, that guy was never an early riser, to make sure he was at the game on time. Now the Holy Rosary Club guys always had money, they come down to the neighborhood really cocky with all their money, and we were having trouble covering. They had $700 we only had $300, so we needed more. They kept saying, "that's all you got?" Our money man Patsy Credit was at a picnic that morning, so we couldn't get the money from him. We went into the Ravenite Café and grubbed the money we needed from the shylocks that hung out there.

Eddie at bat

So anyway, we start the first game, we ripped them 9-2. I had five hits that game. We won the money on the first game. We doubled our bet for the second game. Play the second game, and again we beat them, score was 6-3. Vinny Head had two homeruns in this game. We win that money!

Now by the time we started the third game, some of our regular guys had to go, so we had some scribing's (lousy players, Ed.) playing for us --- even almost had to ask the Priest to play with us. We still figured we could beat them. We decide to triple our bet for the 3rd game. This game was closer, but we still beat them 7-6. Those Holy Rosary guys struck out four times!! We had four and five hits each in this last game. Albee, who was a guy on their team, was fit to be tied, if he had a gun, he would have shot us. A great day to smile on Mulberry Street.

So the games are all over, and now who comes marching around

Home Plate, Batting order. The solid line was the limit of advance while batting

the corner but Patsy Credit. He started cursing me because he thought I would have put money up for him, so he would have won big too (Vinny Head told me not to do it, I listened to him). Patsy Credit was walking around like a maniac yelling "you think that son-of-a-bitch wins three games and they didn't put money down for me!!"

So that was our Labor Day that year, after all the games Vinny Head goes home and had an argument with his wife Chicky, she was real mad, wanted to know why he had to play ball instead of leaving for his honeymoon.

One of the incidents we had was there was a big game that we were going to play in, around 6:00pm. We needed $16,000 apiece. Georgie the cop bet his own money on us. We went ahead in the game. Wouldn't you know in the 5th inning low and behold it started pouring rain. We wanted to keep playing no matter what. We had to call the game though because it kept raining and raining so hard. The guys we were playing ran away like ducks.

Sonny Perrone adds a little color to the character, Patsy Credit:

Patsy was a really big guy. So one night we are in a club down Mulberry Street and he gets really drunk and falls asleep. We can't leave him there. So we get one of the empty pushcarts and drag him onto it. We then roll it to his building and leave him there on the pushcart in front of the building.

Charlie Saia talks about Eddie and his other idol, his Dad, in an Email:

My Idol— Eddie Morano:

Long before he coached basketball at St Pat's Eddie set an example for me. I served Sunday mass at Our Lady of Loreto's and Eddie was there every Sunday at the 7:00 AM Mass. He left a bit early and walked around the corner to Mott St. to hit balls and sharpen his eye. He had dedication that many others lacked. His Sunday work ethic continued on Mulberry St, long before the big games against Louie Russo, Albee et. al. or the Puerto Ricans from Spanish Harlem.

When the Youth Center was finally built and the PAL ran it, Eddie got us into a CYO (Catholic Youth Organization) league and coached us and kept us thinking about sports instead of anything else. Mikey Oof, Spota, Frankie Rabbit, Frankie Orlando, Charlie DeJaccimo were some of the players. We did well and played our nemesis St Anthony of Padua well-enough.

He ran a tournament at the gym and teams from all over the city came and he raised enough money for glass backboards and bleachers. When you were with him you talked sports, sports, sports. The short-wave radio listening to Bob Prince announce the Pirate games and the parleys, round robins and the static from the radio. Who can forget Prince rooting for Dickie Boy (Stuart) to put it out of the park. Eddie was and will always be my idol growing up on Mulberry St.

My Father, Charlie Saia, started a basketball group at Our Lady of Loreto's gym long before the Youth Center was an idea. Each Monday night a group of us would be allowed to play in the gym as long as Dad was there. We took showers afterwards, and by 10:00 p.m. we were home. Nickie Biletto (at right) and Jerry Sceusa were the stars. When Eddie Morano formed the CYO team Dad and Cosmo DiGiacomo were always in attendance and cars were always needed for away games, these Dads supplied the transportation.

From May 15th to Labor Day it was Coney Island time. Dad would first shop for fruits and vegetables at Balducci's on 8th and 6th Avenue, Then back to Prince St. for sandwiches at Joe Darconte's deli. Ham and Swiss on Monday through Sunday excepting Friday which was Tuna day. There was enough food to feed the multitudes. Next back into the 49 Roadmaster Buick and ELEVEN in the car. When we got to Raven Hall, everybody got in for FREE. How he did I will never know but he did. At 12:00 Carmela Durante rang the chow bell and out came the sandwiches, the strawberries as big as plums, the Crenshaw melons the red ripe tomatoes the honey do's, it was incredible, nobody left hungry.

I miss him.

Red Napoli sends an Email to Eddie:

Ed thought you would appreciate the nice memories Charlie had of you and his dad - I was in that 49 Roadmaster many times in the summer on the way to Raven Hall and of course without you Ed none of us would have participated in any of the sports be it stickball, basketball, baseball, football etc - you were the catalyst and a greater positive influence on so many lives that you may never realize - for that I will always be grateful. See you soon. Red

A Stickball Tale

By Richie

I personally will never forget one game we played among neighborhood guys. It was almost like a game between college rivals because on one side you had the "elitist" Fordham crowd and on the other the guys that went to other schools or none at all. There was generally an inverse relationship between the perceived quality of the school and the degree of athletic skill of the participants. To make things a little more even, Eddie organized the game by including Joe "Black" Russo on our team and Joe was among the great hitters. We also had my pal Anthony Viglietta, a Fordham student and a good ballplayer, a hustler and my stoopball partner. Having played on several occasions with his partner Allie Zito against me and Anthony, Eddie knew that we had good hands for stoopball, and judged that we might be able to handle the line drives and ground balls of stickball. We also hustled and moved quickly in any game.

So Eddie put me on third, the critical spot, and I proved him dead wrong in his calculations. Eddie himself played second, as a backup to any grounders that might escape the first line of defense, and he had a lot of action on that count. Now Marty Scorsese was around, and as he once said, he and his buddy Joe Morale might play once in a while for comic relief, and besides, they wore suits a lot and would not want to get them messed up. In this case we didn't need him. We did our own awkward comedy routine and were behind by a lot of runs after a few innings. Anyway, if Marty had played, I'm sure he would have attacked the ball with his thumb and index fingers joined into that little square used by movie directors to judge the right frame for a camera shot.

But we had hope and Joe Black was at bat with a couple of us on base. And Joe hit one so hard that it went over the deepest fielder and bounced to Houston Street where it was hit by a car , which moved it to Mott and Houston, a block east of Mulberry Street. Good fielders never give up. So they chased it. By this time Joe, not a speedy runner, to be charitable, arrived at first base. At that point one of the fielders retrieved the ball and threw it to Mulberry and Houston. By that time Joe was half way to second. Now the fielders had about 400 feet to make up in relaying the ball to the vicinity of the bases. They did get the ball to Jersey Alley by time Joe was on third and nearly got him out at home. Hooray for the scrubs. We had three runs. We lost of course, by a ridiculously big number, but we made it up by going to the movies with Marty with however little money we had left.

Vinny LaBarbera adds some more sports memories:
Of course the basketball game St. Patrick vs. St Anthony--priceless, the stick ball games on Mulberry St. vs. Holy Rosary and I remember my dear friend who I grew up with across the street Nunzio Bonviso when he dramatically hit a home run at the bottom of the 9th with two outs winning the game, which was probably one of the more expensive games bet, about $18,000, according to Eddie who kept count on the monies.  And who could forget the Youth Center and the times you spent on Mulberry Street where all games were played every minute and every hour of the day. And I believe the year was 1955 when they started playing against the James Center guys from Hester St. There were some great plays and great ball players at that game.

And Peter Caterina:
I remember our team—The Jets-Blue and Gold Shirts—Some names-Frank De Angelo, Nicky Biletto, Jerry Sceusa, Michael Laurino, JB, Bobby Brown—We used to play the 5th Street Little Five when the big guys played the Big Five.

"LET'S GET READY TO RUMBLE"

By Catherine Miceli

*Joe at right with pal
Carmine Guidetti*

JOE MICELI, WAS BORN IN JANUARY 8, 1929 the oldest son of Nancy and Joe Miceli Sr's five children. Growing up came fast. His high school education ended after his third year. He now has to earn a living at a young age to help support his family. He was a very caring brother to Dom, Marie, Johnny and Frankie. They all had a close relationship and love of family. When they would get together, they all had a common bond, playing cards.

Living and growing up in New York's lower eastside, at 16 years old wasn't easy for him. He worked a couple of jobs, making $28.00 a week, but they didn't last too long. Whenever there were fights in the neighborhood, they would call Joe to help them.

1946-1947

It was at this time, at 17 years old, when his father, Joe Mitch saw his son's fighting ability and let him pursue his possible dream. He started training and fought 16 amateur bouts. If he won the fight, he would get a wristwatch. He would then sell any award he won to support his family.

1948-1949-1950

He turns pro in 1948 and makes his first dollar as a fighter. It was just enough to buy his first full suit of clothes and continues to help his family. His first year as pro certainly started with a knockout career.

Bobby Nelson, his manager, decided to convert this left-handed boy. This conversion made him become one of the greatest left upper cut artist of his time. He had 17 fights. KO'd 7, Won 4 and had 1 Draw. In 1949, he KO's 3, Won 8 and Lost 3. In 1950, he fights Kid Gavilan at Madison Square Garden and looses by 1 point. He then, KO's 5, Won 2, Lost 3 and had 1 Draw. His career flourishes for a while, and then------

1951-1952-1953

The US Army interrupts his career. He is now drafted in February 1951 through to March 1953. This does not stop him from fighting. His Captain Reynolds loved the sport and

1952 versus Johnny Bratton

transfers him to special services. With his Captain and manager's help, he gets to fight while in the Army. During this time, he fights Joey Giardello to a draw. He's KO'd by Luther Rawlings in the 2nd Round, beats Pierre Langlois. He's TKO'd by Ted Murray and then TKO'd by Johnny Bratton and Gil Turner.

1954

Upon his return home from the Army, his main interest now is to marry his neighborhood sweetheart, Catherine Tuzzo. We were married at St. Patrick's Old Cathedral on September 26, 1954 and later blessed with two sons, Anthony and Joseph.

St. Patrick's Old Cathedral

1955-1956-1957-1958

He defeats Art Aragon in California. In 1956, defeats Arthur King and Danny Giovanelli. In 1957, he looses to Isaac Logart. In 1958, he KO's Jay Fullmer in the 3rd round, only later to be vengefully stopped by, Gene Fullmer, Jay's brother, who fought Joe dirty with constant rabbit punches. He then beats the Champ, Ike Williams 2 out of 3 fights, but these bouts were never for the title.

1959-1960

As much as he tries to do his best, it's just not happening. Out of the 10 fights during these two years, he only wins 2 and ties 1.

Most sports writers always wrote that Miceli was one of the most popular fighters of the boxing television era, and had the most televised bouts in the 1950's. He was known for a vicious left hook, that when delivered on target, meant "goodnight" for his opponent. Primarily a welterweight, he fought the best of three divisions.

He was born too soon, too late. The boxer's of today only have a few fights a year and then become champs. Sometimes Joe would fight two fights in one month. He fought 110 fights, which included fighting 12 world champs, but never fought for the title. It just wasn't meant to be. His record shows 60 wins, 42 losses and 8 draws. He was written up in all Ringside Magazines, ranked third in the welterweight division and put on the cover of Boxing and Wrestling. His career slowly plunges downhill and he has to put all his dreams of being a champ behind him. It was good while it lasted. He admits his mistakes, blamed no one but himself and constantly would tell you, that if he had to do it all over again, he naturally would have trained better and taken the fight game more seriously.

He never believed he was as good as he was, and yet considered one of the best uppercut fighters of his time. I am sure you will agree, that in our eyes, he is OUR UNCROWNED CHAMP.

HIS LATER YEARS

Now that his career is over in 1961, what is he to do? He's now 32, having no trade to fall back on, made the beginning of the rest of his life quite difficult. Many people had promised jobs, but to no avail. He tried just about everything, from being a bar tender to a bouncer. He now realizes that he needs a steady job to support his family. He becomes a truck driver for a short time, then a jail guard at the Riverhead jail. That doesn't work out too well, so he then becomes a check at Hills warehouse. After seven years, Hills closes and then Joe becomes a Rigger at Fairchild Republic. Well, this seemed to be

Rigger at Fairchild Republic

it. He liked the job but unfortunately, after working there 8 years, this too ended. Fairchild plant was also shut down. He's now 59 and semi-retired. He works part time as a packer for a short time and decides to call it quits at 61 years old in 1990.

In November of 1993, he has a heart attack from four clogged arteries. He has open-heart surgery and does very well. God gives him a new lease on life, and to everyone's amazement, he finally stops smoking.

BOXERS HELPING BOXERS

He was a member of The International Veteran Boxers Organization – Ring 8, a boxing organization throughout the country. They are Boxers helping Boxers. They go to great lengths to help those boxers who are in great need. At every Ring 8's Christmas party, the honorees are boxers, referees, judges, boxing writers and historians who all took a great part in the boxing world, letting them know they are never forgotten. They all meet at the Waterfront Crab House on Borden Ave, Long Island City, once a month. Joe was so proud to be not only a member, but also on Ring 8's board of directors. If anyone likes the fight game, just visit the Waterfront Crab House, not only for it's good food, but it will also take you down memory lane. See Tony, the owner, a great guy. Please note: This year, 2011, Ring 8 is proud to announce that it will

sponsor the NEW – New York State Boxing Hall of Fame – at the Historic Waterfront Crab House.

On April 24, 1997, Joe was inducted into the Suffolk Sports Hall of Fame in Patchogue, Long Island. My son Joseph and

I were invited to the Grand opening of the new building in 2010. We couldn't believe how they presented Joe in the boxing area. It's certainly a must see.

Through the years, many newspaper reporters and writers interviewed Joe. They would come to the house and had a good time listening to all his stories, some of which would amaze you. Knowing he had 2 boys, they asked if he would let them fight? "No sir, it's too dangerous. It's the most dangerous sport out there. If they wanna fight, they gotta beat me up first and that day will never come." Lucky for us, they were only interested in playing baseball and very good at it. Go Yankees.

Ron Ross, a good friend, a prominent boxing historian and writer of two boxing books spoke well of Joe. He wrote that he was duly impressed by this fun loving, always smiling, former ring predator who brought joy and happiness to so many hearts.

Thanks to another good friend and boxing historian, Sal Rappa. As a special favor to Joe, Sal would contact everyone he knew who had Joe's fights on film. He was kind enough to put them on VCR tapes. Without Sal, we would not have all these great memories of Joe.

Sal is also a long time member of Ring 8. Living a short distance from us here in Long Island, Sal, Joe and another great fighter Vinnie Cidone would meet and go to the Ring 8 meetings together. Sal recently told me that it's not the same without them and truly misses his two friends.

Our grandson. Tristan, was asked to write a school paper about someone who was a special person in his life. He wrote, "his grandfather (Papa) was a big influence in his life as an athlete. That he was the most interesting family member he had. Despite Papa's age, he always loved to entertain people with his jokes and amazing card tricks. He liked nothing more than to put a smile on everyone's face."

Grandson Tristan and Papa Joe

On March 26, 2011 Tristan Miceli became a Chropractic Doctor. His Papa would have been so proud of his grandson, the Doctor!

"THOSE WE HAVE LOVED NEVER LEAVE US
THEY LIVE ON FOREVER IN OUR HEARTS'
IN MEMORY OF MY LOVING HUSBAND
DEVOTED FATHER OF ANTHONY, JOSEPH
AND FOUR GRANDCHILDREN

Before leaving boxing, Steve Riggio must be mentioned. He was a good friend of Dom and Josephine Viglietta, and Dom was best man at the wedding of Steve to Lena. He also hung out with Joe Miceli and was with him when Joe met Catherine at a dance. His son, Leonard Riggio, who founded Barnes & Noble, Inc., talked about his father in a "Mentoring U.S.A. Essay" in Wisdom for a Young CEO by Dave Barry: "He was a...great athlete....a highly ranked  prizefighter...twice defeating Rocky Graziano, who had never been defeated twice before." Leonard also notes that his father advocated senior fitness, a good message for many of us. Ed.

Entertainment and Social Life

By Richard J. Rinaldo and Friends

Social life in the neighborhood was both formal and informal. Some of it centered on church activities including dances, testimonials, and fund raisers. Some of these were at Webster Hall. It is still there as a night club. Wedding receptions also took place there, some of which were called "football weddings" because of the passing or throwing of different sandwiches in trades around the tables.

Augie Buffa tells us that they would cater some weddings with 10,000 of those sandwiches. The picture on page 216 is from the wedding reception for my Uncle Thomas Quaranta and his wife, Madeline in 1945. This was a sit-down dinner affair since it was a relatively small group.

School plays, such as the ones pictured on page 217, were a big deal, and parents, relatives and friends attended in force. They took place at a theatre on the grounds of the Church of Our Lady of Loreto, and today there is an effort underway to reinstitute some form of Repertory Theatre there. The history of theater and opera in the neighborhood is rich, and much of that is documented by Dr. Emelise Aleandri (See her biographical information in the The Neighborhood chapter). However, except for some forays to Broadway with Father Principe and the Melting Pot Repertory Group. Inc., that was not the main experience of our generation. The Melting Pot outfit featured several of our neighborhood aspiring actors like John V. Bivona and Robert Uricola. They performed at the Center for Homeless Men on Elizabeth and Bleecker, in our Youth Center, and other places in the city. They rehearsed at one time or another in graveyards, on roofs, and in cellars.

In the late '50s and early '60s we enjoyed walks to Greenwich Village, where we would often stop for ice cream at the Howard Johnson's on 6th Avenue (now Avenue of the Americas) and 8th Street. Like local yokels we were all awestruck by the variety of flavors, being used to vanilla, chocolate, strawberry or pistachio in our local stores. Sometimes we would browse the book stores on 8th Street between 5th and 6th avenues, where, for somewhat callow adolescent boys especially, art books with nudes were fascinating. The traditional art shows of spring were also a big treat with the great variety of work adorning whatever fence or wall was available along 6th Avenue

During the '40s there was radio, and most of us listened to the many famous programs, such as *The Shadow Knows*, *The FBI in Peace and War* and *The Lone Ranger*. I even sent away for a Junior FBI badge.

Movies were a main attraction in our earliest days, even absent Martin Scorsese's influence. We would range far and wide, despite our tender ages. On Saturdays we'd go to the New Delaney Theater for 40 cartoons, three movies, especially adventure or cowboy movies, and several serials, like *Gangbusters*. We later learned that the style of these would be the inspiration for movies of the Indiana Jones genre, where the hero always gets into trouble, which he overcomes in the next scene. As youngsters we were also mischievous and the matron would get even by coming down the aisle with her flit gun, spraying us with DDT. How did we survive? We'd hike to the RKO Skouras on 14th Street as well or the St. Mark's Theater on 2nd Avenue near St. Mark's Place, maybe getting a special "Egg Cream" from the famous newsstand on the corner. Supposedly Frank Sinatra once brought Sophia Loren there for a taste of the secret formula they used.

John Buffa told us this story about movie-going:
I got caught in unscrewing a seat in the front roll and people were falling over. They brought a bunch of us to the office where they e knew that the guys were laughing the loudest were the ones that did it. I gave my real name and the right address. They called my Dad, and he wasn't mad as much at what I did but because I gave my right name and address. He said don't ever give your right name or phone number.

The St. Marx was also near the N.Y. Public Library where some of us went to get books using the Dewey Decimal System Card Catalogue. Both were in what was once a German district, and the library still bears the inscription *Freie Bibliotek Lesehall* (reading hall and library in photo.) Germans fled this area, a part of *Kleinedeutschland* (Little Germany), to Yorkville, after the General Slocum steamship fire of 1904 killed so many of them, suffusing the place with sadness. Our journey across Houston

Street and up 2nd Avenue was also the occasion to sample a Charlotte Russe for a nickel or a dime. This was a dessert with whipped cream and a cherry on the top and sponge cake on the bottom. It came in a cardboard wrapper and could be pushed up from the bottom. Naturally, some of us ate the top part and discarded the rest. We might also get a knish or a kosher hot dog, since that area was basically Jewish at the time. There is nothing like food to garner tolerance or even affection for other ethnic groups! And we had hearty appetites. We liked bagels with lox, blintzes, and kosher pickles from the barrel. We liked Dim Sum and chicken in cellophane. We liked white fish chubs and sturgeon, and corn beef on club from Katz's with a Dr. Brown Celery Soda. As we grew older, we'd go to

Lindy's for cheesecake or late night to Ratner's for dairy breakfast food. After all, we were New Yorker's. We liked our own specialties too, *gelato* and lemon ice, *capozella* (half a lambs head baked), *calamari* (squid), *Polpo* (octopus) and pizza, of course, but with anchovies!

In that period visits to used book shops on 4th Avenue were also  a treat for some of us. Called "Book Row," at one time there were 48 stores there. You could find paperback classics for a nickel or old *National Geographic* magazines. Some of the latter treasures are still with me after more  than 50 years and include one with an advertisement for a gold pen my father gave me before he passed on. The paperbacks included many on the study list for aspiring high school junior year honor students, who wanted to score high on the test for New York State Regent Scholarships as seniors. Today the famous Strand Bookstore on 12th Street and Broadway, is the last vestige of that great used bookstore district.

We also loved comic books. They made great trading materials. For guys *Superman* or other adventure  types would be more desirable than *Betty and Veronica*, of course, with *Archie* and *Jughead* being in neutral territory. And *Classics Illustrated* brought us the great stories in an easily digestible form.

Pat Montana discusses some other pastimes:

The thing I remember most about living at 247 Mulberry Street was the chicken market on the corner of Mulberry and Prince. There were three steps at the entrance to the chicken market where we played "tops" when the market was closed. In fact, one of my friends and I became tops champions. We also used to play cards on these steps ("brisk," "nines," "rummy") and we would even pitch pennies against the bottom step. We played "kick the can" with three bases on that same corner.

Our family probably had one of the first black and white televisions, an Emerson, and we used to invite people in the building to view programs. We watched "Howdy Doody"-- it was a big show at that time as was the Milton Berle Show on Tuesday evenings. As kids, we would go to the New Delancey Theater. We would see four movies for a nickel (sometimes we would even sneak in). You could have a headache by the time you came back home! In the summer we'd walk to the west side (Greenwich Village) to a swim at a pool on Leroy Street (Chelsea Pool). You could get a hamburger for a dime and a soda to go with it for a nickel at a store there. Sometimes we hitched the trolley for fun on The Bowery. Take me back to the chicken market on that corner where we started all of our stickball games or stoop ball games against the cemetery wall of St. Patrick's Old Cathedral Church on the opposite corner. We even played games inside the cemetery walls like "jumping over tombstones" and "scaling the cemetery wall."

Entertainment also included the local feasts, discussed further in this chapter and the Religiosity chapter with all their warts—big crowds, garbage, and traffic. But the allure of great food and the excitement of the games and events, parades and even opera music was compelling.

All that was exciting and fun. But the really big time entertainment for many of us, as we grew older, was the nightclubs. These included the famed Copacabana, the Pepper Mint Lounge, and others.

Pictures of different generations at these places attest to their enduring appeal. Less glamorous, but nevertheless popular, were the numerous clubs in the neighborhood that operated long into the evening hours. These were locally owned and any legal transgressions often overlooked by the police, some of whom apparently took tributes for their leniency. They had simple arrangements, a bar, a juke box with a lot of Sinatra music, maybe a dance floor, tables and chairs and low light.

Joe Morale reminded me that among our friends was a big German-American red-haired fellow from Brooklyn. He often wore a dark blue suit, which we called his detective suit. In this suit, with white shirt and a preppy tie, he certainly looked like a N.Y.C. police detective. He loved to hang out in the neighborhood, and one night Joe took him to some of the after hour "joints." He was known to us and often visited one of the places we frequented without problem. But that one night they decided to go someplace where he was not known at all. On our entrance, the crowd in that club scurried away like cockroaches caught in the light. After a while some local detectives peeked in and seeing but not recognizing him, they just as quickly left the premises fearing, we guessed, that he was from internal affairs.

Vinny LaBarbera adds some memories:

First of all the Raven Hall swimming pool and sports complex in Coney Island Brooklyn NY , the Copacabana Night Club on 60 th in NYC-- that's where the elite would meet. Leighton Clothes for Men on 47th and Broadway was the best place to buy clothes and get alligator shoes. And of course some of the discos that we would frequent were the Peppermint Lounge, the Wagon Wheel and Tony's place, The Gingerbread, in the Village. My favorite restaurant was Chateau Henry IV at 64th between Madison and Park. That was a real class place. Then there was late night dinner in Chinatown. These are memories that will last forever.

Summer work
From Richie

We were in college and naturally we liked to work in the summer. So they needed summer help at a Ford plant in Jersey get into cars and move it them to kind of a staging area where professional drivers loaded them onto trucks. There must have been six or seven of us. Joe Black was one, and he didn't know how to drive. He was very nervous, and it was very hot and the doors and windows of the cars were closed. Joe gets in the cars, and being nervous about it, he would grip the hot steering wheel and hold on as long as he could. At the end of the day his hands were as big as a baseball glove.

Pen on Paper © Ron Crawford

THE FEAST

By Angel Marinaccio

The following is extracted by permission from Angel Marinaccio's wonderful book, **Be Home on Time When I Put The Water Up For Pasta** *published by the Beckham Publishing Group, Inc. Angel's biography below adds further color and flavor to our book.*

IT'S MID-OCTOBER ON A RAINY SATURDAY AFTERNOON. I sit at my kitchen table listening to the drizzle and thinking about the Feast of Saint Genarro, which ended a month ago already. The feast is New York City's oldest, the first being held in 1926; it's held to honor the Patron Saint of Naples, and it lasts for ten days! So, it is not the sort of thing you dash off to for a day and then go home. No, it is a true event; something to be shared and enjoyed with friends and family. I've been to fifty-nine of them, and plan never to miss one.

Some people might read that and say, "But wait, after a while, doesn't it become mundane, ordinary? How can you get excited about something you've been to so many times?"

But for me, September wouldn't be the same without it. Neither would Little Italy. These traditional aspects of our life and society are fun to re-visit, and introduce new friends and family to. Seeing the feast through the eyes of my grandchildren, to see the awe and wonder reflected in their eyes; ah, that makes it new and fresh to me every year!

Then there are always new elements; the feast has changed over the years. There used to be a greased pole climbing contest on Hester Street between Mulberry and Baxter that drew enormous crowds. Teams of young men would try to climb to the top to win a prize. It was so much fun, and so funny to watch them; climb and slide, climb and slide, grease flying everywhere. Now, it's gone.

Famous Italian singers, like Jerry Vale and Connie Francis, sang their hearts out on the bandstand back in the 50s and 60s. Now DJs like Brooklyn's Own Joe Cause play the music, and sometimes they'll have a doo-wop show that gets people dancing in the streets.

There also used to be amusement park rides and games; the ride were the usual things-like you'd see at any fair-a Ferris wheel, the whip, and a merry-go-round (to name but a few) but they were special to us. One of the games was a coin toss, where, if your nickel landed on a dish, you won the dish. Almost every house in Little Italy ate pasta off those dishes. Every kid had a penny jar. It was a large pickle jar full with water with a whiskey glass placed at the bottom center of the jar. You dropped a penny in a slit in the lid. If it landed in the whiskey glass, you won all the coins in the jar. That jar was always filled with pennies, and you rarely saw someone win.

On every corner stood a balloon man selling large balloons filled with rice. When you held the handle and shook it up and down, it would make a loud *shake, shake, shake* noise.

The Religious Procession is my favorite part of the feast. A statue of Saint Genarro is paraded down Mulberry and Mott Streets accompanied by an old fashioned Italian band. Every year, when the band passes, I get goose bumps. More recently they've added beautiful floats.

When they take the feast lights down, I always become a little melancholy. As the saying goes, "When the feast is over, the holidays are on their way." Everything about the feast, especially the smells, takes me back to my childhood. It's loud, it's messy, and I love every minute of it.

Further information on Angel:

Angel was born 1950 in New York's Little Italy to first generation Italian Americans.

She was the second child born to parents Nino and Gussie. Her sister Josephine was always there for her growing up like every big sister would be. They are close and so are their children. Her grandparents on both sides of her family came over in the 1900's from Sciacia, Sicily, and settled on Elizabeth Street. Back in those days all the Sicilians lived on Elizabeth Street. From Hester Street to Broom Street it was known as the Sciaccadon blocks. As a kid she played in James Center on the corner of Hester and Elizabeth Street, where all the kids in the neighborhood would be in the winter time and in the summer time they played in the park. She remembers summer evenings when all the moms would be sitting with their chairs that they carried from a walk up apartment to be in front of their buildings watching all the kids play. Don't forget that not everyone had an air condition in those days; their fire escapes were like a terrace for them. It was a wonderful time and a wonderful place to grow up. She married her first love when they both were teens. Her husband's family also came from Sciacia. They lived just a block away from each other. She has two children, a daughter Ann Marie and son Gerard, both of whom were raised in Little Italy. They went to Saint Patrick's Old Cathedral School on Prince and Mott Street, and they both went to college. The Streets of Little Italy were just as safe for their children as it was for her growing up. In her neighborhood everyone knows one another. If you were good they would say what a good kid. If you did something wrong your parents would know soon enough. That's how it was back then. Her children are married, and she has two wonderful grandchildren, Genna and Michael. They live nearby to Little Italy and are very close to the family. Her grandchildren inspired her to write her family history down so they would know where the family came from. Her daughter read it, and she showed it to a friend, playwright Charles Messina. He in turn sent it to Barry Beckham a publisher, and it was published in June 2010. The book, *Be Home on Time When I Put The Water Up For Pasta*, is a memoir of her life growing up in Little Italy. On Sundays, in keeping with the Italian traditions, Angel makes a large pot of gravy with sausage and meatballs, and a large bowl of pasta, and the family eats early, continental style at 3 p.m. It lasts all day with family and friends. She said "after four generations living in Little Italy I can't see myself living anywhere else, what more can I say Little Italy is my home."

PIGEON FLYING

From Zina Saunders' Overlooked New York

"ARTHUR, age 49, grew up in Little Italy, where nearly every rooftop was capped by a pigeon coop. His dream is to buy a brownstone in the neighborhood; not for the space or the status, but to have his own roof where he could put a pigeon coop."

There was pigeons on my roof as long as I can remember. There was a pigeon coop on every other roof in our neighborhood ... in a five block radius, in Little Italy, there must've been about 5,000 pigeons.

As a kid, I would clean up the coop and carry up the feed to roof, cause it was a six-story walk-up. We had 500 birds on the roof, so I'd be carrying up 50-lb. bags of feed.

When we'd see a bird on our roof from a different coop, it was a whole sport to catch them and sell 'em back. When we got another guy's birds, he had an option of coming back and buying it (we had a dollar-a-catch back then), and if the guy thought it was worth another shot, then he got it back. If he didn't, we'd bring it down to the bird store and trade it for feed. If you'd go down to the bird store with 15 birds that you caught that day, that 15 birds would buy you a sack of seed.

There was a guy right around the corner, we used to call him Uncle, he used to catch our birds, and it was like a Soft-Catch, it was a Quarter-Catch. So we'd go up there and he'd have like five of my birds, and I'd give him a dollar and a quarter to get my birds back.

And then there were bad guys that had Catch-Kill. That was when they catch your bird, they just kill it on you on spite.

I actually put a coop back on my roof about 10 years ago, without the owner of the building knowing about it. He had made us take the coop down about 20 years ago, 'cause it was a violation.

But I put another little coop up there, that wasn't so conspicuous. I had racing homers. I put racing homers on the roof for one reason: when you let a racing homer out, it's not a bird like a flight bird, that hangs around the roof all day. When you let a racing homer out, they disappear. And when they come back, they don't hang around the roof, they go right in to the coop. So it was just a matter of convenience for me. I could get over on the landlord, and I still had my pigeons on the roof. But the landlord found out and I had to take it down.

You know what my dream is? To buy a brownstone and put a pigeon coop on the roof."

 *Zina Saunders has been a writer-illustrator for more than 15 years, regularly contributing to a variety of periodicals including The Wall Street Journal, Mother Jones, The Progressive, The Nation, and The New Republic. The portrait and interview with rooftop pigeon coop guy, Arthur, is a part of her Overlooked New York project which can be seen at www.overlookednewyork.com. Zina lives and works in New York City, where she grew up and attended Music and Art High School and The Cooper Union. She left Manhattan in her teens to be a levitating lady with a traveling circus in upstate New York, but eventually returned to her senses and her beloved city.*

PART 7

CELEBRITY

CELEBRITY

Editor's Note:

YOU MAY THINK THAT CELEBRITY IS A STATUS that requires a featured role on television, in film, or in People magazine, but celebrity is a broad term. The people we describe in this chapter are some of our celebrities, and in fact they all enjoy more than just local recognition.

In Fame and Obscurity, Gay Talese included a short piece, "New York City Is a City of the Anonymous." Fair enough as far as his descriptions go— the pretty girl on the subway, the bus driver, shoe shine boys and so on. But even Talese acknowledges their names in some cases. We acknowledge here some of the names we raise among ourselves to celebrity status and we expect some day to see them featured in film, on television, or in People magazine.

VINCENT BIVONA

VINCENT BIVONA IS AN ACTOR. He received the Jean Dalyrimple Award- 2011 Best Comedic Performance "Comedy of Errors" at the American Theater of Actors.

Vincent grew up in New Jersey as a member of the "Diaspora" family of John and Anne Bivona. He has appeared in TV, film, theater, and commercials, including, "The Departed," "The Cowboy," "Cloths of Heaven," "The New Yorkers," "The Years of the Locusts," "Henry V," "You're a Good Man Charlie Brown," "The Waiting," "Pericles," "Shakespeare Tribute," "Taming of the Shrew," "A Midsummer Night's Dream," "A Comedy of Errors," "Divinity," "Waiting for Lefty," "Hamlet," the "Doc Elliot Show," and "MTV'S Rock the Vote."

His training includes studies with The American Academy of Dramatic Arts, Ramapo College, Brooke Bundy (Nustars), The Gene Frankel Theatre and Film Workshop, the Madelyn Burns Studio), and The Robert X. Modica Studio. He studied The Alexander Technique with Leland Val.

He is married to Antonella, who is from Naples, Italy

We asked Vincent a few questions:

Q. Vincent, as the great grandson of Italian immigrants, do you consider yourself Italian-America, American- Italian, just American, or an Italian of American descent?

A. I am very proud of my Italian heritage and consider myself an American of Italian descent. I am proud also of my great grandparent's origins in Sicily.

Q. How do you think that this heritage influenced the way you are to-day?

A. I think that it especially gives me a love for entertaining and giving others something worthwhile through my acting. It also gives me great respect for sociability and camaraderie. Also living in the moment—*carpe diem*-an old Roman idea, along with the idea of working diligently to achieve your goals and persevering through hardship, but enjoying the struggle. Also (laughing), I don't think I could ever eat poorly, and Italian food hopefully will always be a part of my life.

Q. Have you been to Little Italy in the past and recently? Any thoughts about it?

A. Of course. I loved it too, especially those stickball re-unions, the sense of friendship among all the participants and their families. I am very proud that my Mom and Dad have maintained their ties with the wonderful friends that they had from even Kindergarten. They are truly an extended family. This is a wonderful legacy for my genera-tion. I hope we can do that. It was great to see the old cathedral, now a basilica, and the family bakery, now under a different name, but still a bakery. And the colorful Italian restaurant area.

VINCENT CAPUCCIO

VINCENT CAPUCCIO (VINNIE STIGMA) grew up in the neighborhood, living on Mott Street and he still lives there. He is a guitarist and a founding and original member of Agnostic Front, an internationally famous punk rock band, with hugely attended performances throughout the world. They are considered "The Godfathers of New York Hardcore."

Agnostic Front live 2007, Vinnie Stigma centered in the background

According to Wikipedia, "Their debut EP *United Blood*, released in 1983 on an indie label, has since become a collector's item....The follow-up, *Victim in Pain* (1984), is regarded as a seminal New York hardcore release."

Vinnie and Agnostic Front continue to perform in the city and the metropolitan area and in many other states in the U.S. International appear-

ances have been in numerous countries in Europe and Latin America. He also has a shop, New York Hardcore Tattoo, on Stanton St. His solo album, *New York Blood* came out in 2008. In 2009 he was the star of a film, *New York Blood,* directed by Nick Oddo, which includes a number of neighborhood scenes as well as a few neighborhood people as actors. Vinnie and his band are effervescent, dynamic musicians who go all out for their adoring audiences in performances that define their genre. They are accessible, humble, indefatigable, and loveable, even if their shows are a bit raucous at times.

Vinnie was interviewed briefly in Virginia Beach, Virginia about the neighborhood and his music just prior to one of the Agnostic Front shows.

Q. Tell me how you got into music? How old were you when you first started?

A. How old was I? I was twelve or thirteen really.

Q. You started playing the guitar?

A. No, I started in the choir in the church. Yeah we practiced where the organ was. My hero then was Enrico Caruso. I really liked the echo in the church. I also got a kick out of the guys doing doo-wops in the hallways of the buildings.

Q. In the neighborhood?

A. Yeah, you know how the kids used to sing "doo-wop" and then some how that time past, and the guitar just got me. Jim Hendrix and you know what I mean. So, I picked up the guitar and I've been playing ever since.

Q. From 12 years old.

A. Yeah.

Q. How did you form a band—for example how did you run into these guys (rest of Agnostic Front)?

A. I don't know, I don't even know. Yeah, I met them walking around, like out here, like it was like hanging out. Hey do you want to be in my band? And that was the end of that. Like this guy here (pointing to singer Roger Mirat.) He was 17 years old. He's 44 now. Oh my God, we will be together 31 years.

Q. Who lives in the neighborhood now besides you?

A. Everybody lives in the neighborhood now. David Bowie lives in the neighborhood. All these big singers, they live a little bit in the suburbs, but they also have these lofts in the neighborhood.

Q. Does the music incite wildness, like we see in the mosh pit?

A. It's like any other music that raises the spirit in some way, like Rock or Swing.

VINCENT LaBARBERA

BORN AND RAISED IN LITTLE ITALY, New York City, impressionist and comedian Vinny La Barbera has been involved in the entertainment field since he was a child. He first appeared on stage at the age of five and became interested in performing impressions of popular TV and movie personalities when he was ten years old, performing for friends in school, hallways—wherever he found a willing listener. He was especially inspired by singers and enjoyed performing impressions of Johnny Ray, Dean Martin, Frankie Laine, the 4 Aces, Lou Monte, the Ink Spots, the Mills Brothers and Lena Horne.

Vinny made his professional debut as an impressionist and singer at the age of twelve, impersonating singer Johnny Ray at the Statler-Hilton in New York. He was offered a record contract immediately following his performance, but his parents refused to even consider the possibility of having him

leave school to work in show business. Nonetheless, Vinny continued to perform impressions of famous personalities informally for friends and family, and eventually brought his act to small clubs in the metropolitan area, including Trumpets Jazz Club, Montclair, New Jersey. The enthusiastic response of his audience encouraged him to develop more impressions, taking his material from popular actors and singers, including Dean Martin, Jerry Lewis, Paul Lynde, Louis Prima, Elvis Presley, Billie

Holiday, Connie Francis, Lou Monte, Tiny Tim, Howard Cosell, Arthur Godrey, Marlon Brando, Sylvestor Stallone, and Tony Bennett.

He began to work at comedy clubs in New York City during the Seventies and headlined at the "Grand Finale" in 1977-1978 and has continued to entertain at private events and business and holiday functions for the past thirty years.

Vinny's ability to honestly depict familiar people and places with a fast, rhythmic, spontaneous delivery delights his audiences. He cites world-renowned comedian and actor Pat Cooper, a mentor and dear friend, as having an important influence on his work. Vinny is a charter member of Ciao, Little Italy

PART 8

PATRIOTISM

Paint on Concrete
© *L. Marinaccio 2010*

My name is Lorrena Lapouge Marinaccio but people call me Lola. I was born in a little town closed to Paris, France, Saint Germain en Laye. I traveled a lot when I was young and lived few years in Sweden, England and Austria. At an early age, my dream was to live in New York. I started to draw at the age of nine, and my favorite practices were the Simpsons and Disney characters. Then I started to make portraits of famous people like Tupac and the Fugees. When I was 15, I attended a special high school for graphic design. At that  time we didn't use computers. Everything was done manually. I learned a lot and made great strides in developing my skills. I become very passionate about my art when I paint and compose. I don't have a particular style as an artist. I'm very eclectic. I get my technical skills from my dad who is a car designer, and my passion for painting from my grandparents, who were very devoted painters. And I probably use a lot of warm and bold colors because of my African ethnic background. Today I am working as a freelance designer. I design logos, websites, customized painting on walls and much more. I also started a handbag line last year called "Boulibag" (still in progress).

I also have another big passion—shooting videos and photos and editing. The more challenging a project is, the more excited I get. I just hate the routine. I am a very scattered artist, but it is because I am very passionate about art in general. It feels like traveling to different places to discover the world.

John Wayne and Chicken with Lemon and Oil

By Richard J. Rinaldo

LOLA'S MURAL ON THE OPPOSITE PAGE is proof of the high regard held in Little Italy for its sons and daughters who served in our Nation's armed forces. It is also a display of loyalty to the Nation. The mural was unveiled on Memorial Day 2010 and is located on a wall in the courtyard of Most Precious Blood Church on Mulberry Street between Canal and Hester streets. A United States Marine Band and Honor Guard were in the ceremony. Previous plaques on the wall commemorate service members from Vietnam and World War I, who were killed in action. The mural and a plaque honoring PFC Frank Vallone, killed in Vietnam on September 11, 1968, were sponsored by the Little Italy Merchants Association.

In Martin Scorsese's *Mean Streets* one of the protagonists of the movie, Charlie, kind of a composite alter ego of Marty and some of his friends (played by Harvey Keitel), is asked by his girlfriend Teresa (played by Amy Robinson), "What do you like, Charlie?" His answer lists John Wayne alongside chicken with lemon and oil. This was one of Catherine Scorsese's (Marty's mother) specialties. And it was delicious as some of us know. So that's quite a tribute to the Duke, who played the lead character of Sergeant John Stryker in *Sands of Iwo Jima*. It is also a tribute to the United States Marine Corps, and by extension, all our Soldiers, Sailors, Airman, and Coast Guard members.

The story of Iwo Jima was not unfamiliar to the neighborhood, even before the movie. Among its relatively unsung heroes was Joseph F. Falcone, Sr., who was killed in action there. His story has to begin with the story of the plaque pictured here:

—— IN HONOR OF ——
WWII VETERANS OF LITTLE ITALY
★ ★ ★ ★

PVT. JOSEPH ADAMO
PVT. ANGELO AGUILINO
PVT. THOMAS AIELLO
PVT. MICHAEL AMATO
PVT. ROSARIO AMICO
PVT. ANCONA
PVT. SEBASTIAN BALLIRO
PVT. ANTONIO BARBERA
USN. NICHOLAS BELLANTONI
PVT. SALVATORE BENAVENTURA
PFC. JOHN BRUNOFORTE
CPL. PHILIP CAMPANELLA
SGT. RICHARD CAMPANELLA
PVT. VINCENT CAPRIA
CPL. DOMINICK CARCIONE
PVT. GERALD CARDELLA
PVT. ARCHIE CARUSO
PVT. ARMANDO CARUTO
PVT. JOSEPH CATALANO
PVT. CALOGERO CELESTE
PVT. PATSY CHIARELLO
PVT. ANTHONY CINQUEGRANA
PVT. NICK COMO
PVT. FRANK CONIGLIO
PVT. FRANK CORNETTO
USMC. LOUIS CUOMO
PVT. JOSEPH CURRERI
PVT. ALFRED D'ANGELICO
PVT. EDWARD D'AVANZO
PVT. WILLIAM D'AVANZO
PVT. LOUIS DE CESARE
USN. JOSEPH DELLATACOMA
PFC. JOSEPH DE MARCO
PVT. THOMAS DE MARCO
SGT. ANTHONY DE MARO
USN. ANTHONY DI COLA
CPL. CAMILLO DI COLA
PVT. DI DOMENICO
PVT. FRANK DICEMBRE
PVT. MICHAEL DICEMBRE
PFC. SIONE DI LIBERTO
LT. DOMINICK DI MAIO
PVT. SALVATORE DI MARTINO
PVT. AUGUST DIMINO
PVT. PATSY DIMINO
PVT. PASQUALE DI NATALE
USN. PETER DI PILATO
PVT. CARLO DI SANTO
PVT. ANTHONY FABRETTI
PVT. ALFRED FALANGA
USMC. JOSEPH FALCONE
PVT. THOMAS FALCONE
USMC. VINCENT FALCONE
PVT. PETER FAMA

USMC. SALVATORE FAMA
USN. CHARLES FAZIO
USMC. PETER FAZZETTI
JOHN FENECK
PVT. PATSY FERRENTINO
PVT. JOHN FICAROTTA
PVT. SABATO FLORIO
PVT. JOSEPH FONTANA
PVT. SILVIO FONTANA
PFC. GASPER FRISCIA
PVT. LOUIS FRISCIA
PVT. ANTHONY GALLETTA
PVT. DOMINICK GALLETTA
PVT. LOUIS GALLO
PVT. DOMINICK GALTIERI
PVT. SALVATORE GANGAROSA
PVT. BALDASSORE GUARDINO
PVT. JOSEPH GUARDINO
PFC. LORENZO GUARDINO
PVT. CATALDO GUINTA
PVT. JOSEPH GUINTA
PVT. SALVATORE GUINTA
USCG. HERMAN GURSKE
PFC. WALTER GUSTAVO
SGT. GEORGE HORVATH
PVT. SALVATORE IETTO
PVT. ANGELO LA ROCCA
PVT. THOMAS LASPADA
CPL. ANTHONY LIBASSI
PVT. VITO LO CICERO
USN. CARLO LONGARDO
PVT. RALPH LUCIBELLA
PVT. S. LUCIBELLA
PVT. ANTHONY MACRINI
CPL. MICHAEL MAFFEI
PVT. CHARLES MALLIA
PVT. CHARLES MANISCALCO
PVT. FRANK MANISCALCO
PVT. DOMINICK MANZONE
USN. ROCCO MANZONE
SGT. WILLIAM MATERA
PVT. JOSEPH MATRA
SGT. PETER MATRA
PVT. PETER MATRECANO
PVT. LEONARD MERCURIO
USMC. JOSEPH MIGNONE
PVT. THOMAS MIRABELLA
TONY MOLINARO
PVT. COSMO MUSOLINO
PVT. VINCENT MUSOLINO
PVT. PATSY ORSINI
PVT. WILLIAM ORSINI
PVT. DOMINICK PADOVANO
USMC. JOSEPH PALERMO

PVT. ARMANDO PARIANTE
PVT. VINCENT PARIANTE
LT. CARMINE PERROTTA
F. PETTA
L. PETTA
PVT. JERRY PIPOLI
PFC. NICHOLAS PIPOLI
SGT. ANTHONY PIZZARELLI
PFC. ANTHONY PIZZARELLI
PVT. DOMINICK PIZZARELLI
PVT. GERALD PIZZARELLI
PVT. LOUIS PIZZARELLI
PVT. SALVATORE PIZZARELLI
PVT. JOSEPH PONTILLO
L. PROVENZANO
PVT. JOSEPH PULICHENE
PVT. ROCCO REGANATO
PFC. JACK ROMEO
SGT. JOSEPH SABELLA
SGT. MICHAEL SANTOMAURO
SGT. SAVINO SANTOMAURO
CPL. MICHAEL SANTORO
PFC. JOSEPH SBOTO
PVT. PETER SBOTO
USN. ANTHONY SCHIUMO
DOMINICK SCHIUMO
PVT. CARMINE SCOGNAMIGLI
PVT. ANTHONY SEGRETO
PVT. MARIO SGARLTA
PVT. THOMAS SGARLTA
PVT. FRANK SORRENTINO
PVT. VINCENT SORRENTINO
PVT. ANTHONY STEVI
PVT. JOHN STEVI
PVT. RICO TACONA
PFC. ANTHONY TEDESCO
PVT. PETER TERESA
PVT. ROCCO TERESA
CPL. EMANUEL TERIZINO
PVT. ANTHONY TERRACIANO
USN. ANTHONY TESORIERE
CPL. CARMINE TESORIERE
PVT. FRANK TESORIERE
PFC. PETER TESORIERE
PFC. NICHOLAS TORASCO
PVT. JOSEPH TREZZA
JIMMY TRUPIA
PVT. LOUIS TUDISCO
PVT. ANTHONY VILLAROLA
PVT. LOUIS VILLAROLA
PVT. JOSEPH VISCUSO
PVT. SEBASTIAN VISCUSO
PVT. YACOVELLI
USN. PAUL ZINNO

★ ★ ★ ★

THEY SERVED FOR FREEDOM
SPEECH · ASSEMBLY · PRESS
RELIGION · LAW · REPRESENTATION

Just a plaque?

Many of us remember the plaque, which was prominently displayed on the east side of Mott Street between Grand and Broome. My mother would take me shopping down Mott Street. On the way back we would stop just north of the plaque for a slice of Sicilian pizza, and I would look at the plaque, which was surrounded by a fresco depicting the Bill of Rights, as suggested by the words at the bottom of it. (See also picture at right taken in 1978.) Lincoln Anderson tells us the story in an article in the *Villager*, "A lost mural symbolizes a vanishing Little Italy" (June, 2008). He says, "For almost 60 years, a memorial honoring 200 local men who served in World War II was affixed to a wall… around the corner from the Di Palo grocery store. It was put up by the Dapper Don S.A., one of the Italian-American social clubs that used to dot almost every block in the neighborhood." An artist added the fresco mural, according to Anderson, in 1961.

But when the building on which it was placed was purchased, the plaque had to be removed, and the mural was covered. So today there is a blank wall. Had it not been for the good will and patriotism of Lou Di Palo and family, owners of Di Palo Fine Foods, the plaque itself might have disappeared. They restored it, and placed it in their store window, across the street from its original location, taking up a lot of showcase space. It is a welcome source of historic preservation of the neighborhood. It also shows appreciation for service to the Nation and the sacrifices of its service members.

But the story of the plaque is not finished. A haphazard Internet search of names on it found Joseph Falcone, Sr. at http://www.c123rd. com/Marines_FalconeSrJoseph.aspx. His son, Joseph Falcone, Jr. had numerous letters from his father and provided them to the website of Company C, 1st Battalion, 23rd Marines, 4th Division, United States Marine Corps WW II. With the help of Sherrie Ferguson of that organization, I finally confirmed that the Falcone family came from Mott Street and Joseph Falcone, Jr. called me. He told me that he gave his father's letters to the organization as a way to preserve his memory and the memory of all those who served their nation and gave the ultimate sacrifice of their lives to it. Joseph told me, "Sixty seven years after my father was killed, the impact on his family to this very day is unbelievable." Here's part of what Joe said to the organization: "As you know, my father was only one of many brave Americans who lost their lives on Iwo Jima. While I never met him, I am fortunate to have known him through over 700 letters which he wrote during his time in the Marine Corps. I have learned from these letters how much he adored his family, never wanted his brothers to serve in the military, and wished for nothing more than to see an end to the war and return home to those he loved. "

There is also in those letters testament to his fathers pride in being a United States Marine, his sense of humor, and a verity about prayer. In February 1943, he wrote: "The Major General is coming tomorrow to inspect our barracks.... If he is going to inspect every barrack, I don't think he'll live through it. If he should die, Hon, maybe they'll make me the General and the first orders that I will give out is to give myself a three month furlough, come back for a day and then have another three month furlough."

In July, 1943 he wrote "I got an invitation to Nellie's wedding but I can't make it because Uncle Sam is too busy. And in August 1944, "...I heard something like a baby crying up ahead....We went over and looked around and we saw a white blanket with someone under it...all of a sudden the baby started crying. We walked over and took the blanket off and it was a Japanese girl about twenty years old holding the baby in her arms. We tried to take the baby away from her but she wouldn't give it up. We had a heck of a time trying to convince her that we wouldn't hurt her or the baby. She couldn't walk because her heel was blown off and I had to carry her out while this guy, Charlie, carried the baby. They finally put her in a jeep and I guess she was taken care of. And what a cute baby it was. It really made me think a heck of a lot about it being like that back home and how thankful we should all be that it isn't. There was a heck of a lot of things worse than that, Hon, but I even hate to think about it.

In September 1944: "... made Corporal.... It felt pretty good be-

ing called out in front of the whole company and having the Captain congratulating us on our good work. Especially when it's from a man that all the guys respect so much. It's really something hard to explain."

In December 1944: "...I went to Midnight Mass. If you remember I never really was a religious guy and never thought of praying much. I used to say if I ever got myself in a tight spot I wouldn't pray to get myself out of it. Well, I was wrong because now that I'm in a tight spot, I do pray, for you and my son. I don't want anything to happen that would hurt you or the baby."

Mentioned earlier in this book was the notion of *Realpolitik* that Italian-Americans inherited from their Italian ancestors. As long as the heart of man harbors jealousy and resentful envy, political and religious intolerance, overweening pride, and ethnic hatred, the security environment will present dangers to the U.S. and it friends. Wherever such threats may emerge, our Nation's military team has always been ready to fight for the Nation. Italian-Americans from  Little Italy know this and honor those loyal men and women. At right an image from one of our grammar school plays. We were singing, "Give me some men who are stout-hearted men, who will fight for the rights they adore." We had them.

Finally this from *Wikipedia, the free encyclopedia*:

As a member of the Axis powers, Italy declared war on the United States in 1941. Any concerns about the loyalty of Italian Americans were quickly dispelled. More than half a million Italian Americans served in the various branches of the military. In spite of this display of loyalty, hundreds of Italians viewed as a potential threat to the country were interned in detention camps, some for up to 2 years. As many as 600,000 others, who had not become citizens, were required to carry identity cards identifying them as "resident alien". Thousands more on the West Coast were required to move inland, often losing their homes and businesses in the process. A number of Italian-language newspapers were forced to close because of their past support of Fascist dictator Benito Mussolini. Two books, *Una Storia Segreta* by Lawrence Di Stasi and *Uncivil Liberties* by Stephen Fox; and a movie, *Prisoners Among Us*, document these World War II developments. Italian Americans served with distinction during the war, and 14 were awarded the Medal of Honor.

BOZO'S JOURNEY

By Robert Uricola

"THESE ARE THE TIMES THAT TRY MEN'S SOULS. The summer soldier and the sunshine patriot will in this crisis, shrink from the service of their country; But he that stands it now, deserves the love and thanks of man and woman."

Thomas Paine wrote those words in December 1776, at night, on a drum head, while Washington's retreating army camped somewhere in New Jersey. Paine's stirring call to action the first in his American Crisis Series rekindled the flame of patriotism. Citizen soldiers re-enlisted and new recruits flocked to join America's fledgling army.

Michael Uricola, my paternal uncle known on the streets of Manhattan's "Little Italy" as "Bozo" is my first memory in life. The remembrance is this. Uncle Bozo is in uniform. I am in his arms. He kisses me. I can feel the coarseness of his hands and face. Anne, my mother sobs as she removes me from his care. The tenement on Mulberry Street is awash with family and friends. Antoinette, Bozo's mother wails as only Italian mothers from Southern Italy can. Her cries follow Bozo out onto the street, towards his destiny.

It is 1943. I am in my first year of life, and war is raging throughout the world.

What possessed Bozo, barely eighteen at the time to enlist in the armed forces? I'd like to believe Thomas Paine's words influenced his decision.

That's wishful thinking on my part. Bozo, like most working class young men of the depression era left school to help provide for their families. Maybe it was the conflict itself. America had been attacked. Fascism was evil. The cause was just.

Bozo's decision was a personal one. He belonged to a society. I don't mean the greater society of the United States of America. I mean the provincial society of New York's Little Italy. This close knit community instilled in him a code of responsible behavior and deep sense of honor. It was this that he would contribute to America's cause.

I recently came across some photographs of Bozo. They were a welcomed discovery. Memories can be deceptive. More often than not they wander into the realm of mythology and receive a distorted image. One photo spoke volumes. It was taken in mid 1941. Bozo was sixteen years of age at the time. The Puck Building, now a Manhattan landmark, is in the background. Bozo was below average height. Not more than 5 feet 5 inches tall. His face is unremarkable, round and soft, with a hint of teenage sweetness. Looking passed the dark wavy hair and protruding ears, my attention was drawn to his eyes. They were dark brown, determined, and in this photograph burned right through you. I wanted to know more about my uncle.

Why Bozo. I asked my father, Sal? The nickname brought to mind the clown of children's books and television fame. That did not work out since "Bozo the Clown" was created in 1946. My father had no idea how the nickname came about. But, he assured me that if his youngest brother found it offensive there would be hell to pay.

Dad went on to say with glowing pride that the innocent young man in the photograph was a terror in the boxing ring. Bozo began his pugilistic career at ten years of age honing his boxing skills at the James Center, a youth organization located on Hester Street. My uncle took his training seriously, placing all of his restless youthful energy into the organized structure of the boxing ring. He competed in numerous inter-borough competitions right up until enlisting in the service. "Bozo did not win every bout he fought" declared my father honestly. "But let me tell you something if you stepped into the ring with my kid brother, you knew you were in a fight. He never went down, and he never gave up."

Bozo's prowess in the ring translated into respect on the tough, unforgiving streets of Little Italy.

The year the photograph was taken, my father worked *as* a parking attendant in a local garage. One sweltering, July afternoon he received a visit from a young local tough guy. He was planning a score and needed a car. He wanted dad to look the other way while he stole one. My father told him to "get lost." He did, but promised to return with some friends. Dad sent for his brothers, John and Mario. Bozo was home alone at the time. He rushed to my father's side.

As promised the young tough returned with two pals. Bozo knew all three, and they knew his reputation. He introduced dad *as* his oldest

brother before taking the three punks off to the side. They talked. My father kept a wary eye on the proceeding. It wasn't long before the trio left minus what they came for. "What happened, asked Dad? "Nothing, it was all a misunderstanding" replied Bozo. I didn't think much of the story until my father elaborated. The three thugs had pistols tucked inside their waistbands. Fascism did not know what it was in for.

Pearl Harbor stunned America. When the shock wore off many of Bozo's friends rushed to join the armed forces. The selective service system, "The Draft," further thinned the ranks of young men from the neighborhood. A small number chose to evade the draft. Bozo had no use for that line of thinking. To him the choice was simple. His friends were over there fighting. He would join them.

Bozo's determination to enlist was frustrated by age. He begged his mother for permission to sign up. Antoinette would not hear of it. It was not that she was unpatriotic, she was simply pragmatic. "When they call, you go" she told her disappointed son.

Antoinette was in her mid-forties when she gave birth to Bozo. Her husband Michael died of heart decease during the pregnancy. The infant named after him was considered nothing short of a miracle. Antoinette doted on this precious child, as did his three older brothers and three sisters. The sun rose and set on Bozo. My grandmother would surrender him to the United States military only when she absolutely had to, and not a second sooner.

The war in Europe and the Pacific intensified. Casualty lists began to trickle in. The mounting toll of young men from the neighborhood played deeply on Bozo's conscience. He would be filled with shame when the mother of a friend inquired as to why he was not in the service.

On the morning of his eighteenth birthday, he rode the IRT, the subway line his father, a construction worker helped to build to Whitehall Street and enlisted into the United States Army.

Bozo, completed basic training at Camp Drum, in upstate New York, and shipped out in mid-1943. He disembarked as part of the newly formed Fifth Army under the command of General Mark W. Clark at Oran, in North Africa.

Letters penned to my mother, Anne were filled with exotic places. Names like Marrakech, Mehdia, Fedala, and Safi filled the pages. The North African people and their mysterious customs fascinated Bozo. The bustling North African bazaars reminding him of the crowded shopping streets of lower Manhattan.

North Africa fell to the allies not long after the Fifth Army landed on its shores. Peace brought with it new problems. Axis prisoners languished in cramped unsanitary POW camps. A displaced population wandered about aimlessly, begging for food, alms, anything that would relieve their suffering. Victory came at a terrible price.

Bozo's letters grew dark over time. Anne wrote Bozo, "This is some fucking hole." It was obvious that the horrors of modem warfare affected the young soldier deeply.

July 10, 1943 the allies invaded Sicily. The Fifth Army did not take part in the operation. Bozo sat out the invasion in Oran. News from the front was optimistic. The allies were receiving light resistance and the operation was moving swiftly towards a climax. In late August, 102,000 axis forces withdrew across the Strait of Messina reinforcing the Italian mainland.

My mother like most Americans followed the progress of the war in the local newspapers. She came to realize that Bozo might be in Sicily, possibly in the vicinity of Marineo, a small Sicilian hill town that my mother's' family originated from. Anne innocently wrote Bozo suggesting he seek out any relatives that could be found. Bozo replied that it would be difficult since "I 'm not traveling first class."

The liberation of Sicily brought the Italians to their senses. They dumped Mussolini, formed a new government and secretly sued for peace. On September 8, 1943 Italy formally surrendered and joined the allied cause.

Germany turned on their former ally with a vengeance. Italy was placed under Occupation. Italians found cooperating with the Allies were liquidated or shipped off to work camps in Germany. Bozo would be a witness to the chaos that soon engulfed the whole of the Italian mainland.

Bozo received the news of Italy's surrender on board a troop ship anchored off the coast of Salerno. In the early morning hours of September 9, 1943, thousands of young Americans from every corner of the United States watched as the fleet's big guns shelled the coastline of Salerno. When the guns fell silent landing craft loaded with green, untested troops made a run for the beach. Crack German infantry and panzer units put up a stiff resistance. The struggle was hard, bloody, and at times desperate. Bozo and his comrades held their ground. The Germans pulled back to form a defensive line further inland.

The Volturno River meandered below Castello Marrone. The citadel held a commanding view of the plain above Napoli. It was a perfect position for German artillery. Shells rained down on stalled segments of the Fifth Army. Air strikes bombed the stronghold to no avail. Italians knew how to construct with stone. German defenders used the rubble to their advantage. Ground assault after ground assault followed. Bozo was killed in this operation. Shrapnel was the cause. Death in modern warfare far from glorious is often indiscriminate.

I 'm sure Bozo would have preferred a more heroic death. Hand to hand against some Nazi fanatic. That was not to be.

Letters from Bozo stopped. Packages sent to him were returned. He was interred at the American Military Cemetery at Caserta.

The family held the news from Antoinette. No one had the courage to tell her. She grew suspicious with time asking about the lack of communication from her much-beloved, youngest boy. With the war in Europe drawing to a close, she had to be told. Antoinette's cries of anguish echoed throughout the tenement. The distraught mother entered into a period of deep mourning. She would just sit for days on end rocking back and forth in a living room chair.

When her grief subsided, she told my father she did not want her son to remain buried in Italy. She wanted him home. There was no talking her out of it. My Uncle John, a functionary in local Republican politics, and a nephew, New York City Appellate Court Judge Rocco Parella saw to Antoinette's wishes.

In 1947 Bozo came home.

Bozo's wake was held at a funeral home on Mott Street between Houston and Prince Streets in Little Italy. I was six at the time and it seemed that the entire neighborhood came to pay their respects. There's a photograph that shows an oversized American flag, a tribute from his friends made entirely out of Red White & Blue flowers. A color portrait of Bozo in full dress uniform sits atop the flag draped coffin. The captain in charge of the burial detail insisted that nothing could be placed atop the flag. The portrait must be removed. My grandmother informed the captain, that her son died defending the flag.

With that, the photograph remained. My father held onto this portrait throughout his long life. No matter where he traveled, the photograph of his kid brother graced the room he slept in.

A Requiem Mass was celebrated on the main altar of Saint Patrick's Old Cathedral. The church was filled to capacity.

The military ceremony at First Calvary cemetery in Queens, New York was memorable. The haunting notes of taps, the final salute, the reverent folding of the flag. Those dramatic sights and sounds remain with you forever.

Antoinette proudly accepted the flag from the captain in charge holding it close to her heart.

Bozo was interred inside the family mausoleum. The burial site sits on an incline from where the Manhattan skyline rises in the distance. Bozo would have enjoyed the view.

Not long ago on a visit to Italy, my wife Winnie and I took a side trip to Castello Marrone. The ancient buildings have been restored. A plaque dedicated to the battle that took place and the lives that were lost can be found there. A strange quiet hung in the air the day I visited. Walking around the citadel I realized a frontal assault was suicidal. Bozo must have sensed the odds. I can't imagine the courage it took to storm that site.

I scanned the valley and could see Caserta below, just beyond the sprawl of Napoli the gleaming Mediterranean. Than it struck me, dead south was Avellino. The province Bozo's parents were from. He had met his end a few kilometers from the family's birthplace. How ironic, this young man sacrificed to the past for the future.

I wonder what would have become of Bozo had he survived the war? The experience would no doubt have changed him. Possibly he would have continued his education. The G.l. bill afforded him the opportunity; maybe he would have returned to the boxing ring. He was good with his fists. Most likely he would have taken a blue collar job, got married, and raised a family. Whatever he chose to do would have been fine. As my father was fond of saying, "He was a good kid."

The inscription at Bozo's burial site reads simply, "Neither Bombs Nor Bursting Shells Shall Disturb The Eternal Slumber Of This Tired Boy" there's the date of birth and death above his name "Michael John Uricola." Antoinette requested one thing, which forever endeared her to my memory. Just in case you did not know her son's proper name, she had "Bozo" chiseled into the cold hard marble. With that simple human gesture my grandmother, and our family, cornered the market on class.

SOME OTHER MOTHER'S SON

By Sarah Ann LoFaso

A Memorial Day tribute to the memory of the thousands of men and women in the U.S. Armed Forces, who died serving our nation. We will never forget you.

The year was 1942, exactly 30 years since my grandmother; Cira Lofaso sailed from Sicily to join her husband in America. They settled on Mulberry Street in New York City's Little Italy where they raised four sons and a daughter. Her husband worked on the railroads while Cira sewed in the garment district.

In World War II, two of Cira's sons joined the U.S. Army. Frank was a private serving in Europe while Salvatore became a sergeant in the Army Air Force in Pakistan and India.

Cira stayed in touch with her boys through letters, photos and even small gifts. She rejoiced when they came home on furlough; she followed the war reports on the radio; and she cried when she learned that a neighborhood boy had been wounded or killed.

Home on furlough, Frank stands between his mother, Cira and sister, Rose. His older brother, Charles, the author's father, is kneeling

One day in 1944, a telegram arrived. Frank, 24, was missing in action during the Battle of Anzio. A year later, the Army found his grave in a military cemetery in Nettuno, Italy. They shipped his body home to the U.S. for burial.

At his large funeral, a military honor guard stood in formation outside the funeral home and then played Taps as Frank was buried in the family plot in Calvary Cemetery. A soldier gave Cira the American flag that had draped Frank's coffin.

As she stood by Frank's grave, a man approached my grandmother. "How do you know that is really your son buried there?" he asked. Cira was silent for a moment and then said, "If it is not my son, then it is some other mother's son."

Many years have passed since that unhappy day. Our nation is again at war, with young men, like Frank, called upon to make the ultimate sacrifice. I pray for them and for their families. Most of all, I pray for an end to all wars.

This article was reprinted courtesy of ITALIAN AMERICA Magazine, the most widely read publication in the United States for Italian Americans. ITALIAN AMERICA Magazine is published by the Sons of Italy. For subscription information, contact ITALIAN AMERICA MAGAZINE, 219 E Street, NE, Washington, DC 20002. (tel: 202/547-2900. Web www.osia.org)

THE DOG HANDLER CRIED

By Richard J. Rinaldo

VIETNAM. WE WERE UNDER INTENSE FIRE from elements of a North Vietnamese Army regiment. Fortunately, much of the time the fire from their rifles and machine guns was high. The trees showered us with pieces of leaves and debris.

The men of my company were stalwarts and heroes. There were three wounded up near the point, and my company medic with complete disregard for his own safety, left his covered position and dashed forward to administer aid to one of them, whom he carried to safety. Then he returned to help the second one and pull him to safety despite wounds from a mortar round. He went forward through the fire again to help the third man. He was shot in the head and killed. He received the Congressional Medal of Honor posthumously.

While he was doing this I was frantically making arrangements for medical evacuations and a score of other things. I had gone well forward, and at one point in the action one of the wounded was beside me in excruciating pain, screaming and moaning for his mother. But evacuation was too late for him.

My radio was a lifeline to hope—for advice, medical evacuation, food, water, ammunition, and replacements. It helped many and saved lives and limbs then and later in my tour of duty. But it did not help that one soldier, whose pitiful murmurs still echo in my ears. He died there while I stood by helplessly. Ten others were also killed that day. And a scout dog died from heat stroke.

This was a nightmare and like Captain Murray, in the movie "Saving Private Ryan," one of the more accurate Hollywood depictions of combat, I cried later for my men. The dog handler cried too.

For this battle our company sustained numerous casualties, both killed and wounded. For their actions members of the unit received, in addition to the Medal of Honor, a Distinguished Service Cross, seven Silver Stars, eight Bronze Stars for Valor, and eight Army Commendation Medals for Valor. Later we also received a Valorous Unit award for another action.

In subsequent years records of several members of the unit were corrected to indicate receipt of a Bronze Star and the coveted Combat Infantryman's Badge. We do not forget our brothers in arms.

Uncle Len's Shoe

By Richard J. Rinaldo

UNCLE LEN REALLY WAS MY COUSIN'S UNCLE. But, I always called him Uncle Len. His surname was LoFrisco. Like some Italian-Americans, maybe he wanted to disguise his ethnic origins or perhaps folks just called him Frisco, as they did his brother, my uncle through marriage. The official story is that they made a mistake when he enlisted in the Navy, since he was a fair-skinned Sicilian type and did not look Italian. So that's what he officially used.

Brothers Jimmy, Frank, Len, Sal, and Joe

Uncle Len was kicked out of Public School 21 in the fifth grade after calling his teacher a "big ham" and throwing his shoe at him. He then worked as a printer press feeder. Then in 1911, Uncle Len enlisted in the Navy at its lowest rank, Forty-one years later he retired as a Rear Admiral. My cousin made sure at every opportunity to advise me how his rank as a Rear Admiral outranked mine!

Uncle Len served in the active Navy during World War I and World War II, rising in the former to the rank of ensign and serving in the latter as Commander of a ship that took part in the Pacific island-hopping campaign, for which he received the Legion of Merit award. In between the wars he served in the merchant marine in various positions. His brother, my Uncle Jimmie, recalled working for him in one capacity or another, a job he found very difficult. Uncle Len treated him worse than other workers to assure no sign of favoritism.

Uncle Len was very-well spoken, but not affected, his long years outside the neighborhood virtually eliminating any hint of a neighborhood accent. He carried himself well, and one could easily see that he would command both respect and admiration. On retirement he became an executive with Black Diamond shipping. Not bad for a fifth grade education.

Epilogue

By Richard J. Rinaldo

Remember, you may in God's mercy have had your day ....
You may live until over it all comes the glamour of the years,
and you may tell the tale so often that you'll hardly be able to
distinguish the fabric from the embroidery....
On the other hand, your challenge may lie ahead....

Douglas Southall Freeman

If the heart and soul of a community is its people and families, it body may be its architecture. Glitz and sheen are now layered onto the grit and grime of the neighborhood, but it still has its variety of architectural styles—Federal, Italianate, Queen Anne, Second Empire, and so forth. The neighborhood is a museum! The National Park Service listed Little Italy in the National Register of Historic Places in February 2011.

The *gemeinschaft*—bonds of sentiment, kinship and intimacy, human connections in a community with a common tradition, is a bit trickier. This is the realm of heart and soul. I believe that the newcomers to Little Italy share in our heritage. They display the same determination and vigor that most of their immigrant predecessors had, perhaps even more so as they come here out of choice, not desperation. Also, their true grit in many cases is already proven in terms of higher education achieved and financial resources.

You can see them at places like McNally Jackson Bookstore on Prince Street or The Deli next door, or maybe in church— well-dressed, bright, confident, affable, and full of hope. They are in sense descendants of the bus and truck drivers, seamstresses, longshoreman, park attendants, and construction workers of our day. Well, maybe they don't know how to cook. So much better for our restaurateurs. But they contribute immensely to the finance industry, media, higher education, religion and the arts of New York City.

The younger set may not have made it yet, but they are making it. And some are actual immigrants, forming for example a Little Australia in what once was Little Italy. They also see clearly, transforming their vision into art, just as Scorsese did in *Mean Streets*. All the artists and photographers listed in our contributors are in that group. They capture what they see for its uniqueness, beauty, or truth, and share it with others. Maybe among them is another Dorothy Day or Louise Nevelson, or Martin Scorsese.

In this group also are priests like Monsignor Donald Sakano and Father Jonathan Morris of the Basilica of St. Patrick's Old Cathedral, who bring organizational skills, vision, good will, and the spiritual and intellectual prowess of the Catholic Church to the game and activities like *Basilica Café, Amo Latinam, Cinema Italiano, Basilica Schola*. Check it all out at the basilica's website.

In February 2011, a *New York Times* headline about the neighborhood blared, "New York's Little Italy, Littler by the Year." Even earlier, well-known writer Bill Tonelli wrote, "Arriverderci Little Italy," for *New York Magazine*. True enough. There are few Italians or Italian-Americans left. But Lou DiPalo, (see also Patriotism) who still has a business on Grand Street discusses the approach he has taken for his specialty food shop: "We decided we're going to take our business and go backwards— focus the way our grandparents and great-grandparents ran their operation: family-oriented hands-on...."

In likewise fashion, Msgr. Sakano of the Basilica and the Two Bridges Neighborhood Council spearheaded numerous initiatives to foster commemorative activities and events in keeping with the historical nature of the area.

So, it isn't the neighborhood we knew. And seeing the fleeting nature of what we held dear, it may gnaw at us. Isn't it better to embrace the new and fit it into the web we weave around us to capture the joys of life and age? And maybe it's the neighborhood we always wanted, still with character and characters, beauty, fun, and most importantly, preserved heritage. Could use a good stickball field though.

Nunzio Bonviso had some relevant thoughts at a get-together:

> The only regrets I have are that the people of our neighborhood did not have the foresight to put capital back into it. If so, we could have stayed here, properly raised our kids, made our living right here. Coming out of this neighborhood has meant so much, but with that foresight we would a dynamic force not only in Manhattan but in the world. I'm so proud to be here today and with neighborhood friends. We had a lot of brothers and sisters growing up. I didn't realize till later when I got older. Everybody in the neighborhood was brothers and sisters. I'm proud of where I came from and who I am and very proud of the people I know. Thank you.

George Catalano adds to these sentiments:

> What a neighborhood—10 city blocks long and four blocks wide. Maybe about 30,000-60,000 people living together and tied together by a common heritage (Italy). Three generations deep— yet everyone knew everyone. Doors were open, windows not barred, kids playing in the hallways on rainy days, mothers sharing coffee and cake with their neighbors in the building on rotating evenings, children taken care of when parents were ill—the aroma of foods cooking when you entered your building-children protected by the invisible web of extended family. We had it all. Why did we leave?

ACKNOWLEDGEMENTS

Maybe I put together this book, but mostly others tell our story. And they are in the book. Regardless, l must say more. Richie

Emelise Aleandri. The peerless expert on "The Neighorhood."

J.J. Anselmo. For blazing a path, becoming a new brother and teacher.

J.C. Bivona. For challenging assumptions and busting chops.

Nunzio Bonviso. Ever the source of respect and good will.

Cousin Theresa Bynum. For loving, understanding, and a pad in the city. Love.

John Buffa. Especially for his hosting. And all who came to tell stories at the Deli.

Cathy Carlson. For editorial expertise, advice and hard work. An uptown lady.

Ciao, Little Italy stalwarts: John V. Bivona, my lifelong pal for his friendship, legal advice, and more. And **Anne** for her photo album. **Virginia Dell'Olio,** from the beginning. **Sarah LoFaso. Catherine Miceli.** I know how to spell it correctly now. **Anthony and Linda Viglietta. Joe and Marie Graziano.** Good troublemakers.

Stan Erwin. For expert photographic help.

Cousin Bill Finnerty. For so much cheerful hard work and artistic talent in design and edits, and for reinvigorating a family link.

Vincent LaBarbera. Assistant to the Editor. A good shepherd. A believer, counselor, coordinator, psychologist, muse, and sounding board. A rainmaker, recruiter, and salesman. An able assistant with special tasks. A publicist and trusted business agent of sorts. His wife **Donna.** Support to him and to the cause. **Kristine Massari.** Donna's cousin, teacher of Italian, musician, singer, owner of Trumpets Jazz Club and Italian-American extraordinaire, who helped us overcome obstacles.

Susan Martini. For being there to help. And **Joseph Morale** in likewise fashion.

Camille and Eddie Morano. For inspiration, support, love, and good example.

Donald Napoli. For fostering alliances and unbounded enthusiasm.

McNally Jackson Booksellers. Advice, competence, talent from **Erin Curler,**

our primary designer, and **Beth Steidel.** That an ordinary person can access the service of self-publishing at reasonable cost with a machine that produces a book in five minutes is a wonder of modern life. A tribute to American entrepreneurship and fair-dealing.

Cousin Marietta Parisi. A listening and understanding sister. Love.

Cousin Ralph Patete. Ever helping others selflessly! Best chauffeur, NYC, of all time.

Hermi Rinaldo. My wife, who loves me all the time, is patient, and a real saint. Love!

Monsignor Donald Sakano. Pastor of the Basilica of St. Patrick's Old Cathedral and all the shepherds of that church past and present. Mentor, catalyst, booster, advisor. A blessing to all in "The Neighborhood," past and present. His helpful staff.

CREDITS

Some are included within the text of the book, and others listed here by order of appearance.

Cover art, design, and Forward Collage: Bill Finnerty. **Headings design™**: Bill Finnerty. **Preface**: Play Street plaque Editor's collection (Ed.C); NYC Mulberry Street, Wikimedia Commons (WC). **Introduction**: Marietta and granddaughter, courtesy William Parisi and Don Beatrice; WC for Lower East Side Tenements; Ed.C; Viglietta collection. **"There are some good Italians"**: Cover, *The Newsstand*, courtesy J.J. Anselmo; Wedding picture, Ed.C. **I Am An Italian-American:** Ed.C except WC for Christoforo Colombo and Declaration of Independence. **Marty: A Reflection:** Ed.C except for Copake photo on last page from J.V. Bivona collection. **History Collage:** Created by Ed; Upper right courtesy L. Bynum; Industrial School, Ed.C, all others Library of Congress (LOC) No known restriction (NKR). **Memories of a simpler lifestyle**: Milk Fund from Graziano collection; Fishmonger from LOC NNK; Iceman, LOC NNK. **Windows**: Tenement, WC; 213 Mott, Ed.C; Uncle Jim, courtesy M. Parisi; S. Antonio, Ed.C; Lady in Window, LOC NNK. **Friends Collage:** Created by Ed.; Photos courtesy J.V. Bivona, V. LaBarbera, D. Napoli, E. Morano. **Friendships Forged in Little Italy**: Joe, Louis, Charles, Ed.C. **It Was Quite A Journey:** Author. **University of Mulberry Street:** Ed.C. **Nobility Collage:** Created by Ed.; Photos courtesy T. Aiello, J.V. Bivona, P. Caterina, Ed.C. **Doctor Nicholas Testa and the Good Lord**: Courtesy of son, Dr. Noel Testa. **Sal the Barber in the Make Believe Ballroom**: Author, Martin Block, San Kenton, WC. **Buffa Collage**: Photos courtesy Buffa family, created by Ed. **Celebration of Charlie**: Morano collection. **Moe the Butcher**: Photos courtesy Susan Martini. **Parks Man**: Ed.C. **Dorothy Day**: Milwaukee Journal, World Telegram and Sun Collection of the Library of Congress, Courtesy of the Department of Special Collections and University Archives, Marquette University Libraries. **A Psychic**: Courtesy F. Andrews; Ed.C; WC. **Church Collage**: Ed.C, created by Ed. **St. Patrick's Church and School**: Ed.C and Dell'Olio collections. **Heavenly Sundays in Little Italy**: Author. **Praying for Tips**: Author. **Phyliss**: Author. Choir photo: Courtesy V. LaBarbera. **St. Patrick's School**: Ed.C.; Holy Name and Cabrini Guild, Viglietta collection. **Memories of St. Parrick's Old Cathedral:** Author, except Mothers Seton and Cabrini, WC. **Old St. Pat-**

rick's School of June 1950: Author. **Riding Shotgun:** Ed.C, Baptism photo courtesy A. Viglietta. **From Mean Street to Play Street:** Author except Jumping on Backs, LOC NKR. **Stickball:** Eddie with plaque, courtesy Morano family; Rules of the game, E. Morano; Photo of Eddie, Morano family; Group of players, Morano family; Gary Lipani, Morano family; Sports highlights, E. Morano; Players, E. Morano, L. Russo, courtesy L. Russo; Eddie at bat, E. Morano; Home plate, E. Morano; N. Biletto, courtesy P. Caterina; **Sports Collage:** Photos from C. Miceli, V. Dell'Olio, Ed., E. Morano, created by Ed. **Stepping Out Collage:** Photos from Buffa family, C. Miceli, ED., D. Napoli, created by Ed. **Let's Get Ready to Rumble:** Author, except photo of Steve Riggio, courtesy of A. Viglietta. **Entertainment and Social Life:** Webster Hal, WC. Bibliotek, Ed.C; National Geographic, WC; Strand Bookstore, WC; Classics Illustrated, WC. **Vincent Bivona**: J.V. Bivona collection. **Vincent Capuccio:** Courtesy Vincent Capuccio. **Vincent LaBarbera,** courtesy V. LaBarbera. **John Wayne and Chicken with Lemon and Oil:** Ed.C except People exiting St. Patrick's Cathedral, LOC NKR. **Bozo's Journey:** Photos courtesy C. Miceli except Mountains near Castello Marrone, U.S. Army. **Some Other Mother's Son:** Author. **The Dog Handler Cried:** Ed.C. **Uncle Len's Shoe:** courtesy M. Parisi. **Epilogue:** 214 Mulberry Street, courtesy Chris Kozcan; Nunzie and George, courtesy D. Napoli. **Contributors:** Ed. C and by permission.

CONTRIBUTORS

 Thomas Aiello grew up on Kenmare St., attended St. Patrick's School, Cardinal Hayes H.S., and Fordham University where he earned a B.A. in Finance and Banking. He worked on Wall St in the financial and banking industry and in real estate in Staten Island and Brooklyn. He was married to the late Mary Anne Mazzocchi for 46 years and has one son, Thomas Jr., and a grandson Thomas. His ancestors are from Naples, Italy.

Emelise Aleandri—See Part 2

 J. J. Anselmo grew up in the heart of New York's Little Italy -- "coming of age," so to speak, in the early '60s. He is a proud graduate of New York City's prestigious Stuyvesant High School and Columbia University. He is a registered professional engineer who specializes in civil engineering, dealing mostly with the design of waterfront and coastal structures. He has been married for over 40 years to the former Mary Puccio and is the father of two. His roots go back to Monreale, Sicily and Scilla, Calabria

Angelo Bianchi—See Part 1

 John V. Bivona, Esq., grew up at 285 Mott St. He is a graduate of Xavier H.S., Fordham College at Rose Hill, and Fordham Law School. He founded the law firm of Bivona & Cohen P.C. and until January 2009 was the firm's Senior Partner. He is a founder of Felix Invest-  ments LLC and a principal of the firm. He is married to Anne and they have two children Vincent and Christopher. His ancestors came from Sicily, and Avelino and his favorite motto is, "Perseverance wins the crown."

Vincent Bivona—See Part 7

Nunzio Bonviso grew up on Elizabeth St. A retired night-club and disco manager, he is also a retired neighborhood amateur athlete. He is now a dedicated husband, father, grandfather and person of interest. He "wakes up each day looking forward to the future." His favorite saying is "Peace, be well."

Vivian (Anselmo) Beltempo grew up in Little Italy, residing at 214 Mulberry Street until 1970, when she married Anthony Beltempo, who is from Elizabeth and Prince Streets. She went to P.S. 21 and finished up at St. Anthony's School. She graduated from St. Anthony's Commercial High School in 1965. She currently resides in Long Branch, NJ. She works at Monmouth University as the Assistant Director of Conference and Event Services. She is the mother of two children and she has four grandchildren.

Theresa Bynum, daughter of Madeline (née Russo) and Thomas (Tommy Forty) Quaranta, grew up at 260 Mott St. and graduated from St. Patrick's School. She is married to retired FDNY Battalion Chief Louis, and they live in  NYC. They have one daughter, Vanessa. Her grandparents come from Campania, Italy and Strasbourg, France.

Augie and John Bufffa—See Part 3; Vincent Capuccio—See Part 7

George Catalano was raised in Little Italy. He is retired from the U.S. Postal Service. Married to Rosamond (Morelli), they have three children, Michael, Albert, and Lillian, and seven grandchildren. He lives in Florida and enjoying retired life, sailing, and playing picklelball. His ancestors come from Calabria, Naples, and Potenza, Italy

Peter Caterina lived on Mott St. He is a graduate of St. Patrick's School and Cardinal Hayes H.S. and served in the U.S. Army. He is a retired elevator builder. He has been married for 39 years to Antionette (nee Marchello) from Elizabeth Street. They have three children, Peter, Jr., Joseph and Toni Ann. They live in Wantagh, N.Y.

Virginia Dell'Olio is single and still resides in New York City. She grew up on Mulberry St. She has two daughters, Andrea & Christina. She is currently working on a series of stories about growing up in Little Italy. Her ancestors come from Italy and Scotland.

Joseph Falcone Jr.— See Part 8

Sherrie Ferguson—for assistance provided with U.S.M.C and Part 8

Vito Gentile—See Part 2

Joseph Guidetti—See Part 4

Marie Elaine Musto and Joseph Anthony Graziano were born and raised in Little Italy. They attended St. Patrick's School, and in 1964 they were married at its church. In 1970 they moved to Connecticut with their two children Denise and Joey. Since retiring they enjoy volunteer work and spending time with their two granddaughters Olivia and Mia who live close by. Even though they moved from the neighborhood long ago, they have not forgotten their roots and have maintained very close relationships with many of their childhood friends. They often return as a group to enjoy and remember the place of their youth.

Vincent LaBarbera—See Part 7 and Acknowledgements

Sarah Lofaso is a freelance writer and a retired FBI analyst. She earned a B.S. in Business Administration from Ramapo College, N.J. and has completed Masters' courses at the Joint Military Intelligence College and Eastern Michigan University. She is a member of the Society of FBI Alumni, The John Carroll Society, NIAF, OSIA, NARFE, and the Ramapo College Alumni Association. Sarah has four daughters and six grandchildren. She lives in Connecticut. Her paternal grandparents were from Marineo, Sicily and her maternal grandparents were from Naples in the Province of Avellino, (Campania region of Italy). Her favorite quote is: "Let us love, since that is what our hearts were made for."(St. Therese, The Little Flower). Sarah (2nd from left, with daughters).

Donald (Red) Napoli retired as a vice president of JPMorgan Chase Bank after 40 years of service. Following the terrorist attack on the World Trade Center on 9/11 he was recalled as a consultant to settle customer claims for contents of bank safe deposit boxes that were damaged or destroyed. He is engaged in community and church activities and takes classes in bible studies. Married to Lillian, their family includes two children and three grandchildren. His grandparents on his mother's side came from two small towns in Southern Italy, Aquara and Ottati, both in the Province of Salerno in the Region

of Campania. His grandparents on his father's side came from Calabria. His favorite saying is "Pray, Hope, and don't worry." St. Padre Pio of Pietrelcina

Anthony Mancini—See Part 2

Catherine Tuzzo Miceli married Joe Miceli in 1954. She is a substitute assistant for The Brentwood School District and for the past 47 years has been a member of the Sweet Adeline International Organization singing barbershop harmony. She has two sons, Anthony and Joseph and four grandchil-

dren. Her father's parents came from Calabria, Italy and her mother's father came from Avelino, Naples, Italy. Her mother's mom was born in New York City.

Angel Marinaccio—See Part 6

Lola Marinaccio—See Part 8

Gerard Marinaccio—See the Introduction

Jim Merlis is a publicist working in Hollywood

Patrick J. Montana resided at 247 Mulberry Street during the 30s, 40s and 50s and most of the 1960s. Dr. Montana is a professor emeritus of Hofstra University

and continues to teach management and golf at Fordham University's Graduate School of Business. He is author of 30 books in management and founder of the National Center of Career Life Planning. He plans on writing a memoir about life at 247 Mulberry Street. His favorite expression is: "Ciò che si mette in voi uscire" meaning "What you put in you get out." His ancestors came from the Naples area and Sicily. (In picture at left, Pat and sisters, Marie (L) and Allie (R) in the 50s. On the right, Pat and sisters Allie (L) and Marie (R) today.)

  Joseph Morale grew up in Little Italy. He worked in the communications industry for 41 years and served in the U.S. Army Reserves for 26 years, retiring as a Sergeant First Class. He is married to Josephine and they have two children, Frank and Stacy. He lives in New York and remains a big film buff and member of the Screen Actors Guild.

 Camille M. Morano (nee Sorrentino), a graduate of Bayonne High School and student of Seton Hall & CSI, is a retired housewife involved in volunteer work for her church and Eger Care Center. She is married to Carmine Morano. They have a daughter Liz and a son-in-law Erik Rogers who are the parents of their beautiful granddaughter Amanda. Camille's forbearers are from Naples & Ireland.

 Eddie Morano grew up in Little Italy and is an icon of sports in the neighborhood. A retired Dam Control Supervisor, he worked for 43 years for the engineering and construction company, Ebasco Services Inc. He played stickball for 30 years and softball until he was 67. He coached Catholic Youth organization (CYO) basketball and was a Public Schools Athletic League (PSAL) football official for 37 years. His favorite saying is: "To Err is human, To forgive divine."

 Ralph Joseph Patete grew up at 265 Lafayette St., the Monroe Building. He graduated from St. Patrick's School, Cardinal Hayes H.S. and Manhattan College, earning a B.S. in Economics. He was a Program Coordinator in the U.S. Census Bureau for 31 years and owned a limousine business for 10 years. He is retired and living in Virginia. He has three children, Marie Angelica, Ralph David, and Ana Irma. His favorite saying is: "Bless you."

Marietta (née Lo Frisco) Parisi is a retired treasurer and currently a consultant with Caspari, Inc. She is a gourmet Italian cook and is married to William. They have two children and a granddaughter.

Richard J. Rinaldo (Richie) grew up at 213 Mott St. A graduate of St. Patrick's School, Cardinal Hayes H.S., Fordham College at Rose Hill, and Hofstra University, he is a retired military officer now living in Newport News, Virginia. He served as a rifle company commander in combat, earning the Distinguished Service Cross and a Purple Heart. He is involved in civic and church activities, takes classes in languages, art, and music at a local university, and competes in master's track and field, earning an All American award for sprinting. He has published numerous articles in various forums. He is married to Hermi. Their family includes four children, nine grandchildren, and five great grandchildren. His forbearers came from Campania and Calabria, Italy and Strasbourg, France. Favorite saying is "Perseverance wins the crown

Joseph Russo— See Part 6; Msgr. Donald Sakano— See Foreword

Ro and Jerry Sceusa— See Parts 2 and 6; Vincent Scilla— See Part 6

Charles Angelo Saia lived at 300 Elizabeth St. across from Our Lady of Loreto Church. He is a graduate of St. Patrick's School, La Salle Academy, and St. John's University. He was a CPA (Sole Proprietor). Retired now, he lives in the Village of Hampstead, NC, enjoying an active lifestyle of racquetball, fishing, and boating. He has three children, Chuck, Lenny, and Suzanne, and two Grand Kids, Ethan and Matty.

Robert B. Uricola grew up on Mulberry Street. He is a graduate of St. Patrick's School and attended Cardinal Hayes H.S. and the School of Visual Arts. He owned his own film production company and is a producer/writer. His ancestors come from Sicily, just outside Palermo. He is married to Winnie.

Salvatore Uricola (Sally GaGa) grew up on Mulberry Street and now lives in Florida. It is widely known that a character in the movie *Mean Streets* is loosely based on him as a young man. He is a proud father and grandfather.

Anthony Viglietta is a graduate of St. Patrick" School, La Salle Academy, and Fordham College. His financial career began as a Certified Public Accountant and he rose to Chief Financial Officer and Treasurer of REIT, listed on the American Stock Exchange. He was also a co-founder of a real estate company that acquired and operated over 1,350,000 square feet of Midtown Manhattan commercial office and retail space. In the early 1990's he joined DLJ, which was later acquired by Credit Suisse First Boston, in the fixed income area. He was involved is all aspects of Commercial Mortgage Securitization. Anthony is married to Linda. They have two married daughters and two grandsons. Anthony is actively involved in local politics, community affairs with People to People and the Order of the Sons of Italy. His Dad's family is from Naples and his Mom's family from Sicily. His favorite saying is: "Be the best you can," and he believes that we should always give youth positive encouragement, since they don't really know how good they are.

SELECTED MATERIALS FOR
FURTHER READING AND ENJOYMENT

There is a wealth of material about Italian-Americans that can be found using the Internet. Not so for Little Italy. The books, films and music here are about our neighborhood, with the exception of those that are great resources to learn more about Italians and the Italian-American experience in general. Those specifically about Little Italy are preceded by an asterisk. Opinion—Barzini and Gambino are must reading for understanding Italians and Italian-Americans.

Non-fiction:

*Aleandri, Emelise. Images of America: *Little Italy*. New York: Arcadia Publishing, 1999.

*Aleandri, Emelise. Images of America: *The Italian-American Immigrant Theatre in New York City*. New York: Arcadia Publishing, 1999.

American Italian Historical Association Publications of Proceedings, New York: American Italian Historical Association, Volumes 1 to 30 from 1968 to 1999.

Barzini, Luigi. *The Italians*. New York: Atheneum Publishers, 1964

Cordasco, Francesco. *Italian Americans: A Guide to Information Sources*. Detroit: Gale Research Co., 1978

Del Giudice, Luisa, ed. *Studies in Italian American Folklore*. Logan, Utah: Utah State Press, 1993.

Gambino, Richard. *Blood of My Blood: The Dilemma of the Italian-Americans*. New York: Anchor Press/Doubleday, 1974.

Giordano, Joseph, ed. *The Italian-American Catalog: A Lavish and Loving Celebration of and Guide to Our Culture, History, Neighborhoods, Family, Food and Drink*. New York: Doubleday and Company, Inc., 1986.

Giordano, Paolo A. and Anthony Julian Tamburri. eds. *Italian Americans in the Third Millennium: Social Histories and Cultural Representations*. New York: American Italian Historical Association, 2009.

Lagumina, Salvatore J. et al. eds. *The Italian American Experience: An Encyclopedia*, New York: Garland Publishing Inc., 2000.

Malpezzi, Frances M. and William M. Clements. *Italian-American Folklore*. Liitle Rock, AR: August House, Inc., 2005.

*Marinaccio, Angel. *Be Home on Time When I Put the Water Up for Pasta*. Silver Spring, MD: The Beckham Publication Group, Inc. 2010.

Moreno, Barry. *Coming to America Italian Americans*. Hauppauge, New York: Barron's Educational Series, Inc. 2003.

Nelli, Humbert S. "Italians", in Stephan Thernstrom, ed. *Harvard Encyclopedia of American Ethnic Groups,* 1980.

*_Petruzzelli, Gus. *Memories of Growing Up in Little Italy*, New York: ExLibris Corporation, 2010

*Riis, Jacob A. *The children of the poor*. New York: C. Scribner's Sons, 1902.

Scarpaci, Vincenza. *The Journey of the Italians in America*. Gretna, LA: Pelican Publishing Company, Inc. 2008.

*Fiction:

Anselmo, J.J. *The Newsstand: A Novel of Little Italy*. New York: Mc-Nally Jackson Books. 2011.

Fabiano, Laurie. *Elizabeth Street: A Novel Based On True Events*. Las Vegas, NV: AmazonEncore, New York: Melchor Media, Inc. 2010.

Graziano Vincent. *Die Laughing*, Lubbock, TX: Winoca Press. 2009.

Mancini, Anthony. *Minnie Santangelo and the Evil Eye*. Greenwich, CT: Fawcett Crest. 1977.

Mancini, Anthony. *Minnie Santangelo's Mortal Sin*. Greenwich, CT: Fawcett Crest. 1975.

Mazzucco, Melania G., Vita, Virginia Jewiss (Translator), N.Y.: Farrar, Straus and Giroux; 1st edition. 2005.

Prose, Francine. *Household Saints: A Novel*. New York: Harper Perennial. 2003.

Roberts, Barbara Marolla. *The Vineyard on Mulberry Street*. New York: ExLibris Corporation. 2006.

Thompson, Victoria. *Murder in Little Italy*. New York: Penguin Group (USA) Inc. 2006.

*Children's Books about Little Italy:

Barton, Elisa, Ted Lewin, Illus., *Peppe the Lamplighter*. New York: HarperCollins. 1997. (Ages 3 and up). Also Barton, Elisa. *American Too*. New York: HarperCollins. 1996. (Ages 4 and up).

Doti, James. *A Christmas Adventure in Little Italy*. Minneapolis, MN: Jabberwocky Books. 2010. (Ages 6 and up).

Grunwell, Jeanne Marie. *Saint Elizabeth Ann Seton Daughter of*

America Boston, MA: Pauline Books & Media. 1999. (Ages 9 and up).

Keyes, Frances Parkinson. *Mother Cabrini: Missionary to the World.* San Francisco, CA: Ignatius Press 1997. (Ages 9 and up).

Napoli, Donna Jo, *The King of Mulberry Street.* New York: Wendy Lamb Books. 2005. (Ages 8 and up).

Seuss, Dr. *And to Think That I Saw It on Mulberry Street.* New York: Random House Books for Young Readers. 1989. (Ages 6 and up).

Walters, Julie. Patrick Kelley, Illus., *Elizabeth Ann Seton: Saint for a New Nation.* Mahwah, NJ: Paulist Press. 2002. (Ages 11 and up).

*Feature Films about Little Italy:
> *China Girl*
> *Household Saints*
> *Mean Streets*
> *New York Blood*

*Documentaries about Little Italy:
> *ItalianAmerican* Directed By: Martin Scorsese.
> *Little Italy: Past, Present, and Future.* Medici Television. Directed by Federica Martino
> *The Neighborhood (2001)* Directed By: Martin Scorsese.

Music of Little Italy:
> Little Italy Bell'Aria, Bell'Aria CD

Some general websites:
> http://en.wikipedia.org/wiki/Italian_American
> http://www.niaf.org/National Italian American Foundation
> http://www.columbuscitizensfd.org/
> modernitalian@modernitalian.org
> http://www.unico.org/ UNICO
> http://www.osia.org/ Order of Sons of Italy in America
> http://www.italiamerica.org/id49.htm
> www.italianamericanmuseum.org
> http://www.qc.cuny.edu/calandra John D. Calandra Italian-American Institute
> Candida Martinelli's Italophile Site. http://italophiles.com/